Children and Consumer Culture in American Society

Recent Titles in
Children and Youth: History and Culture
Miriam Forman-Brunell, Series Editor

Children and Youth in Sickness and in Health: A Historical Handbook and Guide
Janet Golden, Richard A. Meckel, and Heather Munro Prescott

Asian American Children: A Historical Handbook and Guide
Benson Tong, editor

Children and Youth in Adoption, Orphanages, and Foster Care: A Historical
Handbook and Guide
Lori Askeland, editor

Disabled Children in America: A Historical Handbook and Guide
Philip L. Safford and Elizabeth J. Safford, editors

Adolescent Sexuality: A Historical Handbook and Guide
Carolyn Cocca, editor

Children and Consumer Culture in American Society

A Historical Handbook and Guide

EDITED BY LISA JACOBSON

Children and Youth: History and Culture
Miriam Forman-Brunell, Series Editor

Westport, Connecticut
London

Library of Congress Cataloging-in-Publication Data

Children and consumer culture in American society : a historical handbook and guide / edited by Lisa Jacobson.
    p. cm. — (Children and youth : history and culture, ISSN 1546–6752)
    Includes bibliographical references and index.
    ISBN: 978–0–313–33140–4 (alk. paper)
    1. Child consumers—United States—History—20th century.   2. Children—Family relationships—United States—History—20th century.   3. Consumption (Economics)—United States—History—20th century.   4. Social influence—United States—History—20th century.   I. Jacobson, Lisa, 1962–
HF5415.33.U6C53 2008
339.4'70830973–dc22   2007035421

British Library Cataloguing in Publication Data is available.

Library of Congress Catalog Card Number: 2007035421
ISBN: 978–0–313–33140–4
ISSN: 1546–6752

First published in 2008

Praeger Publishers, 88 Post Road West, Westport, CT 06881
An imprint of Greenwood Publishing Group, Inc.
www.praeger.com

Printed in the United States of America

The paper used in this book complies with the
Permanent Paper Standard issued by the National
Information Standards Organization (Z39.48–1984).

10 9 8 7 6 5 4 3 2 1

Copyright Acknowledgments

The editor and publisher gratefully acknowledge permission to excerpt passages from the following sources:

Anthony Hotchner, *King of the Hill* (New York: Harper & Row, 1972), 85–86. © 1972 by A. E. Hotchner. Reprinted by permission of William Morris Agency, LLC on behalf of the author.

Sidonie Gruenberg, "Children and Money," *Federation for Child Study Bulletin* 1 (January 1924): 1–3. Reproduced by permission of Goddard Riverside Community Center, New York, New York.

Robert Lynd and Helen Lynd, "Child-rearing," in *Middletown: A Study in American Culture* (New York: Harcourt, Brace, and World, 1929), 140–148. Reproduced by permission of Harcourt, Inc. and Staughton Lynd.

Robert Lynd and Helen Lynd, "Food, Clothing, and Housework," in *Middletown: A Study in American Culture* (New York: Harcourt, Brace, and World, 1929), 162–164. Reproduced by permission of Harcourt, Inc. and Staughton Lynd.

Gay Head, "Boy Dates Girl: One Girl's Family," *Scholastic Magazine* (November 25, 1940): 39–40. Copyright © 1940 by Scholastic Inc. Reprinted by permission.

Every reasonable effort has been made to trace the owners of copyrighted materials in this book, but in some instances this has proven impossible. The editor and publisher will be glad to receive information leading to more complete acknowledgments in subsequent printings of the book and in the meantime extend their apologies for any omissions.

Contents

Part II Documents

Part III   Bibliography

Series Foreword

Pocahontas, a legendary figure in American history, was just a pre-adolescent when she challenged two cultures at odds to cooperate instead of to compete. While Pocahontas forged peace, many more now forgotten Native American, Anglo-American, African American, and other children contributed to their families' survival, communities' development, and America's history in just as legitimate, though perhaps less legendary ways. Contracts and correspondence from colonial Chesapeake reveal that even seventeenth-century toddlers labored. But the historical agency of the vast majority of children and adolescents has been under-valued and overlooked in dominant historical narratives. Instead, generations of Americans have credited fathers and other hoary leaders for their actions and achievements, all the while disregarding pivotal boyhood experiences that shaped skills and ideals. Reflecting these androcentric, Eurocentric, and age-based biases that have framed the nation's history, American history texts have reinforced the historical invisibility of girls and boys for centuries. For students searching libraries for scholarly sources and primary documents about children and adolescents in various historical contexts, this near absence of information in master narratives has vexed their research.

The absence of children in standard history books has not only obscured children's history but also the work of scholars who have been investigating youth's histories and interrogating their cultures since the turn of the last century. A new curiosity about children in times past was generated by the Progressive Era agenda which sought to educate, acculturate, and elevate American children through child study and child welfare. In *Child Life in*

Colonial Days (1899), "amateur historian" Alice Morse Earl drew upon archival sources and material culture in order to examine the social history of Puritan girls and boys. Children were also included in Arthur W. Calhoun's *A Social History of the American Family* (1917) and in Edmund S. Morgan's *The Puritan Family: Religion and Domestic Relations in Seventeenth Century New England* (1944), but few other professional historians within the male-dominated profession considered children worthy of study. Those children who made appearances in historical accounts were typically the privileged daughters and sons of white men of means and might.

In the 1960s, larger social, cultural, and political transformations refocused scholarly attention. The influence of sixties' youth culture and second wave feminism and renewed interest in the agency of "ordinary people," youth in particular, laid the foundation for a "new" social history. The confluence of a renewed interest in youth and the development of new methodological approaches led French demographer and social historian Philippe Ariès to study a nation's youngest population. Challenging a dominant assumption that childhood was transhistorical in *Centuries of Childhood: A Social History of Family Life* (1962), Ariès argued that over time, changing cultures and societies redefined notions of childhood and transformed children's experiences. Ariès's work on European children was soon followed by Bernard Wishy's *The Child and the Republic: The Dawn of American Child Nurture* (1968), which explored the changing nature of child rearing advice in the United States.

Despite important inroads made by these and other scholars (e.g., Robert Bremner), the history of childhood became embedded within historical sub-fields during the 1970s. The history of childhood was briefly associated with psychohistory due to the controversial work of Lloyd deMause who founded *The History of Childhood Quarterly*. It was largely historians of the family (e.g., John Demos, Philip Greven Jr.) and those in the history of education (who refocused attention away from the school and onto the student) who broke new ground. Essays appeared in scholarly journals in the 1970s but were not reprinted until the following decade when *Growing Up in America: Children in Historical Perspective* (1985) brought new visibility to the "vitality and scope of this emerging field" (preface). That important collection edited by historians Joseph M. Hawes and N. Ray Hiner, along with their *American Childhood: A Research Guide and Historical Handbook* (1985), served to promote research among an up-and-coming generation of historians whose work would be included in another path-breaking anthology. By placing children at the center of historical inquiry, privileging gender as a critical factor in childhood socialization, and expanding social history to include cultural history, historians in *Small Worlds: Children and Adolescents in America, 1850–1950* (1992) demonstrated that the relationships between childhood and adulthood and kids and culture were historically significant. By privileging previously overlooked and disregarded historical sources, "reading" material culture artifacts as historical texts, and applying gender, race, and class analyses to an age-based one, these historians continued the mapping of childhood's terrain. Creatively and methodically, they traced childhood ideals and children's experiences within cultures and over centuries.

In the early to mid 1990s, those in the fields of psychology and education initiated a scholarly debate about the dangers that popular culture posed to the healthy development of female adolescents in contemporary America. Those scholars influenced by a different scholarly trajectory—cultural studies and feminist theory—saw agency instead, illuminating the many ways in which girls and female adolescents (as other youth) resist, contest, subvert, and reappropriate dominant cultural forms. Moreover, scholars such as Kimberly Roberts brought to light the discursive nature of the contemporary "girl crisis" debate just as others have uncovered numerous other discourses that create, reflect, and reinforce the cultural norms of girlhood, boyhood, female and male adolescence. Trained in fields other than history (e.g., American Studies, communications studies, English, Rhetoric and Composition), the latest generation of scholars has blurred the boundaries and forged new fields. Informed by the work of cultural studies scholar Angela McRobbie, "girl's culture" aimed to balance the boy-centered biases of the older "youth studies." Nevertheless, such late twentieth-century anthologies as *The Children's Culture Reader* (1998), *Delinquents & Debutantes: Twentieth-Century American Girls' Cultures* (1998) and *Generations of Youth: Youth Cultures and History in Twentieth-Century America* (1998) reflect a new multi- and inter-disciplinarity in the study of children and youth which utilizes textual and representational analyses (as opposed to social history) to study the subcultures that children and youth have constructed within larger historical contexts. By developing new methods of inquiry and widening subjects of study, scholars have been able to examine "lived experiences" and "subjectivities," though most of the recent work focuses on teenagers in the twentieth century.

Today, there is an abundance of scholarly works (e.g., monographs, anthologies, and encyclopedias), book series on children (e.g., The Girls' History & Culture Series), national, regional, and local conferences, major academic journals, and in 2000, The Society for the History of Children and Youth, was finally founded by two of the field's pioneers, Joseph M. Hawes and N. Ray Hiner. That professional organization draws together the many college and university professors who teach courses on the history of children and youth, girlhood and female adolescence regularly offered in schools of education, departments of history, psychology, political science, sociology, and in programs on Women's Studies, Media/Communications Studies, and American Studies. But the history of children and adolescents has an even broader audience as media attention on bad boys and mean girls (e.g., "Queenbees") generates new questions and a search for answers in historical antecedents.

To meet the research needs of students of all ages, this accessibly written work—as the others in the series—surveys and synthesizes centuries of scholarship on children and adolescents of different classes, races, genders, regions, religions, sexualities, and abilities. Some topics in the series have a gendered, racial, or regional focus while others (e.g., sickness and health, work and play, etc.) utilize a larger multicultural perspective. Whichever their focus, each and every book is organized into three equal parts to provide researchers with immediate access to historical overviews, primary source documents, and scholarly sources. Part I consists of synthetic essays written by experts in the field whose surveys are chronological and contextual. Part II provides access to hard-to-find primary source documents, in part or whole. Explanatory head notes illuminate themes, generate further understanding, and expedite inquiry. Part III is an extensive up-to-date bibliography of cited sources as well as those critical for further research.

The goal of the Children and Youth: History and Culture reference book series is not simply a utilitarian one but also to ultimately situate girls and boys of all ages more centrally in dominant historical narratives.

Miriam Forman-Brunell, Series Editor
University of Missouri, Kansas City

Preface

By all accounts, children play a crucial role in today's economy. According to some estimates, children spend or influence the spending of up to $500 billion annually. Children's expanding role in consumer spending even prompted an August 6, 2001, *Time* magazine cover story to ask, "Do Kids Have Too Much Power?" While seeming to point to new developments, such trend journalism actually echoes long-standing historical debates over the meanings of childhood, the sanctity of the family, and the authority of the marketplace. Since the late nineteenth century, American children have often been lightning rods for a host of anxieties and aspirations that accompanied the growth of modern consumer capitalism.

In many respects these historical debates over the promises and perils of children's consumer culture mirror the ambivalence and outrage that often surface in scholarly studies. Writing of contemporary consumer culture in *Rethinking Childhood* (Rutgers University Press 2004), Enola Aird charges that today's corporations practice a form of "market authoritarianism" that leaves "children too little room, too little space, within which to grow and develop their own identities." Others view consumer culture as a creative and liberating realm in which children forge identities, cement relationships, and assert their independence. Such arguments parallel larger fault lines in scholarly debates about consumer culture's role in American society. Is consumer culture an agent of homogenization that stifles individuality or is it an avenue for personal expression? If mass marketers and consumers both participate in shaping the meaning of consumption, how much power do mass marketers really have to create new wants and how much autonomy do consumers really have in exercising consumer "choice"?

This book does not attempt to resolve these debates but instead attempts to place them in historical perspective. The children studied in this volume range from toddlers to older adolescents, but the analysis concentrates on the groups of children—from grade-schoolers to high-school students—that most interested mass marketers. Focusing primarily on the period from the Gilded Age through the twentieth century, the volume examines how and why children and adolescents acquired new economic roles as consumers, and how these new roles both reflected and produced dynamic changes in family life and the culture of childhood and youth. It discusses how a variety of historical actors—advertisers, juvenile magazines, merchandisers, parents, child experts, school teachers and school administrators—have attempted to socialize children as consumers. Children, too, of course, have had a hand in shaping children's consumer culture and this research guide explores how children and adolescents have used consumer goods to define personal identities and peer relationships.

This book is divided into three parts. The four original essays in part I address major topics within the history of children's consumer culture. Each synthesizes key themes and findings in the burgeoning literature on children, youth, and consumer culture. A wide-ranging topic, children's consumer culture provides a fascinating lens through which to understand historical transformations in the family, capitalism and business practices, gender roles and gender ideology, and childhood and youth. The essays in this volume draw upon interdisciplinary scholarship in history, sociology, and cultural studies to illuminate these multifaceted developments.

The first essay examines why advertisers and mass merchandisers began to imagine children as consumers in the early twentieth century and assesses the strategies they have used—often with the explicit cooperation of magazine publishers, movie producers, and public schools—to cultivate brand consciousness and brand loyalty. In the second chapter, Amanda Bruce, who recently completed her dissertation, entitled "Strangers in the Living Room: Debating Radio and Early Television for Family," analyzes the often-contentious moral debates that swirled around children's consumption of new media and mass commercial amusements. She argues that these debates reflected much broader struggles for cultural authority among middle-class reformers, media watchdogs, producers of mass media, and children themselves. The third chapter, written by Paul Ringel, an assistant professor of history at High Point University in North Carolina, analyzes institutional responses to children's consumer practices. Adults feared that consumer culture might lead children astray, or worse still, would drag them down the path toward juvenile delinquency. Ringel evaluates the effectiveness of media censorship, juvenile courts, working-girl clubs, school savings banks, and World War II teen canteens in regulating and restraining children's consumption. He also reveals how children and youth sometimes circumvented such reforms and used them toward their own ends. The final essay examines how consumer culture has transformed relations of power and authority within American families. It illuminates the varied strategies—including the use of allowances and children's playtime—that parents and children from diverse class, ethnic, and racial backgrounds have adopted to define the boundaries of children's consumer freedoms and children's family obligations.

Part II features primary sources that address several recurring themes and issues in the history of children's consumer culture. Chapters 5 and 6 present a series of promotional advertisements by children's magazines and articles that appeared in the advertising trade press. These documents highlight the perspectives of advertising authorities and children's magazine publishers, arguably the two groups most invested in nurturing children's consumer desires. The next three chapters deal with several controversial and highly contested dimensions of children's consumer culture and consumer training. The documents in chapter 7 feature classic critiques and defenses of children's consumption of mass media and mass amusements, while those in chapters 8 and 9 reveal the often-contradictory ways that public schools have responded to children's social and economic roles as consumers. Chapter 10 presents the writings of sociologists, child experts, and a teen advice columnist, each of whom assessed how families managed (or ought to manage) conflicts over children's consumption. A headnote setting the documents in context introduces the primary sources in each chapter. Owing to the obstacles of obtaining copyright permissions, the documents in part II are heavily weighted to the first half of the twentieth century. The headnotes suggest Web sites where readers can find additional primary sources that illuminate trends in the late twentieth- and early twenty-first centuries.

Part III consists of a bibliography of secondary sources, divided into three major sections: children, youth, and consumer culture; general works on consumer culture; and general works on the history of childhood, childrearing, and the family.

This book offers students and scholars a starting point for further research. While debates over the pleasures and dangers of children's consumer culture show no sign of abating, they too often occur in a historical vacuum. If we really want to understand why the mass market has gained so much influence in children's lives, we need to put a wider array of groups under the historical microscope—not just retailers and mass marketers. We need to better understand the ways in which parents, child experts, educators, and youth organizations—the very groups who might exert a countervailing influence—have often helped to strengthen children's ties to the mass market. We also need to understand the emotional needs and aspirations

Acknowledgments

The editor would like to thank several individuals who provided crucial assistance on this project. Roger Pryor and Megan Bowan scanned and transcribed the documents in this collection and dispatched this onerous task with great care and efficiency. Roger was also a terrific help with the bibliography. Amanda Bruce, a contributor in this volume, was especially resourceful in suggesting and locating documents that tied in with her essay on children and the mass media. My biggest debt of gratitude is to my husband John Majewski for his willingness to read multiple drafts, his judicious comments, and his pragmatic advice throughout the process of producing this volume. My son Sam, now eight years old, had his own insights to offer on the subject of this book. Through his eyes I glimpsed both the wondrous satisfactions and the bitter disappointments that children's consumer culture often delivers. It is to John and Sam, whose love and support sustain me, that I dedicate this book.

Lisa Jacobson
Department of History
University of California, Santa Barbara

I Essays

1 Advertising, Mass Merchandising, and the Creation of Children's Consumer Culture

Lisa Jacobson

In 2004, mass marketers spent $15 billion on advertising directed at children—and for good reason (Schor 2004). Children spend an estimated $100 billion on consumer goods, and this just represents the money children have accrued from personal earnings, allowances, and gifts. Children's influence on family spending decisions accounts for another $188 billion of annual household purchases (McNeal 1992). Eager to tap children's vast collective spending power, businesses employ teams of market researchers to track children's buying habits and scout trends in fashion and popular culture that reflect what today's youth define as cool. Mass marketers even manufacture trends by hiring teens (or posing as them) to shill for their products in Internet chat rooms.

The aggressive pursuit of child consumers has generated vigorous criticism as well as handsome corporate profits. Just consider the titles of some recently published books: *Stealing Innocence: Corporate Culture's War on Children, Kinderculture: The Corporate Construction of Childhood,* and *Consuming Kids: The Hostile Takeover of Childhood* (Giroux 2000; Steinberg and Kincheloe 1998; Linn 2004). Critics charge that mass marketers have colonized children's imagination and usurped parental authority by filling children with wants and desires that strain family incomes and corrupt family values. Critics also condemn the hypocrisy of mass marketers who routinely exploit children's gullibility even as they claim to empower children by catering to their needs and tastes.

Sociologists, psychologists, and media reformers often present such developments as a recent fall from grace. Some time between the age of television and the age of the Internet, the argument goes, the mass market increasingly overwhelmed efforts to regulate or restrain its corrupting influence on children. In truth, however, neither the baby boomers (the large group of children born between 1945 and 1964) nor subsequent generations numbered among the first children to encounter aggressive marketing. Marketing directly to children has much deeper historical roots. As early as the 1890s, businesses envisioned advertising as a means to build children's brand awareness and shape their future adult buying habits. By the 1910s and 1920s, advertisers and retailers had made an even bigger conceptual leap. They increasingly saw children not only as the shoppers of tomorrow but also as the shoppers of today who could grease the wheels of parental spending.

This essay explores how and why Americans began to imagine children as consumers in the early twentieth century. It then traces how marketing strategies have evolved in response to transformations in the economy, the democratization of the family, and the changing contours of children's peer culture. Finally, this essay assesses the consequences of mass marketers' growing investment in expanding and shaping children's consumer culture. How has the cultivation of child consumers transformed the balance of power and authority within the family and children's relationships with their peers? What have children gained and lost in the bargain?

CREATING A NEW CHILD WORLD: NATIONAL ADVERTISERS AND MASS RETAILERS IN THE EARLY TWENTIETH CENTURY

The years between 1890 and 1940 witnessed a revolution in mass merchandising and juvenile advertising that, in William Leach's words, placed "the 'child world' on par with the adult in strategic marketing importance" (Leach 1993a). Mass marketers' interest in attracting child consumers partly stemmed from the dramatic expansion of mass-produced consumer goods in the last quarter of the nineteenth century. Mechanization of factories made it possible for businesses to produce goods both more quickly and more cheaply. Because mass production often outpaced existing consumer demand, businesses sought to develop new markets for their goods. Advertising helped manufacturers create national markets for goods that had previously been sold in smaller regional or local markets. The quest for new markets, however, did not simply entail expanding manufacturers' geographic reach. It also led businesses to seek out previously neglected demographic groups, including children (Strasser 1989).

Mass production contributed to the explosive growth in the variety and supply of children's toys and children's clothing between 1890 and 1920. Before 1890, few American children owned enough toys to stock a tiny toy chest and most of those would have been homemade. Even well-to-do families considered manufactured toys a luxury. A few department stores sold toys, but they regarded children's playthings as a seasonal business and mounted toy displays only during the Christmas holidays. By the 1910s, however, department stores were dedicating entire floors to toys and year-round toy departments had become customary. American toy makers nearly tripled their production between 1913 and 1919, when high tariffs and World War I cut off the supply of toys from Germany, which until then had dominated the American industry. Toy retailers sold a dazzling array of toys, including teddy bears, dolls, dollhouses, toy cars, electric trains, erector sets, blocks, bikes and trikes, and other sporting goods (Leach 1993a; Cross 1997).

The increasing variety and availability of ready-made children's clothing paralleled the development of the American toy industry. Before 1890 only one factory specialized in children's clothes and mass merchandisers often stocked children's clothing with adult clothing in various departments throughout the store. Clothing, in other words, was organized by type rather than age (Cook 2004). High school girls were especially constrained: they could choose between larger-sized children's clothes or smaller-sized women's clothes (Schrum 2004). George Earnshaw, publisher of the trade journal *Infants' Department,* played a pivotal role in pressing retailers to devote floor space and specially trained salesclerks to children's departments. This strategy first gained traction in infants' departments, which courted the loyalty of mothers by hosting talks about infant care and staging baby contests during the U.S. Children's Bureau's "Baby Week" campaigns in the 1910s. By the late 1920s, department stores and chains like Sears and Montgomery Ward began including children's departments that catered to school-age boys and girls. Most strikingly, in the 1930s children's clothing departments were divided and subdivided into a range of gender and age groupings; toddlers and teenagers had become distinctive merchandising categories. Youthful teen styles now even had a permanent place in the Sears catalog (Cook 2004; Schrum 2004).

Innovative mass merchandisers played a vital role in promoting children's goods and nurturing children's consumer appetites and identities. None did so more effectively than department stores, which began appearing in such big cities as Chicago, New York, Boston, San Francisco, and Philadelphia during the late nineteenth century. With their opulent interiors, tempting glass display cases, and alluring show windows, department stores transformed the urban landscape into a spectacle of abundance. Known as "palaces of consumption," department stores often occupied several city blocks and reached several stories into the sky (Leach 1993b). Chicago's Marshall Field's store was so gargantuan that four Ford plants could have fit inside it (Jacobs 2005). Rural Americans may have never had the opportunity to step inside a department store, but they too could participate in the fantasy world it created by purchasing goods from mail-order catalogs.

While department stores opened their doors to all Americans—regardless of race, class, ethnicity, or age—access to goods, of course, did not equate with the means to purchase them. Those with slimmer pocketbooks had the option of shopping the bargain basement—or of just looking. But department stores prized even those with mere pocket change: the legions of American children who prowled the store's aisles. In merchants' calculations, children's powers of persuasion mattered far more than their personal buying power. As a 1905 industry trade journal observed, "The idea . . . is not to get [children] to buy things, but to allow them to see what they want. Then they'll go home and torment their parents to the limit until that thing is purchased" (Abelson 1989).

Department stores devised numerous strategies to stimulate children's consumer desires and cement the loyalty of children and their mothers to the store. Some created store playgrounds that functioned as both an amusement zone for kids and a babysitting service for mothers, who could leave their children in supervised care for up to two hours. Stocked with toys, doll houses, and play equipment, store playgrounds fueled consumer spending not only by allowing mothers to shop unencumbered but also by stimulating children's wants for certain playthings, readily available for purchase elsewhere in the store. As one mass retailer noted, "Every attention to the child binds the mother to the store." Department stores spared little expense in doing so. They built fantasy play spaces on a massive scale: one playground, decorated to resemble a giant forest, included an indoor lake stocked with fish. Marshall Field's playground, the largest in the nation, attracted 300 to 400 children a day. At Christmastime, department stores mounted their most lavish spectacles, luring children to their toy departments with circus performers, live animal menageries, indoor parades, and live Santas (Leach 1993a, 1993b). Stores also nurtured children's sense of themselves as prized customers by mailing children letters on their birthday, inviting girls to attend dolls' tea parties at the store, and distributing free copies of in-house children's magazines (Leach 1993a; Formanek-Brunell 1993).

Merchandising strategies continued to evolve in the 1930s, when merchandisers increasingly looked to the child, and not just the mother, as the decisive consumer. Retailers lowered counters and mirrors to convenient child heights, placed clothing within easy grasp, and decorated stores in bold primary colors and with storybook characters. They designated floors and departments with trendy names like the "Hi-School Shop" for 10- to 16-year-olds and the "Gradester's Shop" for 7- to 14-year-olds. Some even put swings in their store and awarded boys subscriptions to *American Boy* when they made a purchase of $10 or more (Cook 2004). Retailers trained salesclerks to treat child customers with the same dignity accorded adults. Noting that children took great pride in "hard won coin," Eastman Kodak instructed its salesmen to avoid the common blunder of addressing child customers as "kid" or by any moniker that smacked of condescension. Sensitive to teenagers' yearnings for autonomy, youthful salesclerks even sided with teens over their mothers (Cook 2004; Jacobson 2004).

While mass merchandisers sought to cultivate children's loyalty to a particular site of consumption, national advertisers sought to cultivate their loyalty to particular brands. Initially national advertisers recognized children less as consumers in their own right than as the buyers of tomorrow, whose brand loyalty could be cultivated through repeated exposure to trademarks and brand names (Jacobson 2004).

Businesses encouraged children to incorporate national advertising into their play and their memory banks through a variety of means. In the 1880s and 1890s, they supplied retailers with collectible trade cards that included a decorative picture on the front (sometimes bearing no relation to the advertised product) and the manufacturer's message on the back. Pasting such trade cards into scrapbooks became a favorite childhood pastime in the early twentieth century (Garvey 1996). Admakers also created alphabet primer books lined with advertising messages and jingle books that incorporated brand names into familiar Mother Goose Rhymes. Advertisers hoped that children too young to read would recognize the nursery rhyme verses as "their own form of story" and demand that the ad be read to them (Jacobson 2004).

In the 1910s *St. Nicholas, American Boy,* and other children's magazine publishers began promoting a broader view of children's marketing significance. Children were not simply the consumers of tomorrow but shoppers with distinct desires and the power to influence the spending of family and peers. Children's magazine publishers sought to persuade prospective advertisers that children were impressionable, loyal, and enthusiastic consumers who studied the ads and learned to "buy by name" (see document 1). *American Boy* championed boys in particular as master persuaders who guided family purchases of goods ranging from breakfast cereals and toothpaste to cars, radios, and cameras (see documents 2–3). Advertisers proved receptive to such arguments. During the mid-1910s, *American Boy* began to swell with ads for bicycles, erector sets, rifles, and breakfast cereals. The 1920s marked an even more significant turning point in the field of juvenile advertising. Enthusiastic articles in the advertising trade press now not only recognized juvenile advertising as a worthy long-term investment in building good will among future buyers, but they also touted the short-term benefits of targeting children. Thanks to a rising standard of living and the emerging practice of giving children allowances, advertisers discovered that they could generate immediate returns not only by enlisting children to badger their parents but also by tapping children's own purchasing power (Jacobson 2004).

Why did advertisers and retailers become so enchanted with the idea of courting child consumers in the 1920s and 1930s? In part, changing conceptions of childhood made it easier for mass marketers to conceive of children as consumers. At the turn of the century Americans still revered childhood innocence, but they also increasingly admired children for their spontaneity, spiritedness, and spunk. The celebrated bad boys who starred in such popular novels as Mark Twain's *Tom Sawyer* and *Huckleberry Finn* and Thomas Aldrich's *The Story of a Bad Boy*, made the naughty, cunning prankster into something of a hero. As Kate Douglas Wiggin, the author of *Rebecca of Sunnybrook Farm* (1903), warned, "We must not expect children to be too good. . . . Beware of hothouse virtue." Turn-of-the-century magazine advertisements and trade cards reflected such idealizations of the spunky, precocious child when they depicted children as product endorsers, discerning shoppers, and voracious consumers. Unlike the passive, dutiful child lionized in Victorian culture, the children who inhabited early twentieth-century advertising were far more decisive in asserting their will and their pleasures. Consider, for example, the tyrannical tot in a 1913 ad who shouts, "NO MORE EXCUSES! I Want A Penny *NOW*—FOR WRIGLEY'S SPEARMINT," as he commands his mother to "Buy It by the Box! Then you'll have it when I want it!" Such decidedly unsentimental portraits, intended as satire for adult magazine readers, humorously acknowledged—and even celebrated—the baser passions that animated children's interest in branded consumer goods (Jacobson 2004).

It was one thing to *portray* children as discerning consumers in adult magazines, as many advertisements did in the first two decades of the twentieth century. It was quite another to imagine children themselves as a direct, and potentially lucrative, target of advertising. By the 1920s, a variety of parallel social transformations—the democratization of middle-class family life, the increasing salience of children's peer relationships and peer group activities, and the growing independence and assertiveness of children themselves—had convinced many mass marketers that child consumers were worthy targets of their advertising dollars. Commentators in the advertising trade press believed that they were dealing with a new type of child, one more worldly, self-reliant, and style conscious than the previous generation. They delighted in the progressive spirit of youth, noting that trend-setting youths adopted the new more quickly than adults. Mass marketers regarded boys in particular as consumers who eagerly embraced new technologies and fashions and prodded novelty-resistant parents to keep pace with the times (see documents 2–4). As *American Boy* informed prospective advertisers, "The boy today is usually the first to take up the new things, to demand the improvements that have made the American family's standard of living so high" (Jacobson 2004).

The democratization of middle-class families also sparked advertisers' interest in courting child consumers. During the half century between 1880 and 1930, the urban middle-class family underwent a series of changes that came to the fore most dramatically and perceptibly in the 1920s. The trend toward smaller families of one to three children, most notable by 1910 among urban professionals and business groups, expanded children's autonomy as middle-class families focused more intensely on satisfying the emotions of its members. The new, more permissive childrearing practices advocated by child experts in *Parents' Magazine,* government bulletins, and women's periodicals called for "guidance rather than punishment . . . and a sympathetic understanding of children" (Fass 1977). Children nurtured in such environments, in turn, came to expect greater sympathy from their parents. Sociologists Helen and Robert Lynd reported in *Middletown* (1929), their study of Muncie, Indiana, that high school teenagers ranked "respecting children's opinions" high as a desired quality in parents, especially so in fathers, who typically discharged family discipline. Unlike their rural counterparts, urban middle-class children enjoyed greater latitude for self-expression, more unsupervised time with their peers, and often their own share of the family's spending money (see document 28). Greater family democracy translated into very real changes in both the freedoms and expectations of middle-class children (Jacobson 2004).

Advertising authorities and merchandisers recognized these social transformations—owing partly to their own middle-class backgrounds—and often attributed children's consumer clout to the democratization of the modern family. Advertisers expected that children from more egalitarian families would wield considerable influence over family spending. As one advertising authority explained, "the boy and girl in the home occupy a position of respect" and "adults listen carefully to youngsters' preferences," often denying themselves for their children (Jacobson 2004). Thanks partly to childrearing advice that stressed the importance of personality development and considering children's personal desires, mothers increasingly gave children a greater say in selecting their own clothing (Cook 2004). While mothers once "bought according to their own judgment, regardless of the child's opinion," one advertising expert asserted, they now were "very much influenced by the child's desires in the matter of style." In light of such maternal deference to children's wishes, makers of children's undergarments and shoes, who previously confined their selling talk to mothers, shifted the focus of their appeal to children (Jacobson 2004).

Advertisers also saw children as a more definable and viable market in the 1920s and 1930s because childhood had become more peer-oriented. Not only did schooling keep children in age-segregated settings for longer periods, but a host of new youth agencies emerged to help organize children's leisure. The Boy Scouts, the Girl Scouts, and the Camp Fire Girls— each of which published their own ad-filled magazines in the 1920s—inducted children into the alluring world of consumption as well as the outdoors. Advertisers suggested that their products could be used to earn scouting merit badges or enhance camping experiences (Jacobson 2004). The importance of peer-group socialization was especially pronounced for teenagers, who now spent more time in the company of peers free from adult supervision. The spread of mass commercial recreation and teens' greater access to automobiles was one contributing factor. Another was the dramatic expansion of high school attendance, which climbed from around 10 percent in 1900 to nearly 60 percent by the early 1930s, thanks to compulsory education laws, which raised the age limit for school attendance; child labor laws, which forced more working-class youths into the schools; and the rising corporate demand for high school graduates to staff the economy's expanding white-collar sector. Diminished job opportunities for young people during the Depression swelled enrollments even higher by the decade's end, when attendance reached almost 80 percent (Jacobson 2004; Schrum 2004).

High school attendance brought with it new anxieties about fitting into a peer society that had its own complex social pecking order. Sociologists Robert and Helen Lynd reported in their widely read mid-1920s study of Muncie, Indiana, that adolescent girls who did not wear stylish clothing faced dim dating prospects and certain exclusion from the social elite (see document 29). Boys lacking fashionable attire, access to the family car, or the athletic prowess to win a coveted spot on the high school football or basketball team also found themselves relegated to the social sidelines. Advertisers presented themselves to teens as friendly advisors who could help them navigate the trials of high school peer culture. They simultaneously eased and exacerbated teen anxieties by stressing the importance of impression management and offering purchasable solutions to problems of personal appearance and popularity (Jacobson 2004).

CULTIVATING BRAND LOYALTY AND BRAND CONSCIOUSNESS

Advertisers and children's magazine publishers developed numerous games, contests, and instructional aids to nurture children's brand consciousness and brand loyalty. As early as 1904, juvenile magazine publishers worked to gain advertisers' confidence by training children to pay close attention to advertising (Garvey 1996). *Child Life*, for example, staged a "detective contest" in the early 1930s, asking its grade school readers, with the help of their parents, to identify advertised goods shown on a page, write a letter explaining which they liked best, and list the products used by the family. The magazine then announced the results in the advertising trade press as proof that advertising had reached its mark. Similarly, *American Girl* suggested that its Girl Scout readers try a new game at their next troop meeting to determine who could remember the most brand names from a list of thirty-odd household goods (Jacobson 2004).

Advertisers also sought to mold lifelong consumer habits through children's play. Manufacturers offered mothers and children miniature replicas of branded goods—all supplied free upon request. Miniature stoves, dishes, vacuums, and boxes of cereals and soap cakes reportedly enjoyed a "tremendous vogue" among children who used them for dollhouses. The most elaborate miniature was the Junior Store, which came equipped with play money, counter space for nationally advertised goods, and 32 empty packages furnished by the cooperating sponsors. Not only did juvenile play store-owners gain hands-on training in counting change and purchasing products by name, but every month they also received an issue of the *Junior Storekeeper*, which taught apprentice shoppers how to buy on a budget and reminded them to accept no substitutes for their favorite brand (Jacobson 2004).

Advertisers also found ways to get their messages into the public schools. Doing so enabled advertisers to reach much larger groups of children, including millions of immigrant and working-class children who typically did not read juvenile magazines. Advertisers offered teachers free booklets, exhibits, and charts that promised to enliven run-of-the-mill lessons. Commercially sponsored toothbrush drills and Lifebuoy wash-up charts, for example, assisted lessons in health and hygiene. A chart tracing Shredded Wheat's development from harvest through various stages of production and distribution became the foundation of geography lessons. Advertisers also developed enrichment materials to get their messages from the classroom into the home. In the late 1920s, Cream of Wheat supplied teachers in some 70,000 schools across the country with free graded contest devices, prizes, and breakfast charts to encourage regular consumption of hot breakfast cereals. Teachers asked mothers to return a card affirming that their children had eaten a hot breakfast cereal three times a week. Failure to cooperate could prove embarrassing, as some teachers asked for a show of hands each morning to determine how many children had eaten a hot, cooked cereal. Some critics protested the self-interested advertising enrichment materials used in public schools, but teachers on the whole welcomed them because restrictive school budgets limited the purchase of visual aids (Jacobson 2004) (see documents 18–19).

Advertisers' efforts to inculcate brand consciousness even extended to children who had not yet reached school age. To lure such young prospects, advertising agencies hired well-known authors and illustrators of children's books to create advertising story booklets that wove brand names into fairy tales and heroic adventure stories—all in rhymed verse (Jacobson 2004).

DISCERNING CHILDREN'S DESIRES: EARLY MARKET RESEARCH

Advertisers did not simply envision children as passive consumers whose wants could be molded at will. They also attempted to discern their tastes and aspirations. Market research on children's consumer practices and consumer preferences was still rudimentary in the 1920s and 1930s. Market research interviews with children did not appear until the late 1930s, and even then were still uncommon. Instead advertising agencies often relied on crude measures, such as counting coupon returns, to assess consumer receptivity. More often, they sought children's input by sponsoring prize contests for the best testimonial letter or sample advertisement. Daisy Air Rifles, for example, wanted to learn "Why the Daisy is the Favorite Boys' Gun" and offered prizes to boys whose ideas of interesting targets or new shooting games were worthy of passing on to other boys (Jacobson 2004). Gimbel's department store gathered information on teen fashion trends though an essay contest, "What are the Fashion Fads in your school?" (Schrum 2004).

In the absence of more scientific market research data, mass marketers relied on their own theories of kid psychology to craft ads that would appeal to age- and gender-based interests and children's fantasies of empowerment and adventure. The most successful advertisers, articles in the advertising trade press stressed, shunned copy that smacked of condescension and learned to speak to children in their own language (see documents 7–9, 27). Some mass marketers drew upon emerging psychological research that mapped children's changing developmental needs and interests as they progressed from early childhood through adolescence—knowledge that by the late twentieth century had evolved into a marketing science (see document 17).

Early twentieth-century mass marketers also took their cues from children's popular culture in developing new merchandise. During the Depression, licensed character toys based on children's celebrities—Mickey Mouse, Charlie McCarthy, Shirley Temple, and Superman—revitalized toy sales at a time when many toy companies were struggling for survival (Cross 1997). Shirley Temple, whose own stage dresses and retail line of clothing had a toddler look, helped to make the toddler-size style range for girls a viable new merchandising category (Cook 2004). In the mid-1920s, clothing manufacturers observed that teenage girls liked to personalize jackets, skirts, hats, and other belongings by painting slogans or their names on them. They then marketed the trend back to teens by promoting umbrellas that came either predesigned or, as the ad indicated, "plain if you prefer to paint them yourself" (Schrum 2004).

Advertisers were not always successful, however, in sizing up their teenage audience. In the 1930s, teenage movie stars like Deanna Durbin and Judy Garland had their own teen clothing lines, but by ninth grade most teenage girls wanted to emulate adult movie stars like Joan Crawford and Greta Garbo and fawned over Clark Gable and Douglas Fairbanks rather than Mickey Rooney, who played teenage Andy Hardy on screen. The Durbin and Garland clothing lines, in fact, may have appealed more to parents than teens. Among Deanna Durbin's most enthusiastic fans were parents who wished their own daughters were still as sweetly innocent as the wholesome teen Durbin played on screen (Schrum 2004).

Early twentieth-century juvenile marketers placed greater emphasis on trickle-down theories of consumption than rigorous market research in their quest for child consumers. Much as today's mass marketers rely on trendsetting teens to popularize new brands and revitalize old ones, advertisers in the 1920s and 1930s hoped to build brand loyalty by winning over the key boy. If advertisers could sell the "gang leader," as they sometimes called him, one advertising authority reasoned, "the trick is turned, for he is pretty sure to sell the members of his gang. This may mean five or more sales instead of [just] one" (Lambert 1920) (see document 7). Courting middle-class white boys was especially important because advertisers assumed that such boys could sway the consumer loyalties not just of family members but of other children as well, especially girls and less affluent boys. Kodak, for example, ran special advertising contests in *Boys' Life*, the staunchly middle-class scouting magazine, on the grounds that Boy Scouts were "the best and liveliest boys in town" and as such sure to set enviable examples for others. Advertisers also concentrated primarily on boys and boy culture because they thought girls were far more flexible and boys far more rigid in their gender identification (see document 10). As advertising authority Evalyn Grumbine observed, "Girls admire and enjoy boys' books and many boys' activities. Boys, however, do not reciprocate in their feelings about girls' activities" (Jacobson 2004).

PARENTS AND CHILDREN WITHIN THE CONSUMER HOUSEHOLD

Discerning children's wants and needs was not the only marketing challenge advertisers faced. As one advertising authority put it, marketers also had to master the art of winning "juvenile good will" without losing "the good will of the parent" (Larrabee 1938) (see documents 10–11). The impact of mass marketing on relations of power and authority within the family has been a matter of historical debate. Some historians have argued that age-segmented marketing undermined the family's authority and pitted children against parents (Leach 1993; Ewen 1976; Schor 2004). Most would agree that advertisers' willingness to capitalize on children's growing independence and assertiveness stretched and tested the egalitarian boundaries of the emerging companionate family. But, as other historians have argued, the notion that mass marketers sought to erode parental authority and pit children against adults oversimplifies both the motives of mass marketers and the impact of mass marketing. At least in the first three decades of the twentieth century, mass marketers remained mindful of the tenuous balance between parents' concerns and children's desires, even as they tested the limits of family democracy. Romancing the companionate family often worked more to their advantage than dividing family allegiances

(Jacobson 2004). As children's advertising shifted from print media to radio in the 1930s, however, advertisers often gained the upper hand in guiding negotiations over consumption between parents and children.

Early twentieth-century advertisers struggled to address parents' concerns even as they appealed to children's desires. Overt parental appeals that linked children's consumption to nutrition and achievement often appeared in children's advertising, in sharp contrast to the utopian emphasis on pleasure and anti-authoritarian values that predominated in late twentieth-century children's advertising (Kline 1993; Seiter 1993) (see document 10). Early twentieth-century advertisers often courted children as seekers of parental companionship rather than as rebels against parental authority. A 1932 electric trains catalog, for instance, urged boys to "Take Your Dad into Partnership [and] Make Him Your Pal" by getting his help in building a fully accessorized Lionel railroad system. Clearly, however, expensive train sets required that boys seek a financial partnership with their father in addition to father-son fellowship in play (Jacobson 2004).

In many respects, juvenile advertising in the 1920s and 1930s was remarkably bold in its efforts to empower children within a consumer democracy. Advertisements in children's magazines literally instructed children how to lobby their parents for new purchases, supplying them with sales ammunition that appealed to pressing parental concerns. An advertisement for Structo engineering toys, for example, put a boy's manhood and future success on the line when it instructed boys to "Tell Dad you want STRUCTO because it will teach you to think for yourself, to create ideas of your own, to make you think as *men* think" (Jacobson 2004).

While advertising trade guidelines in the late twentieth century advised advertisers not to urge children "to ask parents or others to buy products," early twentieth-century advertisers exhibited no such compunctions. With boldfaced headlines like "Please—Father—Please" screaming from the top of the page, advertisements routinely sanctioned begging and the old child-hood standby—buttering up mom and dad. Advertisers would not have encouraged such behavior had children's requests not already become an accepted part of middle-class family dynamics. Even so, advertisers' detailed instructions to children on how to make their pitch to mom and dad suggest that advertisers may have needed to stretch the boundaries of the democratic family further than was customary. Carefully scripted sales pitches gave children permission and encouragement to pester their parents and made parental resistance harder to sustain (Jacobson 2004).

Advertisers also went to great lengths to enlist children's pester power when they began airing commercials on children's radio programs in the early 1930s. Sponsors hit upon a winning formula with their promise of free premiums and club memberships in exchange for proofs of purchase. Millions of children joined radio-inspired clubs like Little Orphan Annie's Secret Circle or Post Toasties' Junior Detective Corps for the honor and perquisites of membership: secret passwords and decoding devices that admitted children into the inner circle of their favorite radio heroes and heroines. Sponsors linked premiums and decoding devices to plot lines, making them essential for a fully interactive radio experience. For example, fans of *Jolly Bill and Jane* who had consumed enough Cream of Wheat to earn the club's map of the moon could track the wanderings of Uncle Bill and his companions as they trekked across the Lunera to the evil Bolta's Palace. Commercials tantalized children with the prospect of earning additional premiums and higher ranks within the club if they got their mothers to buy more of the sponsor's product and submitted more box tops (see documents 9–11). Like advertising in the public schools, children's radio clubs helped to make children's consumer culture a national culture that reached children of all races and classes. Broadening consumer culture's reach, however, did not mean that all children participated as equals, as many poor and working-class children often could not scrounge up enough box tops to join radio clubs (Jacobson 2004).

Though popular with many children, radio clubs came under fire from child experts, mother's groups, and PTAs. Critics objected to advertisers' manipulation of children's gullibility with their misleading promises of absolutely free prizes and incessant plugging of their product. Critics particularly resented radio advertising for teaching children "how to argue with their parents" over family purchases (see documents 10–11). Although many parents caved into children's demands, children often became disillusioned when long-awaited, chintzy premiums failed to live up to advertisers' hype (Jacobson 2004).

Aside from the indignant protests against children's radio advertising, early twentieth-century children's advertising on the whole failed to arouse substantial *organized* opposition. Despite its shameless encouragement of begging, despite its invasion of the schoolroom, and despite its efforts to mold even the tiniest tots into brand loyal consumers, children's advertising was often embraced and accepted. Why did so few challenge this dramatic expansion of corporate power? Part of the answer is that advertisers successfully aligned themselves with the very institutions of early twentieth-century childhood that had traditionally protected children's innocence and sequestered childhood as a wholesome, play-centered stage of life. Advertisers secured the cooperation of the public schools in promoting advertising-based instruction in health and hygiene. They supported the Boy Scouts, Girl Scouts, and Camp Fire Girls by allotting much-needed advertising dollars to their magazines and promoting branded goods as adjuncts to scouting activities.

Most critically, advertisers wore down parental resistance by celebrating the companionate family and associating their products with children's developmental needs. The changing responses to advertising on children's radio offer perhaps the best testament to the power of such advertising claims. In the mid-1930s, some child experts came to the defense of radio clubs, arguing that they fulfilled children's developmental needs for "substitute experiences and adventure." Children's desires for chintzy premiums were best understood, child experts contended, as a passing fancy or developmental phase that would quickly wane when children discovered that advertisers could not live up to their hype. By 1945, the Child Study Association recommended that parents learn to cope with "the annoyance" of children's desires for advertising premiums on the grounds that "such things stir youngsters to activity and participation, both of which are wholesome and desirable" (Jacobson 2004).

CHILDREN'S MARKETING IN THE SECOND HALF OF THE TWENTIETH CENTURY

During the postwar years, the spread of affluence and permissive child-rearing gave the baby boom generation greater economic power, while the advent of television gave advertisers new means to reach children en masse. Despite some initial doubts about television's viability as an advertising medium, advertisers enthusiastically took to the airwaves once they became convinced that popular programs like *The Howdy Doody Show* and *The Mickey Mouse Club* could deliver a captivated audience (Downing 2004). Television advertisers built on the practice, first perfected on radio, of weaving product endorsements into children's entertainment programming. Just as possessing a secret decoding device allowed children to become active participants in the unfolding drama of their favorite radio serial, *Winky Dink and You*, a popular 1950s animated TV show, made enjoyment of the show dependent upon those advertised products. With the purchase of a special kit of rub-off crayons and a plastic "magic window" that covered the TV, children could draw in scenery or features on the cartoon characters' faces to help complete story lines (Spigel 1998). Radio and magazines remained the favored venue in the mid-1950s for reaching the typical teenager, who on average spent $555 annually on such goods as records, cosmetics, and training bras (Mintz and Kellogg 1988). Film studios in the 1950s, hit hard by competition from television's growing popularity, also tapped the buying power of teens by producing low-budget teenpics that featured aberrant juvenile delinquents, wholesome California youths, and horrifying sci-fi creatures (May 2002; Doherty 2002).

Confidence in children's purchasing power grew as mass marketers developed more scientific techniques for sizing up their audience. Eugene Gilbert, the self-anointed "George Gallup of Teenagers," recognized that effective marketing hinged on improving marketers' knowledge of teen interests and desires. In the mid-1940s he built a successful marketing research firm on his promise to "translate" teenage desires to businesses like Quaker Oats, Maybelline, and Studebaker. He did so by paying high school students to gather market research data on teenagers throughout the country. Similarly, *Seventeen* magazine regularly conducted market research on its teenage girl readers to learn more about their tastes and buying habits and convince clothing manufacturers, cosmetics firms, and department stores that their messages would reach a style- and beauty-conscious audience. *Seventeen*'s promotional literature presented Teena, the prototypical teenage girl, as a serious shopper, ready and willing to spend her allowance and babysitting money on the fashionable goods featured in her favorite magazine (see document 5). Teena's value as a consumer extended beyond the goods she purchased to meet her own wants. Much as *American Boy* had presented the archetypal adolescent boy as a master persuader in the 1910s and 1920s (see documents 2–3), *Seventeen* presented Teena as a consumer with considerable leverage over family spending decisions (see document 6). By 1948, just four years after the magazine's inaugural issue hit the stands, *Seventeen* could boast that advertisers had invested nearly $12 million to date in getting their products before *Seventeen* readers (see document 5) (Schrum 1998; Palladino 1996; Devlin 2005).

The postwar years also saw greater age segmentation within the children's market. In the 1940s and 1950s, retailers became savvier in appealing to preteen and teenage girls. Department stores recruited popular high school girls to serve on fashion boards and model merchandise in store fashion shows. Storeowners regarded these popular teens as translators of youth culture and expected that other teens would follow their fashion lead. Retailers also took care to make the new teen departments visually and spatially distinctive from younger children's areas. Locating teen departments far from baby departments and next to the college shop appealed to teenage girls who studiously avoided appearing too young and often took their fashion cues from college-aged women (Cook 2004).

CHILDREN'S MARKETING AND THE CONQUEST OF COOL IN THE LATE TWENTIETH CENTURY

In the last two decades of the twentieth century, mass marketing to children became not only more pervasive but also more inventive—and manipulative—in discerning and molding children's desires. Companies expend considerable sums gathering data about children's consumption habits and preferences by testing commercials, conducting focus groups, and surveying kids at the mall. Market researchers have even adopted the ethnographic techniques of anthropologists, gleaning crucial information on kid culture by observing children and teenagers in their own natural habitats. MTV dispatches market researchers to visit fans in their own bedrooms to gain insights into how teenagers think and live. If companies hope to win teens' brand loyalty, market researchers reason, then they will also have to learn to speak teens' language (*Merchants of Cool* 2001). Some market researchers have even hosted slumber parties to learn what makes 9- to 12-year-old girls spend (Schor 2004). In the 1990s, the Internet also became an important market research tool. Web sites required children to provide critical personal data (including name, sex, age, email address, favorite television show and musical group) before they entered certain Web sites. In exchange, Web sites offered children prizes, even cash, with the promise of more if children filled out other surveys.

Market researchers work especially hard to identify and study the so-called alpha pups—the trendsetters or early adopters who influence what their peers do and buy (Schor 2004). (Early twentieth-century advertisers used the term "gang leaders.") These "cool" kids are hardly representative —perhaps only 20 percent of teens would qualify—but marketers value their opinions because cool sells. Ironically, hunting for cool launches teen market researchers on a never ending quest, because cool itself is a moving target: as soon as marketers mainstream cool for popular consumption, cool moves onto something else (*Merchants of Cool* 2001).

Tough as it is to pin down, cool also helps mass marketers gain the affections of younger children, who often aspire to be more like their teen brothers and sisters. The Limited Too, a clothing store for 6- to 14-year-old girls, achieved enormous success with tweens by carrying modestly cut minis and hip huggers styled after teen fashions (Schrum 2004). To stay on the cutting edge of cool, however, marketers have also been willing to risk offending adult tastes and sensibilities. Abercrombie and Fitch did so when it marketed thong underwear to 10-year-olds and then upped the ante by embellishing the underwear with sexually suggestive slogans like "Wink Wink" and "Eye Candy" (Linn 2004). The cool kids who populate food and toy ads aimed at grade schoolers also promote edgy styles and antiadult sensibilities. These kids invariably outwit teachers and parents and often adopt the fashions and mannerisms associated with hip-hop and African American culture (Schor 2004).

Mass marketers have also perfected buzz marketing, a practice by which they seed new products with trendsetters to fuel consumer demand. Not only do companies distribute free shoes and clothes to rappers, actors, athletes, and other cool people, but they also infiltrate chat rooms with their own paid representatives to generate hype for their brand. The marketing firm Girls Intelligence Agency (GIA), founded in 2002, employs a network of some 40,000 girls between 8 and 18 to create buzz for products—either by chatting the products up with friends online or by doling out samples at slumber parties and college bashes. GIA also asks its girl agents to provide feedback on what brands, bands, and fashions their friends think are hot. As critics have noted, such marketing practices corrupt the very notion of friendship by asking girl agents to gather market research data on their friends and sell them goods, often without their knowledge or consent (Schor 2004).

Advertising became an even more pervasive force in public schools during the late twentieth- and early twenty-first centuries. For advertisers, the appeal is easy to grasp: public schools provide a captive audience who cannot zoom past commercials with a flick of the remote or a click of the mouse. For public schools, opening the doors to more advertising has become a matter of necessity. Thanks to the anti-tax movement of the past quarter century and voters' reluctance to approve school bond measures, cash-strapped public schools have increasingly relied upon advertising revenues to make ends meet. An exclusive contract with a soda company can net millions for school districts, while a restricted arrangement with a computer company can yield a new supply of computers. In return for their largesse, corporations gain an advertising venue that reaches masses of children far more cheaply than television (Manning 1999).

Like their early twentieth-century predecessors, contemporary school advertisers produce posters, booklets, magazines, videos, and other sponsored educational materials that claim to be strictly educational but, as *Consumer Reports* has observed, such materials often relay "biased or incomplete information" that "favors the company or its economic agenda" (Manning 1999). Exxon's energy curriculum, for example, downplays the environmental costs of fossil fuels and characterizes alternative energy as expensive and unfeasible (Schor 2004). That self-serving corporate messages bear the imprimatur of the public schools makes them all the more galling. Consider, for example, Kellogg's breakfast curriculum, which urges students to select cereals with lower fat content but fails to discuss the sugar and salt content in its cereals or the importance of fiber. No curricular innovation has sparked more controversy than the Channel One news service shown daily in a quarter of the middle and secondary schools across the nation. First aired in 1989, Channel One exposes children to 2 minutes of commercials and 10 minutes of news. Though purportedly serious news, Channel One devotes more time to sports, weather, and celebrity profiles than current events. Instead of enhancing the curriculum, critics charge, Channel One dumbs it down and robs children of valuable instruction time (Schor 2004; Linn 2004). In 2001, a coalition of progressives and conservatives, which included such seemingly strange political bedfellows as Ralph Nader and Phyllis Schlafly, named banning Channel One "a high-priority educational reform." In a letter urging companies to stop advertising on Channel One, the coalition condemned the in-school marketing program for "misus[ing] the compulsory attendance laws to force children to watch ads," exacerbating the epidemic of childhood obesity by advertising high-calorie junk food, and promoting violent entertainment and materialistic values (Commercial Alert 2001).

Though they often see themselves as innovators, mass marketers in the late twentieth century rely on many marketing strategies developed in the early twentieth century. The practice, so common among fast food chains, of giving away movie-inspired toys to boost hamburger sales and publicize new movie releases harkens back to the Great Depression, when toymakers revitalized sagging sales by creating licensed character toys that revolved around children's celebrity idols such as Mickey Mouse, Shirley Temple, Buck Rogers, and Superman (Cross 1997). Like their predecessors, contemporary marketers also place great faith in what they call the nag factor. If advertising stimulates enough interest, the theory goes, children will pester their parents until mom or dad yields. But where earlier advertisers were more cautious about upsetting the balance of power within the family —winning parental goodwill, after all, was the goal of winning juvenile goodwill—late twentieth-century advertisers have pushed the limits of those boundaries more aggressively. Food advertisers, for example, used to follow what industry insiders called the gatekeeper model: ads aimed at children still needed to convince moms that the product had nutritional value (Schor 2004). That model has increasingly given way to a children's advertising culture in which hedonism, antiauthoritarianism, and kid power reign supreme. Today's kids, as Ellen Seiter puts it, are "sold separately," with appeals designed more to amp the nag factor than to placate the parental gatekeeper (Seiter 1993). In fact, marketers of popular products like Toxic High stickers and the Garbage Pail Kids have learned that children's enjoyment of candy and toys that parents consider inappropriate can dramatically increase their sales potential (Spigel 1998; James 1998).

To acknowledge contemporary marketers' greater investment in creating a distinct children's fantasy culture, however, is not to romanticize the early twentieth century as some utopian moment in children's consumer culture. The Pokemon fad of the 1990s, in fact, can be viewed as a direct descendant of the children's radio clubs of the 1930s. Just as the promise of special premiums from Little Orphan Annie and Jack Armstrong got children to pester their parents for more Cocomalt or Wheaties, the Pokemon craze led children to pester their parents for the precious trading cards that would help them capture all 150 Pokemons, the mythical pocket monster creatures featured in the popular animated kids' television show and video game. While in each case clever market tie-ins with radio idols or popular television shows provided the building blocks for the craze, the appeal of joining a distinct kids' world, impervious to adult comprehension, fueled the fad. Radio club members decoded secret messages to which only their peers were privy, while Pokemon traders became experts in a whole separate world of Pokemon lore, memorizing the names, special fighting skills, and point values of each Pokemon (Jacobson 2004).

Why has the balance of power between advertisers, children, and parents changed so dramatically in the last two decades? One reason might be that children today have more discretionary income than their early twentieth-century counterparts. Advertisers don't need to defer to parental gatekeepers when they can tap children's funds directly. In 1999, the typical weekly allowance for 13- to 15-year-olds, according to the Rand Youth Poll, ranged from $30.50 to $34.25, with girls receiving on average $3.00–$4.00 more than boys. Supplementary earnings typically doubled the weekly yield for teenage boys and girls. Though younger children, aged 10–12, only received a modest $5.00–$6.00 boost to their weekly income from earnings, allowances on average swelled their weekly take by an additional $21.00–$22.00 (Kristof 2000). According to one 1996 estimate, allowances accounted for more than a third of the $89 billion in spending money at children's disposal (Lowry 1996).

Changes within modern families have also helped to give advertisers the upper hand. Parents have more difficulty monitoring and enforcing restrictions on children's media consumption, especially during after-school hours, because in most American families today both parents work outside the home. Parents, though, are hardly blameless. Overworked parents who worry about not spending more time with their children sometimes ease that guilt by give into children's consumer demands (Cross 1997). Parents who succumb to children's nagging convince themselves that doing so is a rational choice. Buying what children want, they reason, makes more sense than wasting money on food they won't eat or toys they won't play with (Schor 2004). Parents have also been slow to adopt new technologies that restrict children's access to unsuitable media. One study found that only one-third of parents with V-chip televisions actually uses the V-chip. Difficulty setting up the device has been a stumbling block for many nonusers; others are simply unaware that the technology exists (Jordan and Woodward 2003). Nevertheless, one might wonder if many Americans parents even attempt to monitor children's media consumption when two-thirds of 8- to 18-year-olds and nearly one-third of 2- to 7-year-olds have personal TVs in their bedrooms (Linn 2004).

Still, even the most vigilant parents face an uphill battle if they want to limit children's exposure to commercial messages. Public interest groups have called for greater regulation of advertising to children on the airwaves and in the public schools, arguing that children are more vulnerable than adults to manipulation by advertisers. The Children's Advertising Review Unit of the Better Business Bureau established voluntary guidelines prohibiting host selling and celebrity endorsers on children's television programs. It also banned advertising that encouraged children to nag their parents for products or suggested that owning such a product was essential for peer acceptance (Schor 2004). By and large, such regulations have done little to level the playing field. Today's advertisers may pat themselves on the back for having more scruples than their early-twentieth-century predecessors, who *actively* encouraged begging. But the reality is that contemporary advertisers don't need to be as heavy handed because child begging has become so deeply entrenched in modern families (Kline 1993). Children's television viewing habits also undermine efforts to regulate their exposure to advertising, since more than half of the television programs children watch are adult shows. Further, network compliance with these voluntary guidelines has diminished because their more loosely regulated Internet and cable competitors have little incentive to comply, thus fueling a race to the bottom (Schor 2004).

Deference to concerns about infringements on free markets and commercial free speech has also weakened government regulations. During the 1980s, when deregulation was in full swing, the federal government lifted a 1974 Federal Trade Commission (FTC) ban on host selling—a practice that obliterates the line between commercials and programs. The result was predictable: advertisers flooded the airwaves again with toy-based television programs like *The Smurfs, Strawberry Shortcake*, and *He-Man*—a marketing ploy the toy industry cynically defended by asserting that children needed pre-formulated story lines to help them play (Cross 1997). In the past decade, however, federal, state, and local governments have taken modest steps to restrain mass marketers. Parents and consumer activists scored a victory against unscrupulous online marketer researchers when the FTC made it illegal under the Children's Online Privacy Act (1998) to solicit personal information online from preteens without parental permission. A few state legislatures have banned Channel One in response to protests from the National PTA, the National Education Association, and the American Federation of Teachers (Schor 2004). Some school districts, mindful of the growing problem of childhood obesity, have banned sales of soft drinks and candy on campus, but lobbyists for soft drink companies and sugar producers have successfully defeated bills that would permit the federal government to prohibit sales of such products in public schools. Even national associations of school boards and school principals, which might be expected to place a greater premium on children's health, have also opposed such legislation on grounds that it would deprive schools of a crucial revenue stream (Linn 2004).

In the absence of stronger public restraints on the advertising industry, child consumers have crafted their own forms of resistance. For many baby boomer fans of *Mad* magazine, a publication beloved for its parodies of advertisements, outsmarting the advertisers was not nearly as satisfying as mocking their foolish pretensions. The *Whatsit*, a four-page children's newspaper that appeared in a major working-class tabloid during the Great Depression, provided a similar function for kids who lacked the purchasing power to gain membership in that era's wildly popular radio clubs. Not only did the kids' paper mock the excesses of radio advertising, but it also offered children a more tantalizing choice of rewards for submitting jokes and solutions to puzzles. Children who had wised up to advertisers' cheap ploys typically chose the dollar bill over a premium that might disappoint (Jacobson 2004). The *Defender Junior*, a children's column in the African American newspaper the *Chicago Defender*, took a similar tack in the 1930s by offering black children free buttons and free membership in its own Bud Billiken club (Hinderer 2007). In a decade when consumer culture had become an increasingly larger part of the public culture of childhood, the simple, non-monetary requirements for membership in the clubs sponsored by the *Whatsit* and the *Defender Junior* provided comforting reassurance that consumption was not the only marker of belonging. Rejected child consumers made their own stand against consumer culture by rejecting its materialistic requirements for belonging.

More recently, children have turned consumerism into a language of protest, marketing their own anti-corporate sentiments through self-styled fashions and Internet zines. Even some graffiti artists assume the role of an anti-consumer rebel by painting over billboards and transforming them into sites for personal expression. Though less overtly defiant, other children have embraced their responsibility as critical consumers by reading *Zillions*, a magazine published by Consumer Reports that teaches children the basics of product testing and comparative shopping.

Though jaded teens may be more attuned to advertising's manipulations, they are hardly immune to its cultural power to fuel trends and reinforce various forms of social inequality. Advertising's more subtle and recurring messages may, in fact, be its most powerful ones. Consumption, we are repeatedly told, is the essence of the good life and the most satisfying means of fashioning the self (Schudson 1984). Throughout the twentieth century such lessons have been especially painful for poor and working-class children, both white and minority, who not only lacked the means to participate fully in a consumer-capitalist economy but also rarely saw their own lived experiences reflected in the mass media. Though mass marketers no longer ignore minority youth, as they did in the early twentieth century, many value poor and working-class minority youth less as a market than as commodified symbols of cool. A sad irony of modern capitalism is that economic disadvantage often works to increase children's exposure to mass marketing rather than insulate them from it. Public schools in the poorest districts with the least resources, after all, are the most likely to subscribe to Channel One and the most likely to rely on corporate-sponsored educational materials (Schor 2004; Linn 2004). The proliferation of mass-mediated images of abundance in children's daily lives makes it impossible for such children to escape reminders of the limits of their own consumer horizons.

WORKS CITED

Abelson, Elaine. 1989. *When Ladies Go A-Thieving: Middle-Class Shoplifters in the Victorian Department Store*. New York: Oxford University Press.

"Commercial Alert, Coalition Launches Campaign Against Primedia's Channel One," press release, June 11, 2001, www.commercialalert.org/issues/educa tion/channel-one.

Cook, Daniel Thomas. 2004. *The Commodification of Childhood: The Children's Wear Industry and the Rise of the Child-Consumer, 1917–1962*. Durham, NC: Duke University Press.

Cross, Gary. 1997. *Kids' Stuff: Toys and the Changing World of American Childhood.* Cambridge, MA: Harvard University Press.

Devlin, Rachel. 2005. *Relative Intimacy: Fathers, Adolescent Daughters, and Postwar American Culture.* Chapel Hill: University of North Carolina Press.

Doherty, Thomas. 2002. *Teenagers and Teenpics: The Juvenilization of American Movies in the 1950s.* Philadelphia: Temple University Press.

Downing, Spencer. 2004. "What TV Taught: Children's Television and Consumer Culture from Howdy Doody to Sesame Street." Ph.D. diss., University of North Carolina, Chapel Hill.

Ewen, Stuart. 1976. *Captains of Consciousness: Advertising and the Social Roots of the Consumer Culture.* New York: McGraw-Hill Book Company.

Fass, Paula. 1977. *The Damned and the Beautiful: American Youth in the 1920s.* New York: Oxford University Press.

Formanek-Brunell, Miriam. 1993. *Made to Play House: Dolls and the Commercialization of American Girlhood, 1830–1930.* New Haven: Yale University Press.

Garvey, Ellen. 1996. *The Adman in the Parlor: Magazines and the Gendering of Consumer Culture, 1880s to 1910s.* New York: Oxford University Press.

Giroux, Henry A. 2000. *Stealing Innocence: Corporate Culture's War on Children.* New York: Palgrave.

Hinderer, Moira. 2007. "Making Africa-American Childhood: Chicago, 1917–1945." Ph.D. diss., University of Chicago.

Jacobs, Meg. 2005. *Pocketbook Politics: Economic Citizenship in Twentieth-Century America.* Princeton: Princeton University Press.

Jacobson, Lisa. 2004. *Raising Consumers: Children and the American Mass Market in the Early Twentieth Century.* New York: Columbia University Press.

James, Allison. 1998. "Confections, Concoctions, and Conceptions." In *The Children's Culture Reader,* ed. Henry Jenkins, 394–405. New York: New York University Press.

Jordan, Amy, and Emily Woodward. 2003. *Parents' Use of the V-Chip to Supervise Children's Television Use.* Philadelphia: Annenberg Public Policy Center, University of Pennsylvania.

Kline, Stephen. 1993. *Out of the Garden: Toys, TV, and Children's Culture in the Age of Marketing.* London: Verso.

Kristof, Kathy. 2000. "Do Your Kids Know That Money Doesn't Grow on Christmas Trees?" *Los Angeles Times* (December 3): C3.

Lambert, S. C. 1920. "Building a Business on Children's Good Will: A Firm That Makes Express Wagons Finds the Right Appeal in Selling Its Products to Boys." *Printers' Ink* 112 (July 29): 89–91.

Larrabee, C. B. 1938. "Forward." In *Reaching Juvenile Markets: How to Advertise, Sell, and Merchandise through Boys and Girls,* E. Evalyn Grumbine. New York: McGraw-Hill.

Leach, William. 1993a. "Child-World in the Promised Land." In *The Mythmaking Frame of Mind: Social Imagination & American Culture,* ed. James Gilbert, et al., 209–38. Belmont, CA: Wadsworth Publishing Company.

———. 1993b. *Land of Desire: Merchants, Power, and the Rise of a New American Culture.* New York: Pantheon Books.

Linn, Susan. 2004. *Consuming Kids: The Hostile Takeover of Childhood.* New York: The New Press.

Lowry, Katharine. 1996. "The Great Allowance Debate: Experts and Parents Don't Always Agree." *USSA Magazine* (August/September): 12.

Lynd, Robert, and Helen Lynd. 1929. *Middletown: A Study in American Culture.* New York: Harcourt, Brace, and World.

Manning, Steve. 1999. "Students for Sale." *The Nation* 269 (September 27): 11–18.

May, Kirse Granat. 2002. *Golden State, Golden Youth: The California Image in Popular Culture, 1955–1966.* Chapel Hill: University of North Carolina Press.

McNeal, James U. 1992. *Kids as Customers: A Handbook of Marketing to Children.* New York: Lexington Books.

Merchants of Cool. 2001. PBS Frontline Documentary. Directed by Barak Goldman.

Mintz, Steven, and Susan Kellogg. 1988. *Domestic Revolutions: A Social History of American Family Life.* New York: Free Press.

Palladino, Grace. 1996. *Teenagers: An American History.* New York: Basic Books.

Schor, Juliet. 2004. *Born to Buy: The Commercialized Child and the New Consumer Culture.* New York: Scribner.

Schudson, Michael. 1984. *Advertising, The Uneasy Persuasion: Its Dubious Impact on American Society.* New York: Basic Books.

Schrum, Kelly. 1998. "'Teena Means Business': Teenage Girls' Culture and *Seventeen Magazine*, 1944–1950." In *Delinquents and Debutantes: Twentieth-Century American Girls' Cultures,* ed. Sherrie Inness. New York: New York University Press.

———. 2004. *Some Wore Bobby Sox: The Emergence of Teenage Girls' Culture, 1920–1940.* New York: Palgrave Macmillan.

Seiter, Ellen. 1993. *Sold Separately: Parents & Children in Consumer Culture.* New Brunswick, NJ: Rutgers University Press.

Spigel, Lynn. 1998. "Seducing the Innocent: Childhood and Television in Postwar America." In *The Children's Culture Reader,* ed. Henry Jenkins, 110–35. New York and London: New York University.

Steinberg, Shirley R., and Joe L. Kincheloe, eds. 1998. *Kinderculture: The Corporate Construction of Childhood.* Boulder, CO: Westview Press.

Strasser, Susan. 1989. *Satisfaction Guaranteed: The Making of the American Mass Market.* New York: Pantheon Books.

2 Children's Media Consumption and Struggles for Cultural Authority in the Nineteenth and Twentieth Centuries

Amanda Bruce

Americans who grew up in the age of cable television, DVD players, and video games are probably familiar with adult attempts to regulate children's media usage. In the 1990s and early 2000s, numerous articles and television news segments decried the negative effects on children of television and video games like *Grand Theft Auto*. Politicians responded to media activists and parental concerns by passing the Children's Television Act in 1990, and in 1992 Congress pushed the video game industry to adopt a ratings system that alerts parents to objectionable games. Debates over the merits and dangers of children's media usage, however, are hardly new. Since the mid-nineteenth century, children's consumption of mass media has precipitated heated discussions about the nature of childhood, the social responsibilities of media producers, and the proper limits of government regulation and artistic expression.

Debates about children's media usage have been inspired by a desire to protect children's innocence. They also reflect struggles for cultural authority among the various groups—child experts, religious organizations, children's librarians, reformers, media producers, and even children themselves—that are the focus of this chapter. While reformers have stressed children's vulnerability and need for protection from negative media influences, media producers have argued that the media alone does not influence children. Instead, media producers have asserted that if children engage in objectionable behavior, they have likely learned it from other sources, including their families and peers. Casting themselves as children's allies, producers have argued that various media provide children a cathartic outlet for their fears and aggression as well as the entertainment that they crave.

Children have not been passive participants in these struggles for cultural authority. Despite their status as dependents, children have often circumvented efforts to control their access to the mass media—whether by overt defiance or through surreptitious consumption. If media producers, parents, and reformers have had the upper hand in defining the terms of debate over children's media culture, children's quests to define their own independent consumer identities have nonetheless helped to shape the contours of that very culture. This chapter examines how such struggles for cultural authority played out in contests over children's consumption of so-called objectionable reading materials (dime novels, crime stories, and comic books) and potentially corrupting new media (movies, radio, television, and video games).

CHILDREN'S MEDIA CULTURE, 1800–1920

At the heart of debates about children and the media is the modern idea that children are distinct from adults and should be shielded from adult responsibilities and harmful influences. This notion stemmed in part from the writings of Enlightenment philosophers such as John Locke and Jean-Jacques Rousseau, who rejected the Calvinist notion that infants were tainted by original sin and instead saw children as products of their environment. While Locke viewed the child's mind as a blank slate that could be molded for good or evil, Jean-Jacques Rousseau viewed children as inherently good and stressed the need to protect them from the corruptions of society. Such ideas about children's impressionability and malleability began to take root following the Revolutionary War and gained currency among the emerging middle class in the middle third of the nineteenth century. While childrearing practices had previously centered upon forcing children to submit to authority, Locke's theories stressed the importance of education and encouraged parents to rely on gentle admonitions rather than physical punishment and stern rebukes. Falling birthrates also led middle-class families to focus greater emotional attention on individual children and devote more resources to their education. Most children in the nineteenth century, however, did not experience a prolonged and sheltered childhood. Childhood was relatively short for enslaved children, who labored in the fields and the master's household, and for immigrant, free black, and working-class children, whose earnings helped their families make ends meet (Mintz and Kellogg 1988; Zelizer 1985).

The new world of sheltered childhood expanded an already growing market for children's literature. In the first half of the nineteenth century, mass production and new printing methods made children's books and magazines both more affordable and more plentiful. Middle-class parents enthusiastically embraced this explicitly didactic literature as a new tool for inculcating middle-class values and proper gender roles. The American Sunday School Union published hundreds of books, including clergyman

Jacob Abbott's popular books about a boy named Rollo, which stressed the importance of hard work, piety, and honesty. By the mid-nineteenth century, middle-class ideals found expression in stories that romanticized childhood innocence. Popular books by New England authors such as Louisa May Alcott and Susan Warner featured good-hearted children (often orphans), who redeemed the adults around them through their piety and self-sacrifice. Novels like Warner's enormously popular *Wide, Wide World* (1850) told the story of Ellen Montgomery, a young orphan who matures into a refined young lady. In a passage that typifies her proper Christian behavior, Ellen refuses to play a game of charades with her friends on a Sunday. "I think Sunday was meant to be spent in growing better and learning good things . . . and I have a kind of feeling that I ought not to do it" (quoted in Murray 1998).

Children's reading, however, was not always confined to literature approved by the middle class. In the late nineteenth and early twentieth centuries, debates about children's reading became intertwined with larger class tensions, as Protestant reformers sought to fortify their waning cultural authority. Upper- and middle-class Protestants felt increasingly threatened by the growing number of southern and eastern European immigrants who crowded into the cities and challenged middle-class notions of respectability by patronizing saloons and bawdy entertainments. The popularity of dime novels and crime-story papers among working-class children in the 1860s and 1870s especially alarmed reformers. Though initially intended for working-class adults, these cheap publications found an enthusiastic child audience. Dime novels captivated children with their tales of crime and adventure on the western frontier and stories of urban detectives, while crime-story papers like *The Police Gazette* tantalized readers with sensationalized accounts of real-life crime. Dime-novel publishers Beadle and Adams further antagonized reformers when they began to market dime novels directly to children in the 1870s (Parker 1997; West 1988).

Critics like Anthony Comstock, a prominent moral crusader who headed the New York Society for the Suppression of Vice, waged campaigns to limit children's access to so-called objectionable reading material. In the 1870s and 1880s, Comstock argued that "The secular press, by the sickening details of loathsome and reeking crimes, is invading our homes with matters which blast the finer sensibilities and spread the pestilent seeds of crime and vice" (Comstock 1891). In Comstock's view, children's malleable nature made them more likely to imitate the lurid and violent acts they read about (see document 12). Vice societies in other cities echoed Comstock's arguments and campaigned for reforms and regulations that would uplift working-class children and protect middle-class children from unwholesome working-class influences. Legislatures in several states censored dime novels at the point of distribution by banning their sale (West 1988). Similarly, the Women's Christian Temperance Union (WCTU) pressured state legislatures to ban the sale of crime-story papers and worked with local police to ensure that such laws were enforced. The WCTU also offered up wholesome alternatives by producing its own temperance-flavored children's fiction. Librarians, a new type of child expert, did their part by refusing to allow dime novels on library shelves (Parker 1997). In the early twentieth century, some children's librarians even refused to purchase new adventure serials like the *Rover Boys* and *Bobbsey Twins,* published by the Stratemeyer Syndicate, on grounds that the books lacked literary merit and featured heroes and heroines who, although virtuous, embarked on adventures without adult guidance (Murray 1998).

At the turn of the twentieth century, new mass commercial amusements like penny arcades and amusement parks sometimes drew reformers' ire, but none created more anxiety nor aroused more indignant appeals for reform than the movies. Silent films were especially popular with working-class and immigrant children, who made up anywhere from one-third to three-quarters of the audience in nickelodeons and movie theaters. Like dime-novel critics, Progressive-Era reformers viewed the movies as a poor moral guide and worried that impressionable children would mimic examples of crime, violence, and indecent sexuality depicted in the movies. In reformers' eyes, the movies induced working-class children either to squander their meager earnings from selling newspapers and shining shoes or to steal money to gain admission (Nasaw 1985).

Protestant clergy, the WCTU, and other antivice crusaders lobbied for national film censorship laws based on the harm they believed films posed to children. Such arguments also armed white, middle-class reformers with a powerful rhetorical tool that bolstered their broader goal of censoring movies for adult audiences, which were composed mostly of immigrants and working-class patrons. Filmmakers attempted to temper criticisms by engaging in voluntary industry self-regulation. Industry film boards reviewed films and determined if scenes needed to be cut. Despite this attempt to make films palatable to middle-class sensibilities, many cities and states created their own censorship boards that either banned films or cut objectionable scenes (Sklar 1994; West 1988). Some states and municipalities also forbade children from attending movies unless accompanied by an adult. Other reformers arranged adult-supervised children's matinees that featured movies deemed acceptable for young viewers (deCordova 1990).

Despite reformers' best efforts to restrict children from consuming media that flouted middle-class norms, children often contested and circumvented adult agendas. Children of all classes challenged the very category of "child" by accessing material intended for adults. They purchased cheap dime novels from newspaper stands and surreptitiously attended movies without adult guardians. In addition, children often rejected the media alternatives offered up by reformers. One boy explained his disdain for the adult-approved children's matinees: "There won't be any shooting or dynamiting in those kid pictures. What's the use of seeing them?" A little girl added,

"We like to see them making love and going off in automobiles" (quoted in deCordova 1990). While children strove to be treated like adults, they also developed independent tastes that defied adult standards. To the consternation of librarians and educators, children eagerly consumed adventure serials, boosting the profits of publishers like the Stratemeyer Syndicate. Consequently, more media producers followed suit and began producing specialized children's media that catered to children's tastes.

CHILDREN'S MEDIA CULTURE, 1920–1960

During the Progressive Era, the most seemingly pernicious innovations in children's media had originated in working-class culture. By the 1920s, however, working-class and middle-class children increasingly participated in a shared national children's media culture. Middle-class children joined their working-class counterparts at Saturday matinees, which now included movie serials and animated cartoons created for children. Children's radio programs, which began airing in the early 1930s, enthralled the millions of children who tuned into programs like *Little Orphan Annie* and *Dick Tracy*. Children also followed the exploits of heroes like Superman in children's comic books, which became widespread by the late 1930s (Wright 2001).

Several larger developments contributed to the expansion of children's media in the 1920s and 1930s. Thanks to child labor and compulsory school attendance laws, children increasingly spent more time in the company of their peers than with adults (Hawes 1997). As a result, media producers began to view children as a demographic category with distinct tastes. Manufacturers now capitalized on the popularity of children's media heroes and heroines by developing licensed character toys such as Mickey Mouse watches and Shirley Temple dolls (Cross 2004; deCordova 1994). Various manufacturers, including producers of snack foods, breakfast cereals, sporting goods, and toiletries, also began to use children's radio and children's magazines more aggressively to advertise directly to children (Jacobson 2004). Among these new media forms, children's radio programs were the most explicitly commercial, since they were created by advertising agencies for the sole purpose of selling products. *Little Orphan Annie* encouraged children to drink Ovaltine "with meals and in-between," and *Jack Armstrong* hawked Wheaties cereal on every program. *Jack Armstrong's* announcer instructed children: "You'll want to be sure that there's a good supply of Wheaties on hand for you all the time . . . if the supply is running a little low now, remind Mother to put Wheaties right at the top of tomorrow's shopping list" (Bruce 2007).

Children attached their own meanings to these media forms and merchandise. They transformed Saturday matinees into boisterous affairs, and they created systems for swapping comic books. Children also gained a sense of importance and belonging by joining clubs associated with film and radio heroes, such as Captain Midnight's Flight Patrol. Radio clubs sent children membership badges and secret messages that could be deciphered with special decoder rings, available only to club members who submitted proof of purchasing the sponsor's product. In addition, children used media to build camaraderie with their peers, as they recounted the exploits of their favorite film, radio, and comic heroes at school (Jacobson 2004). Boys and girls largely shared the same media culture, which, with the exception of popular heroines like Shirley Temple and Little Orphan Annie, generally revolved around male heroes such as Tom Mix and the Lone Ranger. Print media, however, allowed for greater gender segmentation. While publishers produced magazines and comic books intended for boys, they also fostered a separate girl's culture with romance comics such as *Young Romance* or series books like the Nancy Drew mysteries (Wright 2001; MacLeod 1994).

Children may have enjoyed these forms of entertainment, but adults, once again, resented their own lack of control over these new media. Like earlier critics, women's organizations and educators in the decades between 1920 and 1960 voiced aesthetic and moral objections to children's media. They criticized children's preference for formulaic media over adult-approved literature, lamented children's tendency to imitate slang from the movies and radio, and lambasted media producers for glamorizing criminal behavior and exposing children to storylines and characters borrowed from adult pulp fiction. Commenting on *Little Orphan Annie,* one writer grumbled that "Annie, the leading character, is an orphan, and the escapades which comprise the child's day-by-day life approximate a high degree of sadism. She has been kidnapped, chloroformed, rendered unconscious by a deliberate blow on the head, held prisoner several times, pursued over the countryside by the law, imprisoned in barns and hovels and freight cars" (Mann 1934). Organizations like the National Congress of Parents and Teachers (later known as the PTA) also worried about the negative psychological and physical effects of children's media and blamed overstimulating movies and radio programs for causing children's nightmares. In a typical complaint, one parent asserted that his son "now imagines footsteps in the dark, kidnappers lurking in every corner and ghosts appearing and disappearing everywhere and emitting their blood-curdling noises" (Whinston 1933). A New Jersey family even blamed the radio for causing their 10-year-old's death, after he broke his neck re-enacting a scene from a western program. Critics further charged that radio advertisers preyed upon children's gullibility with promises of so-called free prizes in exchange for cereal box tops and other proofs of purchase. "Appealing to children over the heads of parents is keenly resented in most homes," one clubwoman protested. "The reaction is 'I'll decide whether or not Bobby may drink that—not Bobby'" (Women's National Radio Committee 1935; Cross 2004; Jacobson 2004; Bruce 2007).

Reformers who tried to regulate these new media forms achieved mixed results. Women's organizations lobbied the networks through the 1930s and early 1940s, asking for voluntary reform of children's radio programming. The networks responded to these criticisms by creating advisory boards made up of child experts, and in 1939, the National Association of Broadcasters (NAB) adopted an industry-wide code to govern children's programs. The code required that children's programs display respect for parents and adult authority, and it forbade scenes of torture or horror, the elements believed to cause so-called nervous reactions in children. The NAB and the networks, however, failed to enforce the code. Because sponsors never faced boycotts, the networks did not feel pressured to significantly alter children's programs. In the absence of more substantial reform, women's organizations and children's librarians often became amateur producers of radio programs that encouraged children to read, play musical instruments, or learn new hobbies (Bruce 2007). As one women's organization proclaimed, "A good children's program will combat the growing American disease of spectatoritis by stimulating its hearers to do things for themselves. And this kind of show is far more possible as a locally produced program" (Association of Junior Leagues 1948).

Reformers had greater success regulating movies thanks to the threat of federal intervention and the testimony of child experts and social scientists. Despite the industry's attempts to self-regulate, criticism of the film industry intensified at the end of the 1920s with the advent of sound. Performers like Mae West now pushed the boundary of industry controls by using sexually suggestive voices. In order to curb Hollywood, reformers called upon the federal government to break the industry's monopoly on film production, distribution, and exhibition. In addition, the Catholic Legion of Decency threatened to organize a massive boycott of theaters in 1933 (Maltby 1995). That same year, the concern for children's welfare gained new prominence with the publication of Henry James Forman's *Our Movie Made Children* (see document 15). Forman summarized the findings of the Payne Fund Study, the first major research effort to examine the effect of media on children and youth. Researchers involved with the study reached ambiguous conclusions, arguing that the effect of movies was mediated by other influences, including families and peer group. Yet Forman, a journalist, summarized the most negative findings and reproduced testimony from juvenile delinquents who claimed the movies had influenced their bad behavior (Sklar 1994; Jowett, Jarvie, and Fuller 1996). To head off boycotts and federal intervention, the Hay's Office of the Motion Picture Producers and Distributors of America created a new production code in 1934 and established the Production Code Authority to enforce it. The film studios also produced more so-called family pictures that won parental approval. Walt Disney began his own production of feature-length family films with the release of *Snow White* in 1938 (Sklar 1994).

Threats of boycotts also made the comic book industry vulnerable to censorship, at least on a local level. During the 1940s and early 1950s, a Catholic organization called the National Office of Decent Literature published lists of acceptable comics. Local reformers then threatened to boycott local distributors who continued to carry objectionable comics. In New York, home to the majority of comic book publishers, Governor Thomas Dewey twice vetoed legislation banning comic book distribution, contending that its vague wording would invite legal challenges on free speech grounds. Yet legislators continued to call for a comic book ban. To placate critics, comic book publishers adopted an industry-wide code in 1948 that included prohibitions against denigrating authority figures and depicting sex and unpunished crimes. However, this gesture produced no substantive changes to comic book production, since there was no method for enforcement (Nyberg 1998). In fact, the comic book industry incited more criticism after World War II. Male soldiers had avidly read comic books during the war, so publishers courted this older audience with new genres, including harder-edged crime comics and horror comics like EC Comics' *Tales from the Crypt*. One comic featured a story about a gruesome game of baseball played with human body parts; the cover of another featured a woman's bloody neck and decapitated head. To parents' dismay, children purchased these more explicitly violent comics at newsstands (Wright 2001).

The popularity of these new comics, combined with postwar fears about juvenile delinquency, prompted the federal government to seriously challenge the comic book industry. The Senate Subcommittee on Juvenile Delinquency launched a high-profile set of hearings on the comic book industry in 1954. One of the star witnesses in the investigation was Frederick Wertham, a psychiatrist whose best-selling book, *The Seduction of the Innocent* (see document 16), argued that comic books turned otherwise "normal" children into delinquents (Wright 2001; Nyberg 1998).

In some respects Wertham's testimony represented a departure from the advice of earlier child experts. During the 1930s, many child experts had argued that the mass media did not invariably exert a negative influence on children but could instead provide a positive, cathartic outlet for children's fears and fantasies. Acting as expert witnesses, staff members of the Child Study Association (CSA) argued this point during the Senate investigation. Yet Wertham discredited this analysis by pointing out that the CSA's experts had acted as paid consultants for the comic book industry. Wertham's testimony and Senate pressure spurred the comic book industry to adopt a new code that would govern all comic book production, since there was no system to differentiate adult and child comics. The 1954 code, more comprehensive than its predecessor, forbade comics featuring nudity or salacious sexual content, scenes of horror or torture, or sympathetic depictions of criminals. This time, the code was enforced by a new trade organization, which granted a seal of approval to comics that followed the code.

Most distributors complied with the new code by refusing to carry comics without the seal (Nyberg 1998).

Racial, ethnic, and religious stereotypes in children's media also gained attention in the 1940s and 1950s. Greater awareness of the Holocaust and the burgeoning civil rights movement inspired new storylines about racial and religious tolerance. On the *Superman* radio program, Superman defended an interfaith center against bigoted thugs, and battled southern whites who tried to lynch an innocent black teenager. EC Comics included stories like "The Whipping," in which a father's hatred toward his daughter's Hispanic lover accidentally causes her death. In addition, the Stratemeyer Syndicate expunged racist stereotypes from older editions of its adventure novels like the *Hardy Boys* and *Nancy Drew*. Such reforms were limited, however. Radio programs and comic books still featured virulent anti-Japanese sentiment, and most children's media continued to exclude nonwhites, or to only portray them in foreign settings (Nyberg 1998; Murray 1998; Wright 2001).

The advent of television was arguably the most dramatic innovation in children's media in the postwar period. Like children's radio, its content was largely determined by advertisers' agendas. Sponsors for early children's television included cereal and snack food producers. Yet manufacturers of cleaning products and baby food also sponsored children's programs for the first time, in order to reach the millions of baby boom mothers staying home with their children. These advertisers supported a wide variety of children's programs in the early 1950s, including puppet programs, variety programs with adult hosts like *Howdy Doody*, and western adventures such as *Hopalong Cassidy*. There were even a few educational programs for pre-school age children, like *Ding Dong School* and *Captain Kangaroo*. Most of these children's shows featured host-selling, in which a program host or character urged children to consume the sponsor's product. *Howdy Doody* told viewers that Wonderbread was puppet Howdy Doody's favorite, and Commander Buzz Corry on *Space Patrol* praised Rice Chex cereal (Spigel 1998; Bruce 2007).

Two Disney programs, *Disneyland* (1954) and the *Mickey Mouse Club* (1955), proved the most groundbreaking in their commercial success and effect on children's television. Children loved these programs and eagerly pleaded for associated merchandise, such as the Davy Crockett-inspired coonskin caps, but, in contrast to other children's offerings, Disney's shows also won adult viewers as well. In the wake of Disney's success, large companies like Johnson and Johnson began abandoning the children's variety and puppet programs in favor of western dramas and family programs like *Lassie* that might better attract the whole family (Watts 1997; Bruce 2007).

By the 1960s, advertisers' decisions and other commercial developments reduced the variety of early children's television. Syndicated cartoons like *Huckleberry Hound* and *The Jetsons* became the prevailing form of children's television after the Hanna-Barbera production company originated a system of animation that could be quickly and cheaply produced for the small screen. Cereal and snack food companies still utilized children's television to target children, and toy companies also became major sponsors of children's television. While parents had traditionally given children toys only once or twice a year, the baby boom and a vibrant postwar economy encouraged more frequent toy purchases. Mattel laid the groundwork for television toy advertising through its landmark sponsorship of the *Mickey Mouse Club*, which transformed the small upstart into one of the largest toy companies (Cross 2004; Kline 1993).

Television inspired a host of reactions from parents, educators, and child-rearing authorities in its first two decades. Some embraced television enthusiastically, seeing it as a vehicle for cementing family togetherness, an educational tool, or even a convenient babysitter. Parents particularly applauded innocuous puppet programs like *Kukla, Fran and Ollie*, or educational offerings like the science program, *Mr. Wizard*. Psychologist Bruno Bettelheim asserted that even crime-fighting programs served a positive function by allowing children to vent aggression harmlessly. Others, however, worried that children would become addicted to television, or worse still, imitate the violence on television westerns. Some parents complained that television encouraged children to neglect homework and abandon physical activity. Children's attraction to adult programs also raised alarms. The PTA complained that television gave children access to adult content, such as the ribald humor found on *Milton Berle*, a popular variety show that families often watched together. Television's critics, however, could do little to instigate change. Like radio, television broadcasting was largely insulated from critics because they could not block its distribution at the local level in the way comic book reformers could. In addition, broadcasting networks NBC and CBS were powerful companies with favorable ties to the federal government. The networks did respond to public criticisms, once again, with a set of internal codes, but these produced insubstantial change (Spigel 1992; Bruce 2007).

Regulating children's media consumption in the home met with mixed success. Some parents, by insisting that children complete their homework before watching TV, used children's love for television to gain leverage and reassert control. Other parents imposed limits on how much and which shows children could watch. Children, however, often proved wilier than parents anticipated. Children avoided parental surveillance by watching forbidden television programs at friends' houses, or by furtively reading comic books with a flashlight under their covers. Nor was it easy to contain children's media preferences within the sanctified walls of wholesome children's entertainment. The same children who avidly read children's comic books, for example, listened to *Gangbusters*, an adult radio program that presented true-life crime stories. Children sometimes even became their own advocates, writing letters to a local station to protest the cancellation of a favorite television program (Spigel 1992).

CHILDREN'S MEDIA CULTURE AND FEDERAL REGULATION, 1967–PRESENT

In the last third of the twentieth century the federal government assumed a larger but still modest role in regulating and reforming children's media. Federal funding of public television, established in 1967, created a new venue for educational television programs. *Sesame Street*, which debuted in 1969, was inspired by Head Start, a federal program created to improve the preschool education of impoverished children. Although created for children of all classes, *Sesame Street*'s backers particularly hoped the educational program would help prepare inner-city children for school. *Sesame Street* was unique not only because it was the first program to foster children's cognitive development, but also because social scientists and educators played an instrumental role in designing the program and in testing children's reactions to it. The program appealed to children because it presented cognitive lessons in a style deliberately borrowed from commercial television, including the use of short segments, rapid editing, and fast-paced animation. Some psychologists objected to these elements of *Sesame Street*, while other child experts and parents praised the program's multicultural cast and its ability to teach children their letters and numbers (Hendershot 1998; Morrow 2006).

The social turbulence and reform movements of the 1960s also prodded the federal government to take a firmer hand in regulating children's media. By 1968, through television Americans had witnessed urban riots, the assassination of Senator Robert Kennedy, and the Tet offensive. Some speculated that television violence had contributed to the riots and the assassinations of Kennedy and Martin Luther King, Jr. In response to such public anxiety, the Senate held hearings on television in the late 1960s and early 1970s (Hendershot 1998). In addition, civil rights organizations, working with the United Church of Christ, won a landmark court case that established the public's right to testify at hearings of the Federal Communications Commission (FCC), the government body that regulates broadcasting. This meant that activists and media watchdogs could testify against radio and television stations when their license came up for renewal. Justicia, a Mexican-American civil rights organization, for example, petitioned to deny renewing the licenses of stations that featured little diversity, either on or off camera. Networks and local affiliates, fearful of losing their licenses, began hiring minorities, and they consulted members of feminist, civil rights, and other ethnic organizations. This cooperation produced some changes to media content, such as the withdrawal of commercials featuring the Frito-Bandito, a stereotypical Mexican character (Montgomery 1989).

The greater receptivity to regulatory reform emboldened new media watch groups to focus attention on children's television. Organizations from both the political right and left, including the Coalition for Better

Television and the National Coalition on Television Violence, respectively, condemned the violence in superhero cartoons and other children's fare and threatened to boycott companies that advertised on such programs. The networks responded by requiring producers to insert moral lessons into cartoons and removing scenes that featured imitable acts of violence or reinforced racism and sexism. CBS, for example, trumpeted its program *Fat Albert*, a cartoon about black, inner-city children that promoted racial tolerance. Yet while the networks' standards departments paid greater heed to issues of racism and violence, they generally ignored the gender stereotypes prevalent in most cartoons (Hendershot 1998).

Media watch groups also trained their sights on excessive commercialism in children's television. The Action for Children's Television, a group founded by Boston housewives in 1968, joined other organizations in protesting the 1969 debut of *Hot Wheels*, a children's cartoon designed, first and foremost, to sell the miniature toy cars. The FCC called *Hot Wheels* a "program length commercial," and public pressure caused Mattel to withdraw the program. In 1971, ACT asked the Federal Trade Commission (FTC), which regulates advertising, to forbid advertisements targeting children, arguing that children, unlike adults, could not critically evaluate advertisements. ACT and other organizations also linked advertising to concerns about children's health by criticizing the prevalence of sugared cereal and candy bar advertisements on children's television. ACT's lobbying secured some reform. In 1974 the National Association of Broadcasters and the FCC instituted new guidelines that reduced the number of advertising minutes per children's program and prohibited host selling. Continued pressure from ACT and other groups compelled the FTC to consider banning all advertisements that targeted children under age eight, and all advertisements selling sugared cereals to children. A massive lobbying campaign by advertisers, grocery store retailers, and the sugar industry, however, defeated such a move (Hendershot 1998).

The resurgence of conservatism that propelled President Ronald Reagan into office in 1980 dealt another blow to media reform. In keeping with the Reagan Administration's general deregulation of broadcasting, the FCC and FTC abandoned most of the new rules regulating children's programs and the FCC ceased to criticize program-length commercials for children, also called product-based cartoons. By the mid-1980s, product-based cartoons like *Strawberry Shortcake* and *He-Man* dominated children's network television (Hendershot 1998). Advertising agencies created such cartoons on behalf of their toy-company clients. Many of these programs, such as *My Little Pony*, catered to girls' interests, marking the first time broadcasters and marketers created separate entertainment for girls (Seiter 1993).

Sales of licensed merchandise and videos made children's media entertainment even more profitable in the 1980s and 1990s. The Walt Disney Company and Nickelodeon successfully dominated children's media through their cable networks, theatrical films, and merchandise tie-ins at fast-food restaurants. Some parents applauded these media producers because they managed to balance both children's interests and adult agendas. Nickelodeon's *Rugrats*, for example, appealed to children with its irreverent humor and bathroom jokes, while adults approved the program's lack of violence. Nickelodeon also garnered praise by offering more programs centering on female characters like *Dora the Explorer*, as well as featuring more characters of color. The number of programs targeting preschoolers also expanded, as did their profitability. Cable networks, following the lead of PBS's *Sesame Street* and *Barney*, enjoyed handsome profits from licensed merchandise that delighted child fans of *Bob the Builder*, *Blues Clues*, and *Sponge Bob Square Pants* (Hendershot 2004).

The 1990s ushered in a new wave of media reform. Politicians of both political parties, motivated by concern for children as well as a politically expedient desire to assert their interest in family values, supported passage of the Children's Television Act (1990), which reinstated advertising time limits and required broadcasters to provide educational programs. Lax observance of such regulations spurred Congress in 1996 to require broadcasters to offer three hours of educational broadcasting per week on children's programs. Broadcasters largely avoided the act's intent by suggesting that light-hearted teen sitcoms like *Saved by the Bell* were educational, but some new network programs, including Fox's *Where on Earth is Carmen San Diego?* conveyed educational messages in an entertaining format (Kinder 1999).

Media reform in the 1990s also attempted to give parents more control over children's media consumption. Such reforms, however, often proved more symbolic than effective. The Telecommunications Act (1996) required that new television sets come equipped with the V-chip, a technology that allows parents to block children's access to selected television programs (Kinder 1999). Yet relatively few parents have opted to use the V-chip owing partly to confusion over how the chip operates. Adult efforts to supervise children's music also seemed weak. The Parents Music Resource Center, founded by the wives of several Washington politicians, including Tipper Gore (the spouse of former Vice President Al Gore), had pressured the music industry to adopt a voluntary labeling system that alerted parents to violent and sexually explicit content in 1985. Corporate interest in capturing the youth market, however, often trumped parental concerns, so many companies still failed to use the labels. Cultural fears about music intensified after a series of highly publicized school shootings in the mid- to late-1990s. Media pundits argued that rocker Marilyn Manson's hard-edged music inspired the two students behind a mass shooting, at Columbine High School in Littleton, Colorado (Cross 2004; Sternheimer 2003). The Internet has introduced even more complex obstacles for parents to surmount. Not only is children's Internet use more difficult to monitor, but so is their exposure to sexual knowledge and sexual danger, as pop-ups lead children to pornographic Web sites and sexual predators use chat rooms to meet children. In the 1990s the federal government struggled to construct legislation that would protect children from Internet predators. The Supreme Court, however, struck down both the Communications Decency Act (1996) and the Child Online Protection Act (1998) as violations of free speech. The Child Internet Protection Act (2000), which was upheld by the Supreme Court, attempted to balance protections of free speech and concerns about children's welfare by requiring public libraries to block computer access to pornographic Web sites (Sternheimer 2003).

Media-savvy children, however, once again found ways to subvert adults' cultural restrictions. In their computer conversations, children utilized a short-hand language that stymied parents' supervisory efforts. Children also downloaded patches to add more graphic or sexually explicit material to teen-rated versions of their video games. In addition, Web sites like MySpace provided children with a method of distribution outside of adult control. Children could become their own media producers, and circulate original stories, poems, and music.

The differing expectations of children, child experts, and parents continue to complicate discussions about children's media consumption in the twenty-first century. Children's tastes are, to some degree, more faithfully represented in media products, as producers strive to compete with the models established by *Sesame Street's* creators (The Children's Television Workshop), Disney, and Nickelodeon. New methods for studying children's preferences, combined with greater willingness to tolerate superhuman heroes, bathroom humor, and frenetic puppets have produced a media culture that speaks to children's desires. Yet despite changes in children's media, media producers still largely cater to the preferences of white, middle-class boys. While politicians and parental organizations tend to ignore issues of diversity, they continue to express outrage each time a new media product blurs the boundary between adult and child. Such struggles over childhood innocence continue to resonate in American culture more than one hundred years after the dime novel debates.

WORKS CITED

Association of Junior Leagues of America. 1948. *Reckoning with Radio: A Guide to the Production and Promotion of Local Radio Programs.* College Park, MD: Library of American Broadcasting, University of Maryland.

Bruce, Amanda. 2007. "Strangers in the Living Room: Debating Radio and Early Television for Children." Ph.D. diss., State University of New York at Stony Brook.

Comstock, Anthony. 1891. "Vampire Literature," *North American Review* 153: 160–71.

Cross, Gary. 2004. *The Cute and the Cool: Wondrous Innocence and Modern American Children's Culture.* New York: Oxford University Press.

deCordova, Richard. 1990. "Ethnography and Exhibition: The Child Audience, the Hays Office and Saturday Matinees," *Camera Obscura* 23: 90–107.

———. 1994. "The Mickey in Macy's Window: Childhood, Consumerism, and Disney Animation." In *Disney Discourse: Producing the Magic Kingdom*, ed. Eric Smoodin. New York: Routledge.

Hawes, Joseph M. 1997. *Children Between the Wars: American Childhood, 1920–1940.* New York: Twayne Publishers.

Hendershot, Heather. 1998. *Saturday Morning Censors: Television Regulation before the V-Chip.* Durham, NC: Duke University Press.

———. 2004. "Nickelodeon and the Business of Fun." In *Nickelodeon Nation: The History, Politics, and Economics of America's Only TV Channel for Kids,* ed. Heather Hendershot. New York: New York University Press.

Jacobson, Lisa. 2004. *Raising Consumers: Children and the American Mass Market in the Early Twentieth Century.* New York: Columbia University Press.

Jowett, Garth S., Ian C. Jarvie, and Kathryn H. Fuller, eds. 1996. *Children and the Movies: Media Influence and the Payne Fund Controversy.* Cambridge: Cambridge University Press.

Kinder, Marsha. 1999. "Ranging With Power on the Fox Kids Network: Or, Where on Earth is Children's Educational Television?" In *Kids' Media Culture,* ed. Marsha Kinder. Durham, NC: Duke University Press.

Kline, Stephen. 1993. *Out of the Garden: Toys and Children's Culture in the Age of TV Marketing.* New York: Verso.

MacLeod, Anne Scott. 1994. "Nancy Drew and Her Rivals: No Contest." In *American Childhood: Essays on Children's Literature of the Nineteenth and Twentieth Centuries.* Athens: University of Georgia Press.

Maltby, Richard. 1995. "The Production Code and the Hays Office." In *Grand Design: Hollywood as a Modern Business Enterprise, 1930–1939,* ed. Tino Balio. Berkeley: University of California Press.

Mann, Arthur. 1934. "Children's Crime Programs," *Scribner's Magazine* (October): 244–46.

Mintz, Steven, and Susan Kellogg. 1988. *Domestic Revolutions: A Social History of American Family Life.* New York: Free Press.

Montgomery, Kathryn C. 1989. *Target: Prime Time, Advocacy Groups and the Struggle over Entertainment Television.* New York: Oxford University Press.

Morrow, Robert W. 2006. *Sesame Street and the Reform of Children's Television.* Baltimore: The Johns Hopkins University Press.

Murray, Gail S. 1998. *American Children's Literature and the Construction of Childhood.* New York: Twayne Publishers.

Nasaw, David. 1985. *Children of the City: At Work and At Play.* New York: Oxford University Press.

Nyberg, Amy Kiste. 1998. *Seal of Approval: The History of the Comics Code.* Jackson: University Press of Mississippi.

Parker, Alison M. 1997. *Purifying America: Women, Cultural Reform, and Pro-Censorship Activism, 1873–1933.* Chicago: University of Illinois Press.

Seiter, Ellen. 1993. *Sold Separately: Children and Parents in Consumer Culture.* New Brunswick, NJ: Rutgers University Press.

Sklar, Robert. 1994. *Movie-Made America: A Cultural History of American Movies.* New York: Vintage Books.

Spigel, Lynn. 1992. *Make Room for TV: Television and the Family Ideal in Postwar America.* Chicago: University of Chicago Press.

———. 1998. "Seducing the Innocent: Childhood and Television in Postwar America." In *The Children's Culture Reader,* ed. Henry Jenkins. New York: New York University Press.

Sternheimer, Karen. 2003. *It's Not the Media: The Truth About Pop Culture's Influence on Children.* Boulder, CO: Westview Press.

Watts, Steven. 1997. *The Magic Kingdom: Walt Disney and the American Way of Life.* Columbia: University of Missouri Press.

West, Mark I. 1988. *Children, Culture, and Controversy.* Hamden, CT: Archon Books.

Whinston, Charles W. 1933. "Terror in the Bedtime Stories," *New York Times,* March 12, 10.

"Women's National Radio Committee and the Broadcasting Industry." 1935. In *Proceedings: Thirteenth Annual Convention of the National Association of Broadcasters.* July 8–10, 1935. Colorado Springs, CO. National Association of Broadcasters, Inc. Library of American Broadcasting, University of Maryland, College Park.

Wright, Bradford W. 2001. *Comic Book Nation: The Transformation of Youth Culture in America.* Baltimore, MD: Johns Hopkins University Press.

Zelizer, Viviana. 1985. *Pricing the Priceless Child: The Changing Social Values of Children.* Princeton, NJ: Princeton University Press.

3 Reforming the Delinquent Child Consumer: Institutional Responses to Children's Consumption from the Late Nineteenth Century to the Present

Paul Ringel

Since the 1870s, Americans have created a variety of institutions to regulate both children's spending and their access to mass amusements. Juvenile courts, adult-supervised working girls' societies, school savings banks, and censorship boards have all sought to reform and discipline child and adolescent consumers either by curtailing their spending and restricting their access to allegedly dangerous amusements or by channeling their consumption in more wholesome directions. Such institutions responded to widespread concerns that children needed to be shielded from negative influences that might interfere with their proper moral and physical development. Some adults even feared that consumption of the wrong kinds of fashions and the wrong kinds of media would set children on the path to juvenile delinquency. These institutional responses to children's consumption, however, have yielded at best mixed results. In fact, two of the most significant developments in the history of American childhood in the twentieth century have been the expanding access of young people to the consumer marketplace and the continuing efforts of marketers, advertisers, and manufacturers to subdivide the nation's children into increasingly narrow age groups to sell even more products. Consumer culture has not only changed the experience of being a child in the United States, it has also redefined what many Americans perceive to be the natural progression of the maturation process.

Despite their limited success, if not outright failure, these efforts to restrict the consumer activities of the nation's youth offer insights into why so many Americans feared the growth of consumer culture and how those concerns shifted over time. They also reveal a recurring tension between two competing perspectives of the American child, distinguished largely by the class and religious backgrounds of reformers: a conservative and often evangelical view of youth as a time of great moral and physical peril, and a genteel, liberal belief in the natural innocence and limitless potential of childhood. Conservative reform organizations generally promoted proscriptive measures that attempted to eliminate or restrict young people's access to consumer goods, whereas progressive or liberal reformers often created new institutions designed in part to accommodate youthful enthusiasm about consumer culture by channeling it into more salutary activities.

These two methods of regulating children's consumption have each gained and lost influence during different eras of American history. In the 1870s, the first, largely conservative generation of reformers perhaps naively expected to eliminate children's access to consumer products deemed harmful to their moral and physical development. By the turn of the twentieth century, consumer industries had become so pervasive in the United States that many no longer regarded such a goal as practical. In place of outright censorship and legal prosecution of distributors, Progressive Era reformers created institutions such as settlement houses, juvenile courts, and working-girls' societies that sought to uplift working-class and immigrant children and youth, curb their access to dangerous amusements, and inculcate middle-class values. Like their Gilded Age predecessors, however, some Progressive Era reformers resisted accommodation to the burgeoning consumer society. Advocates of school savings banks, for example, were much more interested in teaching children to save their money than in teaching them to spend it wisely. The increasingly pervasive youth cultures of the post–World War II era, some of which rebelled against the Protestant middle-class values of mainstream America, and the anti-Communist fervor of the early Cold War led to a revival of the proscriptive approach during the 1950s. Politicians' heated rhetoric overshadowed the relatively mild actions taken to curb the excesses of either the young consumers or the industries that marketed to them. As the youth market continued to expand in the last third of the twentieth century, dramatic stands against the corrupting effects of consumer culture on the nation's youth offered many reformers and cultural critics an easy method for gaining political capital but only limited hopes of effecting substantive change.

This chapter examines the development and effectiveness of various institutions that sought to regulate the spending habits and consumer practices of children and adolescents. The essay explores why some reforms succeeded while others failed and why, in some instances, children and adolescents were able to circumvent such reforms. As this chapter demonstrates, the power of the mass market cannot fully account for why institutional responses to children's consumption have generally yielded unspectacular results. Reformers' misunderstandings of children's ostensibly delinquent consumer practices also generated plenty of resistance from children and adolescents themselves. In many cases during the post–World War II decades, decrying the malevolent influences shaping the child consumer has become the simpler and more politically savvy alternative to actually addressing the sources of youthful disaffection.

CONSERVATIVE REFORM IN THE GILDED AGE

When the first efforts to restrict the child consumer arose during the 1870s, the concepts of the teenager, the adolescent, or the tween had not yet become integrated into American culture. Instead, children and young adults were often grouped together under the term youth, which could encompass an age range from seven or eight until the early- or mid-twenties. Children who were allowed to play beyond the sight of their mothers entered this amorphous period of life and would not leave it until as young men they began to earn a living sufficient to support themselves or as young women they married someone who could assume responsibility for their economic well-being.

Many nineteenth-century Americans perceived this period of youth as a particularly hazardous stage of life. Although most religious conservatives no longer openly advocated infant depravity, the Puritan belief that all humans were born with the stain of original sin and could not be saved until they were mature enough to undergo a spiritual conversion, many continued to argue that young people were particularly susceptible to sinful influences. More genteel segments of society adopted the romantic belief that children were born innocent and would lose this natural quality through excessive and premature interaction with the corruptions of commercial interests. Regardless of the ideological source of their concerns, most Americans agreed that youths needed protection from the temptations of a consumer culture that grew increasingly pervasive in the decades after the Civil War. This concern was particularly directed toward children of working-class and immigrant families, who middle-class and wealthy Protestant reformers believed did not receive the moral training necessary to withstand the lure of consumer culture.

Publishers of dime novels, a cheap and largely disreputable form of popular literature, were among the first to attempt to break through this protective barrier and target American youth as consumers independent from their parents. These novels originally were intended for the soldiers of the Union and Confederate armies, but as early as 1864 the industry became aware that boys were buying these books in large numbers and without the consent of adults (Norton 1864). By the late 1870s, dime novel publishers decided to create a product designed to appeal specifically to boys, a tactic that distinguished their merchandise from the majority of goods produced for kids but marketed for the approval of the parents who were presumably the paying customers. Beadle's Half-Dime Novels, the most successful publishers of this genre, offered stories of cowboys, pirates, and detectives that many boys and young men read ravenously. Although these stories maintained a strict moral code in which the hero triumphed and the villain received due punishment, they also contained a level of violence and social and intellectual crudity that dismayed both the adults who perceived American youth as morally suspect and those who viewed children as innocents.

The first groups to raise a significant public outcry against these books generally embraced the more pessimistic view of the nation's youth. Reformers such as Anthony Comstock of the New York Society for the Suppression of Vice perceived these dime novels as just one of the many moral and physical hazards unleashed by the emerging urban, industrial culture. They feared these temptations would lure susceptible young people into situations that would corrupt their inchoate and unguided young minds. Many of these reformers were particularly concerned about the influence of these publications on poor and immigrant children, but Comstock appears to have believed such products could lead any youths toward violent and sexually depraved behaviors (see document 12). In fact, his book *Traps for the Young* suggests that Satan intentionally caused newsstands that sold such papers to be placed "along the pathway of the children (going) from home to school and church." This fear inspired him to call the publishers of dime novels "vermin" and argue that "these publications, like the fishes of the sea, spawn millions of seed, and each year these seeds germinate and spring up to a harvest of death" (Comstock 1883).

This passionate belief led Comstock and his compatriots to call for the proscription of these books. Using the press and his own lectures to publicize his cause, Comstock called for city governments and the national postal service to eradicate this genre of fiction entirely by prohibiting its distribution through the mails and indicting newsstands that carried these books. This effort to restrict children's consumption was part of a larger movement of child protection in urban America that had begun as early as 1854, when the Children's Aid Society of New York City opened lodging houses for newsboys to keep them away from the theaters and grog shops of the Bowery neighborhood. During the Gilded Age, the New York Society for the Prevention of Cruelty to Children intensified this effort by convincing the city's police department to empower private agents nicknamed Gerrymen (named after the society's president, Elbridge Gerry) to keep child workers away from immoral environments such as theaters, amusement parks, penny arcades, and the streets of nearly any poor or immigrant neighborhood of the city. While these men, whom urban children nicknamed the Gerries, did manage to chase many young actors out of Manhattan theaters and occasionally execute a successful raid on young street traders, most children were able to elude efforts to thwart their activities by combining forces (even with children from rival neighborhoods or gangs) to warn each other about the impending arrival of the Gerries or, in a pinch, by outrunning their pursuers. In general, these efforts failed because reformers lacked the resources and police lacked the interest required to prevent determined youths from plying their trades (Nasaw 1985).

While the majority of reformers of this era attempted, in the words of one historian, to "quarantine the susceptible" children of the nation's cities, a few extremists such as Comstock pursued the even more implausible goal of creating an insurmountable barrier between youths and potentially hazardous commodities (Nasaw 1985). Comstock's solution was to remove the dangerous goods, while other child savers took the even bolder step of removing susceptible children from the city altogether. The Children's Aid Society of New York City, for example, adopted the latter approach, loading thousands of poor and immigrant children each year onto what became known as orphan trains and shipping them to rural areas where primarily middle-class Protestant families assumed responsibility for them. The Children's Aid Society hoped that placing children in such rural families would not only restore the virtue that corrupting urban amusements had stolen from children but would also help immigrant children from Catholic and Jewish families assimilate mainstream Protestant values. Anxieties about children's consumption thus often were intertwined with anxieties about the destabilizing potential of class and ethnic differences. Unlike Comstock's crusade, the orphan train movement was specifically class based. Many of the children transported on these trains were not orphans but simply children of impoverished families; in fact, some of them had been left only in the temporary custody of state or church agencies while their families attempted to establish an income sufficient to care for them (Holt 1992).

The conservative reforms of Comstock and the Children's Aid Society had a measurable, though limited, impact. Over the course of his 42-year long career, Comstock claimed he obtained the arrests of more than 3,600 men, women, and children for violating obscenity statutes (Comstock 1883). The orphan trains relocated over 100,000 children between 1854 and 1929, when they ceased operation. Such efforts, however, could not stem the flow of mass commercial recreations that enticed children and youth to spend their earnings. By the turn of the twentieth century, a new generation of reformers had adopted a very different set of strategies to meet the challenges posed by a mass consumer society.

REFORMS IN THE PROGRESSIVE ERA AND INTERWAR YEARS

During the Progressive Era, a period that spanned roughly from 1890 to 1919, consumer industries began pursuing the disposable income of young people with increasing vigor. For example, while the popularity of dime novels had begun to lag by this time, this decline occurred largely because new forms of entertainment such as vaudeville theaters, dance halls, nickelodeons, and the toy sections of department stores enticed young readers away from their books. Such entertainment opportunities grew in tandem with the nation's cities, and thus attracted the concern of a new generation of reformers seeking to provide solutions for the social problems created by urban growth.

These middle- and upper-middle-class activists, part of a loosely bound movement known as Progressivism, worried about the corrupting influence of consumer culture on American youth. In this respect Progressive reformers shared much in common with their Gilded Age predecessors. Progressives, however, were far from united in the strategies they used to regulate children's consumption. While advocates of school savings banks, like Gilded Age reformers, sought to isolate children from consumer temptations, other Progressives worked to provide wholesome alternatives to mass commercial amusements and teach children and youth middle-class notions of respectable consumption. This latter group differed radically from earlier reformers such as Comstock and Gerry, who believed youths were morally unprepared to cope with the temptations of consumerism and thus sought to create the most extensive possible barriers between the nation's young people and these enticements.

By contrast, Progressives, many of whom had received college educations, possessed a nearly unshakeable faith in the power of social science to cure society's ailments. They shared an inherent optimism about mankind's, and by extension children's, ability to overcome any moral and physical obstacles with the proper expert guidance. The problem, from their perspective, was not human nature but social environments. Thus if the reformers could construct the proper surroundings for young people, the temptations of consumer culture, even if occasionally sampled, would no longer prove harmful.

Two developments at the turn of the twentieth century—the rise of mass commercial amusements and the emergence of a new public culture of dating—especially alarmed Progressive reformers. When not working or in school, working-class children and youth increasingly spent their time and money in movie theaters, amusement parks, penny arcades, dance halls, and pool halls—all forms of mass commercial recreation that reformers regarded as morally corrupting and fraught with sexual danger for vulnerable adolescent girls. To make matters worse, young people frequently enjoyed these activities in the company of their peers and outside the watchful eyes of their parents. Many working-class youths had abandoned traditional courtship rituals of formal introductions and chaperoned get-togethers and had instead taken up dating—a new practice in which men would treat women to an evening or afternoon of entertainment with the implicit expectation of some return payment in the form of sexual exchange. Reformers worried that the new mass commercial recreations—the primary sites of dating—not only encouraged female sexual independence but also set up women for sexual exploitation (Peiss 1986; Odem 1995). Not surprisingly, Progressives regarded adult supervision as a crucial component of recreation reform.

Progressive reformers created a variety of institutions to combat the allures of mass commercial amusements and restore traditional norms of sexual respectability and courtship. Some of these institutions, such as juvenile courts, schools, and working girls' societies, focused nearly exclusively on the problems of children and young adults; others, including settlement houses and police forces, addressed the subject of the child consumer as part of a larger effort to improve the governance and management of the nation's cities. Regardless of their particular agenda, nearly all of them adopted methods that combined education about proper consumer behavior with activities that simultaneously satisfied children's desires for excitement and promoted their physical, moral, and intellectual development.

Settlement houses were among the first institutions to undertake this task. Organized by middle-class and wealthy reformers in the late nineteenth century as centers to help working-class and immigrant communities to adapt to life in urban, industrial America, these establishments focused much of their attention on training neighborhood youths to cope with modern society. Leaders of the movement such as Jane Addams, who founded Hull House in Chicago in 1889, believed the urban environment created particular difficulties in achieving this goal. She argued that "it seems at times as if a great city almost deliberately increased its perils" for young people: "the newly awakened senses are appealed to by all that is gaudy and sensual, by the flippant street music, the highly colored theater posters, the trashy love stories, the feathered hats, the cheap heroics of the revolvers displayed in pawn-shop windows" (Addams 1909). The National Federation of Settlements worried in particular that department store salesgirls, daily confronted with consumer temptations, would develop tastes for expensive clothes and jewelry beyond their financial reach and would surrender their virtue to acquire them—either by turning to prostitution or by providing sexual favors to men who treated them to new clothes or a night on the town (Odem 1995).

Many Progressives sympathized with the youthful impulse to seek fun and understood that wage-earning adolescents in particular needed to satisfy their natural cravings for mystery, romance, and adventure. "'Looping the loop' amid shrieks of stimulated terror or dancing in disorderly saloon halls, are perhaps the natural reactions to a day spent in noisy factories and in trolley cars whirling through the distracting streets," Addams conceded. "But the city which permits them to be the acme of pleasure and recreation to its young people, commits a grievous mistake" (Addams 1909). Instead of blaming youth, Progressives such as Addams faulted local governments for failing to offer more salutary outlets for the energies of urban youth. Addams noted that ancient governments built theaters and stadiums and that medieval monarchs held tournaments, pageants, dances, and festivals, but "only in the modern city have men concluded that it is no longer necessary for the municipality to provide for the insatiable desire for play." This neglect, along with the unprecedented economic and social independence experienced by urban youth during this era, created "malignant and vicious appetites" for commercial recreations that provided escape but not renewal (Addams 1909). In Addams's view, commercial recreation invited complete surrender of intellect and self-control, making it a perversion of traditional forms of play rather than an extension of them (see document 13).

In lieu of "restrictive measures," Addams and other Progressive reformers created activities and services to fill the vacuum left by local government's abdication of its responsibilities. One of the primary goals of this work was to reintegrate youth and adult leisure. Progressives called for the construction of community recreation centers and endorsed ethnic festivals and pageants to teach immigrant children about their heritage (Addams 1909). Progressives also proposed alternative forms of entertainment through which educated and trained professionals could provide activities to stimulate young people's bodies, minds, and imaginations. For example, while attending the commercial theater might encourage youths toward antisocial acts of violence, theft, and sexual misconduct, Addams believed that participation in community theater productions of classic plays, under the guidance of an experienced and knowledgeable director, would offer youth opportunities for self-expression and adventure. Similarly, she argued that joining a neighborhood baseball team would both provide needed physical exercise and strengthen young people's bonds to their local community (Addams 1909).

Settlement houses and philanthropic organizations such as the Young Women's Christian Association (YWCA) also sponsored working girls' clubs, which offered young wage-earning women wholesome, adult-supervised alternatives to mass commercial amusements. Initially, working girls' clubs provided evening lectures, libraries, sewing and cooking classes, and public parlors in which young women could socialize with friends. The clubs sought to create a homey atmosphere that would sequester girls from corrupting mass amusements and expose them to middle-class standards of decorum and domesticity. The Association of Working Girls' Societies, a consortium of working girls' clubs in New York and other cities, even published a journal which featured short stories and editorials cautioning girls against flirting with men, accepting dates from strangers, and reading cheap story papers (Peiss 1986).

Such efforts to uplift the recreation of youths, however, generated little enthusiasm among young people themselves. Many working-class women found the often didactic entertainments offered at the working girls' clubs poor substitutes for the thrills of dance halls and cheap theaters. Even for working-class women dedicated to improving their economic and social status, the ethnic and class differences that plagued many of these clubs made them an unappealing option. Factory workers felt condescended to by reformers, and immigrants often found middle-class American notions of women's social roles irrelevant to their own experiences. Others placed more hope in cooperative action based on class than in allegiances based on gender, and these women generally found more value in the growing movement of organized labor. At times, the cultural barriers must have seemed insurmountable; for example, during the summer, when work was often hard to find and the clubs might have served the greatest purpose, many clubs closed down as wealthier club officers left the city for vacation resorts (Peiss 1986).

Progressive reformers tried to attract more working-class women to clubs and settlement homes by including more mixed-sex entertainments like fancy dress balls. Although the inclusion of men was a concession to working-class culture, middle-class reformers hoped that sedate music and the presence of adult chaperones would create the respectable atmosphere missing from public dance halls. Yet these half-hearted attempts to replace the excitement of commercial recreations with supervised couple dances achieved few successes. In the eyes of young working-class women, the reformers were hopelessly behind the times.

Reformers fared little better in pressuring amusement entrepreneurs to ban alcohol sales in their establishments and hire adult chaperones to monitor public dances (Peiss 1986). Where moral suasion and moral uplift had failed, however, many activists hoped that state action would succeed. Genteel opponents of modern cultural trends could not combat the allures of commercial recreation and unchaperoned dating, but they could—and did—help enact legislation that sought to protect adolescent girls from sexually predatory men. In 1885, female moral reformers launched campaigns in states across the nation to raise the age of consent in statutory rape laws in order to protect young women from this most-feared consequence of the new mass entertainments. At that time most states set the legal age of consent at 10 or 12, but these women built public support for more stringent age of consent laws by depicting adolescent girls as victims of villainous sexual predators as well as victims of their own consumer desires (Odem 1995).

Reform novels, such as *Pray You, Sir, Whose Daughter?* (1892) by Helen Hamilton Gardener, linked the seductions of mass amusements to the perils of sexual seduction. In Gardener's cautionary tale, a 14-year-old shop girl accepts an enticing invitation from a much older store manager to attend an amusement park. Once there the manager plies her with wine and seduces her. The fallen shop girl is ostracized, while the store manager, who resides in a state with a low age of consent law, escapes criminal prosecution. Thanks to such novels and the persistence of women reformers, by 1920, most states had raised the age of consent to 16 or 18 (Odem 1995).

Progressive reformers also sought to regulate working-class sexuality and consumption through the juvenile courts, which first appeared in 1899 as an instrument for transforming the behavior of young offenders without incarcerating them. Juvenile court judges often sent delinquent girls to reformatories, where they received domestic training, or required them to report to probation officers who monitored their behavior and oversaw their rehabilitation (Odem 1995). The juvenile justice system also helped working-class parents bring wayward sons and daughters back under their control. Working-class sons and daughters understood that their wages were vital to the family's economic survival, but they sometimes defied parental wishes by withholding a larger than customary sum from their paycheck or by spending their earnings on what adults perceived as foolish goods and entertainments. Desperate working-class parents, many of them single mothers, reported their daughters to juvenile courts for keeping company with men and their sons for staying out late or running away—often with the expectation that the juvenile courts would help them settle other parent-child conflicts such as how wage-earning adolescents spent their money and their leisure. Working-class parents could be safely assured that the juvenile courts and probation officers would echo parental demands that daughters wear less makeup, dress less provocatively, and stay away from dance halls, and sons spend less money on urban amusements and dates (Odem 1995).

No amount of legal coercion, however, could sequester adolescents from consumer temptation, and some juvenile court judges began to argue that parents needed to cast aside outmoded customs and values and accommodate youthful stirrings for adventure. One such judge was Ben Lindsey, the juvenile court judge of Denver and a leading advocate of the juvenile court system across the nation. Lindsey heard many youths complain about the outdated social values of American society. Armed with their opinions and his own experience as a mediator between juveniles and adults, Lindsey deflected blame away from the youths and instead chastised adults who refused to acknowledge and adapt to the changes in modern society. In his widely read book *The Revolt of Modern Youth* (1925), Lindsey attacked coercive approaches toward restraining the child consumer, claiming "there is no point in blaming the new conditions, nor in raving that they must be changed by censorship, new laws, more force, more ignorance, more silence, fear and other nonsense." He argued that adults who simply told young people they could not use the "agencies of modern life" such as "the automobile . . . the telephone, the motion picture, the radio . . . (and) jazz music" were ignoring the unprecedented economic independence of the nation's youth that often left them beyond the punitive grasp of their elders (Lindsey and Evans 1925) (see document 14).

Instead of such a proscriptive approach, Lindsey called for frank discussions with both schoolchildren and young adults in which parents not only presented but also explained the motivations behind their value systems and then gave their offspring the opportunity to clarify their objections. This democratic response to child-rearing, which argued that authority worked more effectively when children were given a stake in their life decisions, emerged as a prominent method of the 1920s and 1930s (Jacobson 2004). Indeed, it marked the pinnacle of Progressive methods of shaping an environment designed to train young people to become educated and sophisticated consumers.

Many parents, however, resisted the trend toward greater family democracy and attempted to retain tight control over adolescent daughters. During the interwar years, Mexican American families insisted that chaperones accompany them to dances, movies, and social events where boys and girls mingled. In the eyes of elders, adolescent daughters who failed to uphold traditional standards of decorum and respectability risked not only their own reputations but also their family's standing in the community. Despite such family pressures, Mexican American girls proved quite resourceful in circumventing adult chaperonage. Emboldened by images of heterosexual romance in popular culture and their less restricted Anglo peers, Mexican American daughters snuck out of the house to meet dates or attended dances chaperoned by a sympathetic older brother. The Catholic Church sponsored sex-segregated recreations and screened wholesome movies approved by the Legion of Decency, but the allures of mass culture and dating proved too difficult to surmount (Ruiz 1998).

Many Progressive and interwar reformers sought an accommodation with consumer culture: they wanted to contain its excesses and create wholesome alternatives that could compete with its allures. Advocates of school savings banks, on the other hand, were more interested in teaching children self-denial than how to navigate the temptations of consumer culture. School savings banks, which originated in 1885, sought to make saving a regular habit by requiring elementary and secondary school students to deposit money on a weekly basis. By the first two decades of the twentieth century, school savings banks had taken root in large Eastern, Midwestern, and West Coast cities. Through a combination of peer pressure and inducements such as offering children the same interest rates enjoyed by adult depositors, schools and banks worked together to encourage students to make a deposit, no matter how minimal, each week on Bank Day. While some children found the enticement of their own bank accounts quite powerful, others dreaded Bank Day and the potential humiliation of not having coins to deposit.

School savings banks had a wide range of supporters, not the least of which were the American Bankers Association and the local savings banks that sponsored the school programs to build good will and secure loyal customers. A wide variety of moral reformers and thrift advocates, including home economists and the Women's Christian Temperance Union, also lauded the cause. Like other Progressive reformers, these thrift advocates saw education as a means to combat pauperism, intemperance, and related social ills that accompanied mass immigration, industrialization, and urbanization. They hoped that compulsory saving would discourage children's spendthrift habits, reduce children's access to mass amusements, Americanize immigrants, and cultivate self-supporting citizens. School banking promoters were especially eager to limit opportunities for working-class and immigrant children to squander their nickels and dimes on sweets, cigarettes, penny arcade games, and movie tickets—goods and entertainments that in reformers' view compromised children's health and their morals. To accomplish these ends, many school banking programs instituted policies that discouraged withdrawals, including requiring parental consent on withdrawals larger than a quarter. During the late 1910s and 1920s, when labor unrest and the specter of Bolshevism sparked red scares, thrift advocates hoped that school savings banks would teach the sons and daughters of immigrants and the laboring poor that thrifty habits yielded substantial economic gains under capitalism (see documents 20–21).

School savings bank administrators often boasted of their success in reducing consumption of candy and movies—an accomplishment that won plaudits from many parents. Thrift advocates missed the mark, however, in imagining how school savings banks could be used an instrument of social control. While thrift advocates envisioned school savings banks as a tool to regulate children's spending, working-class children sometimes embraced school banking as a tool to regulate their parents. Aaron Hotchner, who grew up in St. Louis in the 1920s, used his school savings bank account to prevent his intermittently employed father from dipping into his own meager earnings. Just as working-class parents had embraced juvenile courts as an ally in reasserting parental control over children's spending and leisure, working-class children used school savings banks to resist seemingly unjust assertions of parental authority (see document 24). School savings bank proponents also overestimated the value of school banking's value as an Americanization program that would promote thrift to immigrants, as many immigrants—including Italians, Poles, and Eastern European Jews—already ranked higher among the nation's savers than native-born Americans.

In the 1920s some school savings bank programs departed from the rigid emphasis on saving for its own sake and encouraged children to save for a specific purpose—the purchase of a bike, a phonograph, summer camp tuition—that in some way furthered children's development. School savings banks nevertheless encountered opposition from childrearing authorities and some teachers in the 1920s and 1930s who scorned banks for emphasizing accumulation at the expense of teaching children how to spend their money wisely (see document 23). Parents and child experts also criticized school banking for relying too heavily on contests and competitions between classrooms to achieve 100 percent student participation (see document 22). Parents of elementary school children reported that children were far more invested in school spirit and fitting in than in honoring the principles of thrift when they made their deposits.

The Great Depression further undermined faith in the cause of school banking, as many sponsoring banks went bust and lost children's savings (see document 24). Moreover, by the early 1930s the larger movement to restrict or channel young people's consumer impulses had flagged as the economic downturn restrained youthful consumers more effectively than any reform movements ever had. School savings bank programs enjoyed a modest revival after the Second World War but never recovered the popularity they had enjoyed during the 1920s. Sponsoring banks tried to make saving enticing by promoting saving as deferred spending (see document 25), but even these inducements had worn thin by the 1970s, when money-smart students discovered they could earn much fatter interest rates by investing in mutual funds (Jacobson 2004).

WORLD WAR II AND THE DELINQUENT CHILD CONSUMER

During World War II, child consumers, and particularly their even more troubling counterparts—juvenile delinquents—reemerged as a major public concern. The mobilization of the economy for total war created new opportunities for adolescents to earn money but also imposed new restrictions on how youth could spend that money and their leisure time. The government called upon citizens to conserve scarce resources that could help win the war—everything from rubber tires to kitchen fat and scrap metal—and issued ration coupons for the purchase of meat, sugar, butter, coffee, tires, and gasoline. Shortages of cloth transformed wartime fashions, as pleats, cuffs, and men's vests gave way to shorter hems and streamlined silhouettes. Wartime rationing and conservation had a direct impact on teen dating and leisure activities. Insufficient gasoline meant that teenagers had to dispense with joyriding and relocate dates closer to home. High school athletes often lacked team buses to transport them to meets. Funding for community recreation centers quickly dried up, as tax revenues were diverted to the war effort (Duis 1996; Palladino 1996).

At the same time, however, labor shortages on the home front meant that teens also had more opportunities to earn money. The opportunity to earn up to $60 a week in defense jobs compelled many teenagers to drop out of school; between 1940 and 1941, for example, almost half of Boston's 16-year-old boys did so. Other boys and girls dropped out to attend National Youth Administration (NYA) camps that taught them the skills and discipline needed to become effective factory workers. Yet as the war proceeded, the government phased out the NYA camps and attempted to reverse this trend, encouraging students to stay in school and develop both their physiques and their intellects in order to best serve their country. At the government's urging, teens contributed to the war by raising money for war bonds, building scale model planes and ships for naval training exercises, collecting salvage, tending victory gardens, and working on farms during the summer (Palladino 1996).

Whether they dropped out or worked after school, teens soon had more disposable income than most of them had ever had before but fewer places to spend it. This problem contributed to the widespread public perception that juvenile delinquency was on the rise. Thanks to the increased participation of women in the paid workforce, a greater number of teenagers were left unsupervised and to their own devices. Girls flirted with boys in uniform and some, who came to be known as V-girls or Victory girls, were thought to trade sexual favors for a night on the town or a pair of stockings. In Los Angeles, city officials blamed V-girls for the rise of casual sex and increasing rates of venereal disease, which shot up 120 percent among teens during the war (Palladino 1996). Equally troubling were black, Latino, and Filipino adolescents who used their disposable income to build an oppositional culture identified largely by its consumer products and leisure activities. Young men such as Malcolm X used bebop jazz, the lindy hop, the conk haircut, and, above all, the zoot suit, to pronounce their independence from mainstream culture (Kelley 1994). The zoot suit, with its cuffed and baggy trousers and wide shouldered, thigh-length jacket, not only defied middle-class norms of respectability—the look was also popular with gangsters and jazz musicians—but it also ignored government injunctions against excessive usage of fabric. Working-class minority youth wore zoot suits as an emblem of their disaffection from a society in which they faced racial discrimination, police brutality, and limited economic opportunities for advancement. Hipster girls declared their own defiance of mainstream society by wearing dark red lipstick and provocatively tight skirts and sheer blouses. The heightened public profiles of these youths and the interracial mingling that occurred at nightclubs, where youths danced to the accompaniment of swing bands, exacerbated traditional fears about the connection between consumer culture, juvenile violence, and sexual misconduct.

This concern emerged particularly in cities with diverse populations such as Los Angeles, where police and city government activity during and after the war attempted to prevent interracial socializing among the city's white, African American, Latino, and Filipino youth. City officials particularly focused on restricting the activities of the zoot suiters—youth whom officials often derided as *pachucos*. While the meaning of that term varied depending on the user and context, *pachucos* generally became identified more by their fashion than by their ethnicity, as the press and the police lumped all Latino, black, and even white working-class youths who adopted the style of the zoot suit into the same category (Pagán 2003). The tensions created by interracial mixing in nightclubs and defiant fashion statements erupted in violence during the Zoot Suit Riots of 1943, when white service-men and civilians clashed with African American and Latino youths. During the nearly week long riots police and soldiers chose to "de-zoot" these up-starts, stripping them of their suits rather than injuring or killing them and thus rebuking the power of their consumer identity (Pagán 2003). When the worst of the riots had ended, the city government banned the wearing of zoot suits within the city limits (Macías 2004).

Because interracial mixing so often occurred where swing music was played, state and local authorities argued that such music was an induce-ment to delinquency. State officials in the Midwest tried to ban jukeboxes to rid their jurisdictions of swing's influence. Local authorities elsewhere instituted 10 o'clock curfews to keep teens out of juke joints and dance halls (Palladino 1996). Others sought to address the rising specter of teen delinquency by offering wholesome, supervised alternatives to the night-clubs, much as Jane Addams and like-minded reformers had sought to do earlier in the century. In lieu of harsh external controls like curfews and jukebox bans, Mark McCloskey, the recreation director for the Office of Community War Services, proposed the creation of teen canteens. As his Progressive Era predecessors had, McCloskey sympathized with teenagers' quest for adventure and recognized that there were too few wholesome outlets or recreation facilities for teen fun, as many cities during the war had cut back on services such as swimming pools and community centers to save tax revenues and resources (Palladino 1996).

The teen canteens differed, however, from Progressive Era attempts to uplift recreation in one crucial respect: teenagers themselves were integral participants in planning and running the canteens. In stark contrast to the working girls' clubs of the early twentieth century, adults were largely absent from the planning process, though they did sit on joint adult-teen governing boards and provide some chaperonage. With names like "Jive Hive," "Boogie Bar," and "Swing Haven," the canteens bore the imprint of teen culture. Many came equipped with jukeboxes, dance floors, ping-pong tables, and coke bars—thanks in part to the corporate sponsorship of Coca Cola, which hoped to cash in on the youth market. The most elaborate, well-funded canteens had bowling alleys and game rooms. Teen canteens needed to satisfy teen tastes but also to assure adults that swing culture would not violate community standards of behavior. Rules prohibiting drinking, gambling, and pick-up dates and requiring girls to register their plans in advance if they wanted to bring a soldier to a dance satisfied many governing boards (Palladino 1996).

In practice, many, but not all, teen canteens reinforced racial segregation —often by design. Because teen canteens were organized around neighborhood lines, canteens allayed fears that gatherings would become racially or ethnically mixed and get out of control. Some teen canteens, however, embraced the idea of opening their doors to teens of all backgrounds and did so in hopes of furthering understanding and eliminating the sort of social prejudice that smacked of fascist intolerance. In the aftermath of the June 1943 race riots in Detroit, for example, white and black teens joined the same canteens and supported a citywide, biracial youth council. Teenagers in Brooklyn, Iowa, and Indiana undertook similar projects of racial reconciliation. In the hands of some, teen canteens became more than outlets for recreation—they became forums for advancing ideals of cultural pluralism, ideals integral to the nation's professed commitment to protecting democratic freedoms (Palladino 1996).

In the wake of the Zoot Suit Riots, the city of Los Angeles took similar steps to uplift youth recreation and combat juvenile delinquency. In 1944, the city council created the Los Angeles Bureau of Music, an organization designed to suppress unsupervised race mixing by sponsoring choral concerts and community sings and promoting music that city leaders believed deserved to be celebrated. Instead of nurturing a multiracial music culture, the Los Angeles Bureau of Music hoped to bind diverse groups by giving them the opportunity to perform classical music and folk music, but certainly not swing or jazz. These alternative programs marked a departure from the restrictive efforts of law enforcement to separate the races, for at least publicly civic authorities celebrated classical concerts and community sings for creating a constructive environment in which the races could mingle safely (Macías 2004). Nonetheless, while the musical offerings of the Bureau did create performance opportunities for many young Angelenos, they failed to achieve their additional goal of diminishing the influence of the city's growing multi-racial jazz and swing music culture (Macías 2004). In fact, this culture would become increasingly tied to concerns about juvenile delinquency that surged across the nation during the decade after the war.

JUVENILE DELINQUENCY AND CONSUMER CULTURE AFTER WORLD WAR II

In the postwar years, teenagers increasingly became known for their buying power and influence, and a growing number of industries began targeting teens. The tensions caused by this growing connection between the nation's teenagers and consumer industries were heightened by the continued expansion of the oppositional and multiracial culture that had incited conflict in Los Angeles and other cities during World War II. By the early 1950s, the culture of zoot suits and jazz music had begun to grow into a more mainstream culture of youthful rebellion, fueled in part by Hollywood's romanticization of this culture through movie stars such as

Marlon Brando and James Dean. The arrival of rock 'n' roll would further accelerate this process, but even before that moment arrived, many adults became concerned about the negative influence of the media and consumer industries upon young Americans. These critics charged the media and consumer industries with standing between parents and children and thus causing an increase in the rate of American juvenile delinquency. Despite a lack of evidence that teen delinquency was indeed rising, this argument was so popular during the first half of the 1950s that Congress created a subcommittee to study the claim (Gilbert 1986).

These claims were remarkably similar to those made 70 years earlier by moral reformers such as Anthony Comstock. Like his predecessors, Frederic Wertham, a leading critic of comic books and other disreputable forms of media, claimed that reading such materials caused boys and young men to commit acts of violence and sexual depravity and called for a ban or at least a severe regulation of these offensive publications (Wright 2001). Yet Wertham's critique was also quintessentially a product of its time, for at a peak moment of the Cold War he contended that comic books and other media's indoctrination of America's children paralleled the propaganda approach used by totalitarian governments during and after World War II (Wright 2001) (see document 16). In Wertham's view, comic books inured young readers to violence, much as Nazi or Communist propaganda conditioned Germans and Soviets to accept the murderous policies of Hitler and Stalin. In 1953, the Senate convened its Subcommittee to Investigate Juvenile Delinquency and proceeded to spend much of the next three years examining the impact of television, radio, movies, and particularly comic books on the moral development of the nation's children. Ultimately, the committee decided to take no action against the industry after public pressure forced publishers to hire a "comics czar" to oversee the industry's self-regulation. This decision would establish a pattern for the periodic investigations that Congress would launch on this subject over the next half century; while politicians of both parties would gain tremendous publicity from their opposition to such materials, regulation would never extend beyond advisory warning labels or the extraction of promises of more careful self-policing by the industries.

This renewed call for proscription of products specifically directed toward young people was a response to yet another expansion of children's role as consumers in American society. In fact, the fervency of this protest during the 1950s reflected the general futility of institutional opposition to this trend, and the periodic strident but ineffective complaints since that decade about music or video games inspiring youth violence or sexual activity have resulted in very few practical solutions for reversing this growth. As one historian has written, "the market itself has settled the controversy"; four decades after the conclusion of the Senate subcommittee's hearings, the youth market resulted in $89 billion in revenue, an increase of 1000 percent since 1957 (Palladino 1996). Consumer culture has become an integral part of American childhood, and concerns about impeding children's moral, intellectual, and emotional development have proven consistently incapable of altering that economic and social reality.

Efforts to address the problem of juvenile delinquency have also missed their mark because reformers interpret expressions of disaffection in commercial culture as a cause rather than a symptom of adolescent disaffection from mainstream values. Blaming consumer culture and popular culture for delinquent behavior, in fact, has sometimes obscured deeper historical changes and structural transformations in the economy that have generated oppositional youth cultures. The controversy surrounding the popularity of hip-hop culture in the 1990s offers a case in point. In 1994 Congress held hearings on the negative impact of gansta rap on the black community. Many of those who testified, including C. Delores Tucker of the National Political Congress of Black Women, decried rap lyrics for glamorizing violence and drug use and for promoting sexual promiscuity and the mistreatment of women. Such messages, Tucker lamented, explained "why so many of our children are out of control and why we have more black males in jail than we have in college." At the hearings Joseph Madison, a former executive director of the Detroit NAACP, joined Tucker in condemning rappers for failing to seize the gains won by civil rights leaders in the 1950s and 1960s to acquire more education and improve themselves (Lipsitz 1998).

In calling for censorship, however, critics of gansta rap ignored changes in the economy and public policy that made so many African American and Latino youth receptive to rap lyrics and hip-hop style. As real wages fell in the mid-1970s and 1980s and as jobs moved overseas or to distant suburbs inaccessible to residents of the inner cities, black youth unemployment rose sharply, as did the number of children living in poverty. Calls for censorship of rap music fit in neatly with a neoconservative agenda in the 1980s and 1990s that sought to shift the focus of public debate and blame for social problems from structural inequalities to individual moral failings and a debased popular culture. Widely condemned songs such as Ice-T's "Cop Killer" and NWA's "Fuck the Police" might reinforce anti-police sentiment among minority youth, but a long history of police brutality created that sentiment in the first place (Lipsitz 1998). Censoring rap music might temporarily silence disaffection, but it would require a different kind of government involvement—investment in urban renewal, jobs training, and jobs creation, less punitive welfare programs, affordable health care, and support for a living wage—to address the underlying causes of this disaffection. Bill Clinton, who famously condemned the rapper Sister Souljah in his 1992 presidential campaign for stating that she understood the "logic" of the violent response to the verdict exonerating police for beating Rodney King, added his voice to the neoconservative side of the culture wars. As president be advanced modest proposals to fund jobs training but shied away from larger government commitments to alleviating poverty. Clinton took pride in the Personal Responsibility and Work Opportunity Act, popularly known as the welfare reform act of 1996, which fulfilled his promise to "end welfare as we know it." Preferring small-scale initiatives, the Clinton Administration instead proposed midnight basketball to deal with the inner-city "youth problem"—a solution that mirrored so many earlier reform efforts to control delinquency by providing wholesome alternatives to the culture of the streets.

From the early twentieth century to the early twenty-first, efforts to regulate and reform delinquent child consumers have alternated between attempts to channel children's adventure seeking into wholesome outlets and attempts to impose control through censorship and other proscriptive measures. Judged by their more ambitious goals, censorship advocates have probably been less successful owing to the ingenuity of mass marketers in mainstreaming marginalized cultures and coopting the notion of cool. Programs to uplift recreation have enjoyed their greatest success when they incorporated input from adolescents and adapted recreations to youthful tastes and consumer desires. Thanks in part to shared governance by teenagers and adults, teen canteens in World War II attracted far more participants than the early-twentieth-century working girl clubs directed by middle-class elites. The delinquent child consumer has proved a compelling focal point for struggles over cultural authority for the past century and a half. The intensity of the late-twentieth and early-twenty-first century culture wars suggests that children's consumer culture—a source of pleasure for some and angst for others—will continue to shape intergenerational tensions, stimulate public debate, and prompt the formation of new institutions to combat its excesses.

WORKS CITED

Addams, Jane. 1909. *The Spirit of Youth and the City Streets*. New York: Macmillan.

Comstock, Anthony. 1883. *Traps for the Young*. Cambridge, MA: Belknap Press of Harvard University Press, 1967.

Duis, Perry. 1996. "No Time for Privacy: World War II and Chicago's Families." In *The War in American Culture: Society and Consciousness During World War II*, ed. Lewis Erenberg and Susan Hirsch, 17–45. Chicago: University of Chicago Press.

Gilbert, James Burkhart. 1986. *A Cycle of Outrage: America's Reaction to the Juvenile Delinquent in the 1950s*. New York: Oxford University Press.

Holt, Marilyn. 1992. *The Orphan Trains: Placing Out in America*. Lincoln: University of Nebraska Press.

Jacobson, Lisa. 2004. *Raising Consumers: Children and the American Mass Marketing the Early Twentieth Century*. New York: Columbia University Press.

Kelley, Robin D. G. 1994. *Race Rebels: Culture, Politics, and the Black Working Class*. New York: Maxwell Macmillan International.

Lindsey, Ben B., and Wainwright Evans. 1925. *The Revolt of Modern Youth.* New York: Boni & Liveright.

Lipsitz, George. 1998. "The Hip Hop Hearings: Censorship, Social Memory, and Intergenerational Tensions Among African-Americans." In *Generations of Youth: Youth Cultures and History in Twentieth-century America,* ed. Joe Austin and Michael Willard, 395–411. New York: New York University Press.

Macías, Anthony. 2004. "Bringing Music to the People: Race, Urban Culture, and Municipal Politics in Postwar Los Angeles." *American Quarterly* 56: 693–717.

Nasaw, David. 1985. *Children of the City: At Work and At Play.* Garden City, NY: Anchor Press/Doubleday.

Norton, Charles Eliot. 1864. "Dime Novels." *North American Review* 49: 303–9.

Odem, Mary. 1995. *Delinquent Daughters: Protecting and Policing Adolescent Female Sexuality in the United States, 1885–1920.* Chapel Hill: University of North Carolina Press.

Pagán, Eduardo Obregón. 2003. *Murder at the Sleepy Lagoon: Zoot Suits, Race, and Riot in Wartime L.A.* Chapel Hill: The University of North Carolina Press.

Palladino, Grace. 1996. *Teenagers: An American History.* New York: Basic Books.

Peiss, Kathy. 1986. *Cheap Amusements: Working Women and Leisure in Turn-of-the-Century New York.* Philadelphia: Temple University Press.

Ruiz, Vicki. 1998. "The Flapper and the Chaperone Cultural Constructions of Identity and Heterosexual Politics among Adolescent Mexican American Women, 1920–1950." In *Delinquents and Debutantes: Twentieth-Century American Girls' Cultures,* ed. Sherrie A. Inness, 199–226. New York: New York University Press.

Wright, Bradford W. 2001. *Comic Book Nation: The Transformation of Youth Culture in America.* Baltimore: Johns Hopkins University Press.

4 Parents and Children in the Consumer Household: Regulating and Negotiating the Boundaries of Children's Consumer Freedoms and Family Obligations

Lisa Jacobson

Few novels have captured contemporary anxieties about consumer culture's potential to corrupt children and family relationships as well as Roald Dahl's *Charlie and the Chocolate Factory*. In both the popular 1964 novel and the 1971 film, a parade of stock child characters—the gluttonous chocoholic, the spoiled brat, the demanding tyrant, and the media junkie—meet terrible, though ultimately curable, fates thanks to their own consumer excesses and their overindulgent parents. *Charlie and the Chocolate Factory* amuses young and old alike because we can see ourselves in its portrait of overindulgence. Children might be reminded of their own excesses in hounding parents for goods, while parents might blush in recognition of how easily they succumb to children's demands. Yet, Dahl's characters are so over the top that children and parents might also pride themselves on having retained at least some measure of self-control. Dahl's story, in fact, is as much a celebration of consumer culture's power to reenchant the everyday world with fantasy and play, as it is a critique of consumerism run amok. Consumer freedom, if properly channeled, the story seems to say, can be wondrous indeed.

Throughout the twentieth century parents and children have struggled to determine the boundaries of children's consumer freedoms. What children spent their money on and how much spending money they were entitled to were ever-present sources of family conflict. Parents' concerns about their teenage daughter's budding sexuality made conflicts over age-appropriate fashions especially intense (Schrum 2004). Parents and children also butted heads over what constituted worthy uses of children's leisure time and appropriate adult supervision. At stake in these family struggles were broader concerns about the sanctity of the family and the authority of the marketplace in modern capitalist culture. In resolving these conflicts, parents and children were not only negotiating the boundaries of children's consumer freedoms. They were also defining the proper balance between children's autonomy and parental control and between individual entitlement and family obligations. Race, class, gender, and ethnicity all played crucial roles in structuring the outcomes of these family struggles.

REGULATING AND NEGOTIATING CHILDREN'S SPENDING LIMITS IN THE EARLY TWENTIETH CENTURY

The notion that children were impulsive spendthrifts with unquenchable consumer desires circulated widely in the United States at the turn of the twentieth century. "The mind of a child," Carolyn Benedict Burrell wrote in a 1900 issue of *Harper's Bazaar*, "veers between the love of acquiring and the love of spending. It delights to hoard, to shake its bank and feel its increasing weight, and to spend recklessly until it is bankrupt" (Burrell 1900). A 1903 survey of children's spending habits bore out such impressions. Even when exhorted to save their pennies, the survey indicated, children failed to heed parental advice. A 10-year-old boy confessed, "My father advises me to save [ten cents a day], but I say what's the use? I have all I need." Women's magazines, parenting guidebooks, and education journals called for new kinds of training to teach children economic responsibility and respect for money. Some recommended school savings banks, which required children to deposit money on a weekly basis to make saving an ingrained habit. School banking advocates envisioned compulsory saving as a way to reduce children's access to allegedly dangerous public amusements such as movies and pool halls and to instill habits that would make children, especially immigrant and working-class children, disciplined and productive citizens (Jacobson 2004) (see documents 20–21).

Others endorsed giving children an allowance—a fixed weekly sum—to teach children how to spend wisely as well as how to save. The idea of giving children allowances had earlier nineteenth-century precedents but did not really gain steam until the 1920s. The new enthusiasm for children's allowances partly reflected children's heightened sentimental value and a growing egalitarianism within the middle-class family that recognized children's entitlement to a share of the family's resources (Zelizer 1985). Child experts, however, also blamed too much parental sentimentality for children's lack of money sense (Jacobson 2004). As middle-class families became smaller and more child-centered, parents and family experts expressed concerns that the child lavished with care and affection might become the tyrannical child—willful, demanding, and unmanageable. Worse still, such attentive childrearing might produce a generation of children who would become selfish, immature adults, lacking in self-direction and inner-strength (Fass

1977). Allowance proponents sought to discipline parental sentimentality as well as the child spender by replacing parents' haphazard giving of spending money with systematized money training. Absent some regular system, experts contended, children would never learn to handle money wisely or value it appropriately. "If given too lavishly," Burrell argued, "it will mean nothing; if doled out too parsimoniously, it will acquire an abnormal value" (Burrell 1900; Jacobson 2004).

In many respects, the allowance solution adapted behaviorist psychology to children's money training problems. Stressing the virtues of regularity and routine over the careless indulgence that typified sentimental parenting, the roots of behaviorist childrearing could be found in L. Emmett Holt's widely disseminated *The Care and Feeding of Infants* (1896), which went through several editions in the early twentieth century. Holt advised mothers to instill healthy habits by adhering to strict schedules of feeding, sleeping, and toileting. Behaviorists urged mothers to resist picking up a crying baby or feeding it on demand, as these responses would only spoil the child and create a demanding little tyrant. Allowance proponents applied the same attention to rationalizing children's economic habits as the advocates of scientific mothering did to rationalizing their physical habits (Jacobson 2004).

Convincing parents to replace unsystematic giving with allowances was no easy task. A survey of 630 grammar school children, conducted by a woman's club in 1903, suggests that haphazard giving was the norm. Less than one-third of the children received allowances, while the rest collected money in small sums ranging from a penny to a dime "whenever I ask for it" or "most every day or two." Some parents objected to allowances on grounds that a regular provision of spending money would give their children too much liberty. Before the 1920s, such attitudes were especially pronounced in immigrant families, which viewed children's discretionary spending as a threat to the hierarchical basis of family authority. Although wage-earning boys from immigrant families claimed some financial independence, often the only spending money wage-earning daughters enjoyed came from the little they skimmed from their pay envelopes in defiance of parental wishes. By contrast, middle-class parents more commonly rejected allowances as a stingy way to treat their children and equated providing for their children with doling out spending money on demand (Jacobson 2004).

During the 1920s and 1930s, allowance advocates addressed some of these objections by stressing the educational value of allowances. Angelo Patri, whose newspaper columns and radio broadcasts made him a well-known and widely respected childrearing authority during the 1920s and 1930s, insisted that parents who withheld allowances were the stingy ones. Doing so, he argued, deprived children of valuable experience in money management and unnecessarily prolonged their economic dependency. Plus, allowances worked as an educational tool only if they were provided children a small margin over actual needs. Lacking that cushion, Patri wrote, allowances "[became] just another narrow and repressive . . . disciplinary measure." Allowance advocates also warned against "too much regulation" of children's spending choices. Parents could achieve better results if they praised the good purchases and overlooked the bad (Jacobson 2004).

Allowances were less permissive than they might seem at first blush. Child experts calculated that giving children more spending freedom would ultimately help them make wiser spending decisions. Allowances permitted children to make their own spending choices, but they also held children accountable for their own spending mistakes. Sidonie Gruenberg, a leading child expert in the 1920s, assured parents that children learned more from their mistakes than from scolding or "early protection against unwise purchases . . . A stark record of a long succession of ice-cream sodas or short-lived catch-penny toys" may "improve the child's taste or shift his choice of purchases." Eventually, with practice, children learned to "buy daily without regrets" (Jacobson 2004) (see document 26).

This consumer-oriented money training differed sharply from school savings bank programs in both means and ends. Allowance advocates questioned the efficacy of compulsory saving as a means to instill habits of fiscal responsibility. Practice in habitual saving might change children's behavior in the short run, they argued, but it provided no guarantee that children would internalize self-restraint. Practice in spending, by contrast, offered children a superior form of experiential learning. Children learned to save when they wanted a more expensive item than their weekly allowance could afford. Allowance advocates also stressed the importance of adapting children's money training to child ways of learning. "Saving in response to mother's 'you may be thankful for more money someday' carries no meaning to the small child who has little conception of time beyond today," noted one *Parents' Magazine* contributor. Most children could not grasp the concept of saving for a rainy day until they reached their teens. Ultimately, allowance advocates were more invested in producing wise spenders than habitual savers. In recounting allowance success stories, allowance proponents often celebrated children's newfound appreciation of the high cost of living—knowledge that put children in greater sympathy with parents' needs to rein in family spending, especially during the inflationary decades of the 1910s and 1920s. To these writers, the virtues of allowances were clear: child-centered means achieved adult-approved ends (Jacobson 2004).

During the interwar years, children's spending became an arena for complex negotiations over the proper balance of parental control and children's autonomy. Although family conflicts over spending money were hardly new, sociologists and cultural commentators believed they had grown more intense, thanks in large part to the spending pressures spawned by the new public culture of dating and mass recreation (Lynd and Lynd 1929) (see document 28). As that dating culture spread to rural communities in the 1930s, even rural teens, previously a more quiescent group, became interlocked with their parents in "violent, internal" conflict over spending money and the use of the family car (Bell 1933). Likewise, working-class families found it more difficult to lay claim to the wages of their wage-earning children without granting sons and daughters a greater share for their own disposition (Benson 1998).

Family experts blamed spending money disputes on parents' failure to adopt more egalitarian parenting styles. In their view, allowances were a key component of the modern democratic family ideal. Child experts even characterized allowances in highly democratic terms, referring to them as the child's "share in the family's 'luxury spending'" or as "a gradually increasing franchise." Child experts also worried that children would grow resentful of their prolonged dependency and perhaps succumb to delinquency if parents denied them spending money—a conviction supported by the 1934 White House Conference on Child Health and Protection, which found that adolescents without allowances were more likely to rank low on measurements of "personality adjustment" and "moral habits." The most radical expression of democratized family spending was the family firm—a family conference that invited children to participate in family spending decisions. The extent of children's participation and weight of their vote would vary according to the child's age and the matter under discussion. The family firm significantly revised traditional patriarchal arrangements by calling upon fathers to share financial information not only with their wives but also with their children (Jacobson 2004). The ideal father, in historian Robert Griswold's words, was "a kindly, nurturing democrat who shared rather than monopolized power" (Griswold 1993).

The idea of the family firm, first proposed in the mid-1920s, gained more salience during the 1930s, when advocates envisioned financial candor as a means to subdue resentment over limited depression-era family finances (Jacobson 2004) (see document 30). For many working-class and middle-class families, the Depression dealt a severe blow to the rising consumer expectations of the 1920s—a decade that saw an enormous proliferation of new consumer goods and services. These expectations became all the more difficult to contend with because the family itself had become less a consuming unit than a collection of individual personalities, each with competing claims on the family's resources (Wandersee 1991).

To a surprising degree, child experts became even more committed to consumer-oriented money training during the Great Depression. For a variety of reasons, the Depression helped to legitimize consumer spending as a positive social and economic good. Politicians, New Deal planners, and Keynesian economists all pressed Americans to see consumer spending as the cure for unemployment and a flagging economy. Popularizers of Freudian psychology also strengthened the association of consumer desire with regeneration and psychic vitality. Casting aside earlier views of children's spending impulses as dangerous and insatiable, modern psychology encouraged a more sympathetic view of children's desire for things. No longer a sign of moral failure, an abundance of consumer desire instead testified to unmet psychological needs. The child who spent all her money at the candy store was not an incorrigible spendthrift with an overactive sweet tooth but a child who did not receive enough affection from her parents. A five-year-old who stole money from her seven-year-old brother after being denied an allowance of her own was not a thief but a child who succumbed to deep-seated feelings of jealousy. Child experts now worried more about the stifling effects of restraint and viewed excessive thriftiness in children as a potential sign of psychological maladjustment (Jacobson 2004).

What did parents and children think of the new consumer-oriented approach to money training? Many adolescents were quite enthusiastic about allowances. The 16- to 18-year-olds who signed an "Adolescents Want Freedom" manifesto insisted that an allowance was essential for their self-esteem. "Many of us who are decidedly anti-social," the teens explained, "are so only because our parents have not taken care to allow us to dress in conformity with our social standards and so have let us in for so much ridicule that we prefer solitude and shun society" (Jacobson 2004). The growing teen practice of shopping with friends and siblings rather than with mothers reflected teens' expectation that they deserved a greater say in clothing purchases (Schrum 2004). Not all children, however, saw allowances as the road to new spending freedoms. As the sociologists Robert and Helen Lynd reported in their mid-1920s study of Muncie, Indiana, some high school girls preferred not to have an allowance, recognizing that "you can get more without one" (Lynd and Lynd 1929) (see document 28). To these teenagers, the ostensibly hidden mechanisms of control embedded in allowances were all too readily apparent (Jacobson 2004).

As the Muncie teens understood all too well, parents also gained something in the bargain. Allowances granted children greater spending freedom, but they also compelled children to spend within fixed limits. *Parents' Magazine* contributor Marion Canby Dodd seemingly gave her adolescent daughter complete freedom to dispose of her clothing allowance, but the stipulation that she not ask for more money nor buy anything to which her mother strongly objected suggested that adult interests still bounded such freedom (Jacobson 2004). *Parents' Magazine* even encouraged mothers to be more charitable toward teen fashion fads, arguing that any kind of style consciousness was a positive sign that teens cared about their appearance and would develop lifelong habits of good grooming (Schrum 2004). Likewise, while appearing to grant children a greater say, the family firm often enhanced parental authority. In practice, disclosing financial information to children typically moderated children's demands. These democratic reforms nevertheless constituted real gains in the minds and pocketbooks of many adolescents. Although the statistical data on children's allowances varies, a 1936 survey of 825 children, usefully categorized by class, found that 48 percent of children from professional families and 43 percent of children from semi-professional and managerial class families received allowances—an impressive increase over the single-digit percentages that often prevailed at the turn of the century. Allowances were less common among working-class children, but they too experienced significant gains, with 28 percent of workers classified as "semi-skilled" and 12 percent of those classified as "slightly skilled" providing allowances (White House Conference on Child Health and Protection 1936). Just how much these allowances augmented children's spending funds is difficult to know, but opinion surveys suggest that many children equated allowances with greater spending freedom. Most of the 400 high school students who entered *Scholastic Magazine*'s "The Kind of Parent I Hope to Be" contest in 1939 favored democratically run households in which children received allowances from early childhood and in which weekly family councils ironed out budgets for each child (Jacobson 2004).

CHILDREN'S SPENDING AND THE SHIFTING MEANINGS OF INDIVIDUAL ENTITLEMENT AND FAMILY OBLIGATIONS

Family negotiations over children's spending money reveal much about how different families in different eras have sought to balance individual needs and desires with larger family obligations. Race, class, gender, and children's earning power (or lack thereof) have all played crucial roles in determining the outcome of these negotiations. In the late nineteenth and early twentieth centuries, wage-earning children in working-class and immigrant families turned over most, if not all, of their pay to their parents, but retained some say in household spending decisions. Many recent immigrants, African Americans, and working-class families depended for their survival on the supplemental income of children. The ages of wage-earning children ranged widely, depending on family need and the industry that employed them, but most were in their late teens and early twenties thanks to the institution of compulsory education laws. Although parents today regard children's earnings as the property of children, this was not the case a century ago (Moehling 2005). Working-class and immigrant parents often permitted wage-earning sons to retain a small portion of their pay for discretionary spending, but they typically required wage-earning daughters to hand over all their earnings in an unopened pay envelope (Ewen 1985).

Most children complied with these expectations, but not solely out of duty or under threat of punishment. To maximize children's supplemental income, parents also gave children incentives to work. A disgruntled child, parents realized, might work more slowly at piecework or get fired for doing poor work. Older children might take the even more drastic step of moving out and taking their paychecks with them. Parents rewarded working children by allowing them greater input in family spending decisions and subjecting them less to physical punishment than their nonworking siblings. Allocations for clothing give some indication of children's influence on household decisions. Such expenditures were significantly higher for wage-earning children than nonworking siblings—the equivalent of four or more new outfits a year—and these expenditures increased as children's earning power increased (Moehling 2005). Historian Vicki Ruiz has found that Mexican American daughters who held full-time jobs were more likely to challenge or evade chaperonage at mass commercial amusements than non-wage-earning Mexican American adolescents (Ruiz 1998). The bargaining power of wage-earning daughters was especially high in families headed by single mothers, who depended even more on their children's income for economic survival (Odem 1995). While middle-class children relied on their cultural capital as savvy consumers and cherished members of the companionate family to bargain for a greater share of family resources, working-class children leveraged their economic capital, or earning power, to achieve similar ends.

Wage-earning adolescents who asserted too much economic independence, however, sometimes got more than they bargained for. Some working-class parents reported disobedient sons and daughters to the juvenile courts for not contributing enough to the family's income and for spending their earnings foolishly (Odem 1995). In addition, adolescent girls rarely claimed as much control over their earnings as their brothers did during the late nineteenth and early twentieth centuries. Adolescent boys generally retained more of their earnings and enjoyed more leverage in household decisions because they received higher wages. In addition, many considered economic independence part of boys' training for manhood; giving girls some control over their earnings concerned parents less because female economic dependency was constant—both before and after marriage. Immigrant parents also exercised greater control over girls' earnings because they wanted to limit their access to mass commercial amusements—places where potential sexual danger lurked. In parents' minds, limiting the economic independence of adolescent daughters also limited their sexual independence (Ewen 1985). Ironically, financial dependency may have made adolescent girls and young women more vulnerable to sexual exploitation. In the new public culture of dating, men treated women to an evening at the movies or a day at the amusement park, often expecting some form of sexual exchange in return. Not coincidentally, adolescent girls and young women spent most of their discretionary funds on clothing and accessories—the very trappings that would make them more attractive to men and help them secure dates (Peiss 1986).

Notions of feminine self-sacrifice also limited girls' spending freedom. In economic hard times, girls often subordinated their consumer desires (and educational ambitions) in the interest of protecting the family's economic stability. During the Great Depression, teen advice columnists urged girls to chip in for dating expenses and spend less money on clothes so that other family members could fulfill some of their wants and needs. Such advice may have reflected popular Depression-era stereotypes of girls as gold diggers and fashion slaves, but it also reinforced expectations that girls should bear the greater burden in heeding limits on family spending (Jacobson 2004). In the second half of the twentieth century the gender gap in family allocations of spending money began to close. Some parents gave girls larger allowances to compensate for girls' more limited earning opportunities. Even when the disparity between girls' and boys' earnings narrowed in the late twentieth century, girls still received larger allowances. In 1999, girls received on average $3.00–$4.00 more than boys for their allowances—sadly, perhaps a recognition that achieving feminine ideals of beauty and style required greater expenditures (Jacobson 2004).

The spread of the sheltered childhood ideal in the twentieth century added new wrinkles to family negotiations over children's spending money, as it became harder to connect lessons in spending to the experience of earning. Since the nineteenth century, the greater earning power of middle-class breadwinners had enabled middle-class children to experience a prolonged and protected childhood free from the responsibility of work. In Viviana Zelizer's words, children were valued as "economically useless" but "emotionally priceless." Working-class children of all races did not join the nonproductive world of childhood until much later (Zelizer 1985). Some state legislatures banned child labor in the late nineteenth century, but a national ban did not come into effect until 1938, when Congress passed the Fair Labor Standards Act.

Two parallel trends in early twentieth-century childhoods—declining opportunities for earning and rising expectations for some spending freedom—raised new concerns about the nature of family obligations and individual entitlement. Could allowances ease children's resentment of economic dependency without also over-inflating their sense of entitlement? Could they teach children the true value of money if parents did not also require children to work? The ideal of a sheltered childhood compounded these moral dilemmas because children's need for spending money preceded their ability to earn. (Jacobson 2004). The tension between children's entitlement to spending money and their obligations to family came to the fore in debates over the merits of linking allowances to children's fulfillment of household duties. Throughout the twentieth century, many parents have treated allowances as a payment for performing household chores and bringing home good grades. Many childrearing authorities, however, have strenuously objected to this common practice. Using allowances either as a reward or as a punishment, they contend, undermines the value of allowances as an education tool—how can children learn to budget their allowance when its supply is unpredictable? Worse still, such practices, Sidonie Gruenberg wrote in 1923, confuse "the give-and-take of family life with the buy-and-sell of the market place." Instead of learning to respect money, children, some experts feared, would learn to bargain over the worth of each good deed and to calculate the economic risk of each bad deed. To avoid reducing family obligations to a set of cold economic calculations, child experts have often proposed that parents pay children only for tasks the family would normally hire someone else to do. Such earning opportunities give children a fuller appreciation of the value of the dollar without corrupting their sense of family obligation (Jacobson 2004) (see document 26).

Recent studies suggest, however, that children have often developed their own moral calculus in negotiating how and when allowances should be tied to household chores. Some accept the conventional wisdom that children should be paid for extra work but not daily chores. As one kid noted in a USAA survey of 1,000 10- to 13-year-olds, "Kids should clean and take responsibility just because their parents told them to, not because they're going to get an allowance" (Lowry 1996). An undercurrent of calculation, however, sometimes informs such seemingly altruistic attitudes. Some children have learned that doing some additional chores for free on top of their regular chores strengthens their position when bargaining to do bigger jobs for pay. Children have also learned that bargaining power hinges on acquiring knowledge of markets. Many gain leverage in family negotiations by trading information with other kids about the going rates for allowances and for performing extra chores and sharing tips on how to get a raise in their allowance (Zelizer 2002; Lowry 1996).

Race and class often complicate how children come to understand the meanings of individual entitlement and family obligation. Elizabeth Chin's 1999 study of fifth-grade African-American girls in Newhallville, Connecticut —a black working-class neighborhood of renters and homeowners—found that concerns about fulfilling family obligations weighed heavily in children's spending decisions. Unlike their more sheltered middle-class counterparts, Newhallville kids knew at a young age the trials of making ends meet and the costs of rent, groceries, and the birthday gifts they requested. The demanding child consumers who inhabited middle-class suburbs were nowhere to be found in Newhallville, where kids learned early that wheeling and whining for goods would not be tolerated. Unlike middle-class kids, who generally regard allowances as discretionary income to spend as they pleased, Newhallville kids used their own to buy basic necessities like socks and underwear and help fund summer camp. Most of their discretionary income went for inexpensive drinks and snacks purchased at the local grocery store. As part of her ethnographic study, Chin took individual children on a shopping trip and gave each $20 to spend. The Newhallville children compared prices and carefully weighed consumer choices, frequently choosing goods that could be shared with friends and siblings or strengthen family relationships. Children took satisfaction in using their money to purchase gifts for mothers or grandmothers—those female caretakers who often sacrificed personal luxuries to provide for others. Though keenly aware of brands, Newhallville kids cared more about stretching their dollars and often chose practical items like shoes and school supplies when spending on themselves. Children's sense of entitlement often took a back seat to fulfilling family obligations—a duty, Chin writes, that could be "sustaining and joyful but also painful, onerous, and highly charged. I sometimes suspected that the lesson imparted to children and imparted by them was at times a coercive generosity: share or else" (Chin 2001).

In the late twentieth century, Chinese American and Korean American children who grew up working in their immigrant parents' small business also had to negotiate a delicate balance between asserting individual consumer desires and honoring family obligations. Partly because their mom-and-pop business operated on slim profit margins, Asian American immigrant parents often gave their children allowances instead of a paycheck. Parents classified children's work in the family business as a household chore and regarded the allowances as a gift rather than a wage. Many children accepted this arrangement with little grumbling because these allowances generally satisfied their wants and needs. Such gift money, however, often came with strings attached that limited children's autonomy. Parents retained "their authority and control over children's lives," sociologist Lisa Sun-Hee Park writes, "by forcing them to make specific requests for money rather than giving it to them automatically" (Park 2005, 54).

Limited family finances have not always inspired family cooperation. The failure to satisfy children's consumer desires has also placed tremendous strains on family relationships in poor and working-class families. In the Lynds' 1929 study of Muncie, Indiana, a working-class mother of five children complained that her "stuck-up" 11- and 12-year-old daughters refused to wear homemade clothes and forced her to take additional work in order to provide her daughters with what they considered proper school attire. The pressure to conform to the reigning fashion standards was sufficiently high that many working-class daughters threatened to quit school, and often did quit, if their mothers could not outfit them appropriately (Lynd and Lynd 1929) (see document 29). Carl Nightingale's 1993 study of Philadelphia's inner-city poor African American families documented bitter disputes that broke out between parents and children over how income tax refunds and welfare checks would be spent and over whose consumer desires would be gratified (Zelizer 2002; Nightingale 1993). Such disputes help explain why Stephon Marbury, a well-known NBA player, became a hero to kids and parents alike in the fall of 2006 when he introduced a line of sneakers that sell for just $14.98 a pair. Kids who would have never entertained the idea of asking for $70 Air Jordans—Marbury, who grew up on food stamps, was once one of them—could enjoy the cachet of owning a pair of Starbury's while less affluent parents could rejoice in being able to fulfill their children's desires (Adande 2006).

To many observers in the late twentieth and early twenty-first centuries, affluence, aggressive marketing, and permissive parenting all seem to have enhanced middle-class children's sense of entitlement and weakened parental restraints on children's spending. Childrearing authorities have continued to stress the educational value of allowances, noting that allowances develop character, foster regular habits of saving, and raise children's financial literacy. Just how many parents embrace allowances as an educational tool, however, remains an open question. In many instances, allowances function solely as an economic entitlement—an indication perhaps that the tenets of family democracy have trumped concerns about inculcating wise spending. Some parents also seem to have abandoned the use of allowances to exercise indirect control over how children spend their money. Consider the advent of e-wallets—a kind of virtual credit card that allows kids to make purchases online with money their parents have placed in a special account. E-wallets enable parents to limit children's spending to a predetermined sum, but they don't limit where children can spend that money. Parents' willingness to let children surf the seemingly boundless realm of e-commerce suggests that some parents have also willingly relinquished control over children's spending choices (Jacobson 2004).

REGULATING CHILDREN'S CONSUMPTION THROUGH PLAY

Regulating children's expenditures has not been the only way parents have tried to reassert control over children's consumption. During the 1920s and 1930s, child experts recommended that parents adopt more relaxed parenting styles and equip their home with playrooms and educational toys that stimulated the imagination. Parents, of course, had long been encouraged to provide their children with playthings and separate play spaces, but interwar childrearing authorities raised the stakes of failing to do so. By not giving children a room for play and the creative toys to cultivate skills and hobbies, a *Parents' Magazine* contributor asserted, parents ran the risk of turning "children adrift in a world of movies and street excitement," unprepared to resist their demoralizing effects (Jacobson 2004). Interwar proponents of summer camp shared such concerns and promoted camps as an antidote to the cheap thrills and mind-numbing effects of mass culture (Paris 2008).

Child experts envisioned playrooms as essential for children's healthy development and psychological adjustment. Reflecting Freudian psychology's criticism of undue repression, child experts depicted the playroom as an integral feature of a home where, as Emma Kidd Hulbert put it, "restrictions are few" and "don't is a word seldom heard." Simply decorated, fuss-free playrooms, equipped with sturdy furnishings that could withstand rambunctious play, gave spatial expression to the idea that "Free, 'unbossed' play is the most serious business of the child"—a childrearing principle so important that a 1918 international conference on childhood enshrined it in their New Bill of Rights of Childhood (Macleod 1998). Stocking playrooms with the right toys was equally important: art supplies, puppets, costumes for dress-up, blocks, and educational toys that inspired creative effort were all preferable to flashy toys that merely involved the child as a spectator. Toy makers capitalized on parental anguish over children's attraction to potentially corrupting outside amusements by promising to keep children absorbed in wholesome play at home. "You, being a wise parent," a catalog for Buddy "L" dump trucks and machinery noted, "want to satisfy the boy's urge to be doing" and "keep him . . . off the street." Play with the right kinds of toys in the right kinds of spaces was all directed toward a definite end: producing a cultured child, with good taste, the capacity for self-directed play, and a refined appetite for edifying forms of entertainment (Jacobson 2004).

Child experts also promoted more egalitarian parent-child relationships as key to restoring the primacy of family ties and home-centered recreation. Stuffy mothers who appeared too concerned with maintaining household order came under fire. So, too, did impatient, unsympathetic, intolerant, and tyrannical fathers. The new and improved parent no longer obsessed over discipline and responsibility, but instead became understanding companions who related to children on an equal basis, learned their slang, and "made a game out of everyday living" (see document 27). Behind child experts' celebrations of unthwarted play and family fun, however, often lay more conservative goals. Simply put, parents exercised authority more effectively through play and friendship than obedience and discipline. Charles Gates, a social scientist, made the ultimate goal of family companionship explicit: "Only by . . . genuine sympathy with the child can [parents] hope to control the child." Many parents seem to have embraced such advice. In Robert and Helen Lynd's 1929 study of Middletown, mothers from both the business class and working class identified play as the crux of successful modern parenting. "I certainly have a harder job than my mother; everything today tends to weaken the parents' influence," one mother confessed. "But we do it by spending time with our children. I've always been a pal with my daughter, and my husband spends a lot of time with the boy" (Lynd and Lynd 1929) (see document 28).

Parents' actual record of success in using play and playthings to strengthen their influence, however, is more mixed than such confident assessments suggest. Parents have long considered toys as tools that prepared children for adult roles. Doll play supposedly nurtured girls' fashion sensibilities and maternal instincts. Doll tea parties, doll funerals, and doll weddings even taught girls the etiquette of important social rituals (Formanek-Brunell 1993). In the early twentieth century African American parents—hoping that doll play would inculcate race pride, refine taste, and discourage interracial sexual liaisons—insisted that their sons and daughters play with col-ored dolls instead of white dolls. As reform-minded African Americans saw it, doll play was much more than a wholesome child's amusement—it was key to the survival of the race (Mitchell 2004). Similarly parents imagined that boys' play with electric trains, chemistry sets, and Mechano engineer-ing toys would nurture worthy career ambitions and set boys on the path to responsible manhood (Cross 1997).

Children, however, have often resisted such didactic uses of toys. Instead of nurturing their dolls, some girls cut them and subjected them to ex-treme punishments; nineteenth-century doll funerals focused more on the harrowing experience of death than the rituals of mourning (Formanek-Brunell 1993). Parents, too, increasingly confront a modern toy industry that caters more to children's yearnings for rebellion and adventure than to adults' interest in meeting children's educational and developmental needs. Since the 1970s, fantasy toys divorced from the real worlds of fam-ily and work have gained a larger and larger share of the market (Cross 1997).

Other early-twenty-first-century toy marketing developments, critics charge, point to troubling counterrevolutionary trends. Some worry that Bratz dolls, the wildly popular pouty-lipped, bare-midriffed dolls "with a passion for fashion," encourage the "sexualization of childhood"—a trend reinforced by the retailing of "thong underwear emblazoned with sexually suggestive phrases for 6-year-old girls . . . [and] 'pimp' Halloween costumes for little boys" (MacPherson 2005). Toy marketing can also frustrate paren-tal efforts to combat gender stereotypes. How much power, feminist writer Peggy Orenstein wonders, do parents really have to shape what it means to grow up female when the toy industry floods the market with some 25,000 girlie-girl princess products, ranging from princess Barbie dolls and pink princess paraphernalia (sequined purses, bedding, and jewelry) to the ul-timate extravaganza—the Princess-Makeover Birthday Party (Orenstein 2006)?

Despite such challenges, parents have continued to experiment with new institutions and new parenting practices in their quest to reduce children's exposure to mass culture and rampant commercialism. Like earlier genera-tions who sought to temper children's consumer excesses by stimulating their imagination with creative in-home play, some early twenty-first century middle-class parents have launched their own antispoiling crusade to coun-ter commercial values. Simplicity circles in more than 100 cities encourage children to find as much pleasure in the intangible stuff as they do from a trip to the mall or the toy store. One so-inspired mother—fed up with the birthday extravaganzas she once staged for her own preschoolers—began requesting on party invitations that guests only give art supplies. Many in-terwar childrearing authorities would surely have applauded her strategy to make creative play an alluring alternative to a commercial culture run amok (Padgett 2001). Bolder still were the legions of parents who decided to home school their children. The Christian conservatives who currently dominate home schooling might seem miles apart from the secular countercultural leftists who pioneered home schooling in the 1960s, but both groups share a disdain for mainstream consumer culture and a desire to shield children from acquisitive values and degrading images of sex and violence. Many Christian conservatives, in fact, embraced home schooling as an antidote to consumer culture's corrosion of family ties. Just as interwar child experts had hoped that restoring recreation to the family's functions would strengthen the family as a counterweight to the allures of consumer culture, Christian conservatives hope that restoring education to the family will do the same (Talbot 2001).

EXPLAINING CHILDREN'S EXPANDING CONSUMER FREEDOMS: PARENTAL COMPLICITY AND PARENTAL CONSENT

Cultural critics often cast parents and children as passive victims of the invasive forces of the market, powerless to withstand the influence of greedy corporate interests. Yet, to a remarkable degree, parents have actively consented to the dramatic expansion of children's consumer freedoms. Historians have offered several explanations for why this is so. Peter Stearns argues that children's expanding consumer freedoms went hand in hand with opposing trends toward greater control and greater supervision of children. Vigorously enforced school attendance, ever more lengthy and challenging homework assignments, and a widening array of adult-guided after-school activities demanded greater discipline from children. By the same token, however, parents who crowded children's free time with dance lessons, music lessons, and organized sports also sanctioned consumer pleasures and fantasy play as children's just reward (Stearns 2003). The overscheduled child and the overindulged child were often one and the same.

The compensatory satisfactions of children's consumer culture could be just as powerful for adults as they were for children. Gary Cross contends that parents willingly acceded to an expanding children's consumer culture because it allowed adults to participate vicariously in the playful, even primitive, pleasures of childhood that adults had long ago learned to repress and control. By indulging their children with toys and enjoying the sense of wonder that consumer novelty aroused in their children, parents also temporarily satisfied their need to escape the tedium and responsibilities of adulthood and recapture their own lost wonder. Put another way, in yielding to children's consumer desires, parents were also nurturing their own inner child. These vicarious pleasures exacted their own price, however. Instead of fostering deeper emotional connections between parents and children, Cross argues, consumer novelty set children on an endless quest for cool that often put parents and children at odds (Cross 2004).

More benign interpretations of children's impulses have also contributed to greater parental acceptance of children's consumer desires. Early-twentieth-century childrearing advice literature warned mothers not to feed their baby on demand and recommended mechanical restraints to curb thumb sucking and masturbation, fearing that giving into the infant's insatiable impulses would create a tyrant who lacked self-control. By the early 1940s, however, childrearing authorities came to view the baby's impulses as benign and harmless. Viewing the baby's wants as a reflection of the baby's needs, childrearing authorities theorized that indulging babies, rather than depriving them, would make them less demanding as they matured (Wolfenstein 1955). Changing views of children's spending impulses paralleled these changing views of the infant's impulses. Casting aside earlier views of children's spending impulses as dangerous and insatiable, in the 1930s psychologists and Freudian popularizers interpreted children's desire for things as a reflection of unmet, unconscious needs (Jacobson 2004). As more Americans came to associate fun and spending with the good life, fewer parents, in turn, felt compelled to impose excessive restraints on children's consumer desires.

Validating children's consumer desires could also take on larger political meanings during the Great Depression. The *Defender Junior*, a children's column in the African American newspaper the *Chicago Defender*, repeatedly told its young readers that black children, like all other children, deserved respect and equal treatment as consumers. Edited by the fictive Bud Billiken, the column continued to preach the virtues of thrift and respectability, as it had done throughout the 1920s, but stressed children's entitlements as consumers during the 1930s—a decade when African American activism against economic discrimination soared. African American parents reinforced Bud Billiken's equation of children's rights and consumption rights by taking their children to Bud Billiken parties (sponsored by the *Chicago Defender*) where candy, ice cream, lemonade, and toy prizes were in abundant supply and where children could play without fear of social ostracism. To be recognized as a real child, the *Defender Junior* implied, was to be recognized as a consumer who enjoys toys and sweets, and the freedom to play in public spaces (Hinderer 2007).

Other scholars contend that parents have yielded to an expanding children's consumer culture because doing so has made it easier for mothers to accomplish the daily tasks of rearing children and managing a home. Despite the introduction of labor-saving technologies such as washing machines and electrical appliances, the actual time spent on such tasks grew in the early twentieth century. A shortage of household servants, rising standards of cleanliness (fostered in part by advertisers), and more intensive childrearing all placed additional demands on middle-class housewives in the early twentieth century. The demands on mothers' time have continued to escalate as greater numbers of mothers entered the workforce in the second half of the twentieth century. Not surprisingly, busy mothers have often relied on toys, videos, and television to keep children occupied and entertained while they cooked and cleaned (Seiter 1993).

Acknowledging parents' complicity in the expansion of children's consumer freedoms by no means denies the power of the market in shaping and fostering dramatic transformations in relations of power and authority within the household. Nor have the allures of consumer culture invariably entailed a sacrifice of parental authority. Through allowances, playrooms, and educational toys, parents have attempted and sometimes succeeded in reasserting parental control—albeit in more indirect and manipulative ways. Combating rampant commercialism remains an uphill battle, however, because so many modern parenting practices rely on consumer enticements and because mass marketers have so aggressively appropriated those practices to their own ends. Perhaps parents and media critics are so often dismayed by consumer culture's hold on children because it reminds them of the limit to which parents can control childrearing outcomes. Parents are only one of many socializing influences in children's lives, and the mass media, the mass market, and children's peer affiliations make for potent contenders.

WORKS CITED

Adande, J. A. 2006. "The Shoe May Just Make the Man." *Los Angeles Times,* September 14, D1, D9.

Bell, Earl H. 1933. "The Family: Age Group Conflict and Our Changing Culture." *Social Forces* 12 (December): 237–43.

Benson, Susan Porter, 1998. "Gender, Generation, and Consumption in the United States: Working-Class Families in the Interwar Period." In *Getting and Spending: European and American Consumer Societies in the Twentieth Century,* ed. Susan Strasser, Charles McGovern, and Matthias Jundt, 223–40. Washington, DC: German Historical Institute; and New York: Cambridge University Press.

Burrell, Carolyn Benedict. 1900. "The Child and Its World," *Harper's Bazaar* 33 (November 3): 1721–22.

Chin, Elizabeth. 2001. *Purchasing Power: Black Kids and American Consumer Culture.* Minneapolis: University of Minnesota Press.

Cross, Gary. 1997. *Kids' Stuff: Toys and the Changing World of American Childhood.* Cambridge, MA: Harvard University Press.

———. 2004. *The Cute and the Cool: Wondrous Innocence and Modern American Children's Culture.* New York: Oxford University Press.

Ewen, Elizabeth. 1985. *Immigrant Women in the Land of Dollars: Life and Culture on the Lower East Side, 1890–1925.* New York: Monthly Review Press.

Fass, Paula. 1977. *The Damned and the Beautiful: American Youth in the 1920s.* New York: Oxford University Press.

Formanek-Brunell, Miriam. 1993. *Made to Play House: Dolls and the Commercialization of American Girlhood, 1830–1930.* New Haven, CT: Yale University Press.

Griswold, Robert. 1993. *Fatherhood in America: A History.* New York: Basic Books.

Hinderer, Moira. 2007. "Making African-American Childhood: Chicago, 1917–1945." Ph.D. diss., University of Chicago.

Jacobson, Lisa. 2004. *Raising Consumers: Children and the American Mass Market in the Early Twentieth Century.* New York: Columbia University Press.

Lowry, Katharine. 1996. "The Great Allowance Debate: Experts and Parents Don't Always Agree." *USAA Magazine* (August/September): 12–15.

Lynd, Robert, and Helen Lynd. 1929. *Middletown: A Study in American Culture.* New York: Harcourt, Brace, and World.

Macleod, David. 1998. *The Age of the Child: Children in America, 1890–1920.* New York: Twayne Publishers.

MacPherson, Karen. 2005. "Is Childhood Becoming Oversexed?" *Pittsburgh Post-Gazette,* May 8, www.commercialfreechildhood.org/news/articles/childhoodoversexed.htm.

Mitchell, Michele. 2004. *Righteous Propagation: African Americans and the Politics of Racial Destiny after Reconstruction.* Chapel Hill: University of North Carolina Press.

Moehling, Carolyn. 2005. "'She Has Suddenly Become Powerful': Youth Employment and Household Decision Making in the Early Twentieth Century." *Journal of Economic History* (June): 413–37.

Nightingale, Carl H. 1993. *On the Edge.* New York: Basic Books.

Orenstein, Peggy. 2006. "What's Wrong with Cinderella?" *New York Times Magazine* (December 24): Section 6, 34.

Padgett, Tim. 2001. "Keeping It Simple." *Time* 158 (August 6): 48–49.

Paris, Leslie. 2008. *Children's Nature: The Rise of the American Summer Camp.* New York: New York University Press.

Park, Lisa Sun-Hee. 2005. *Consuming Citizenship: Children of Asian Immigrant Entrepreneurs.* Stanford, CA: Stanford University Press.

Peiss, Kathy. 1986. *Cheap Amusements: Working Women and Leisure in Turn-of-the-Century New York.* Philadelphia: Temple University Press.

Ruiz, Vicki. 1998. "The Flapper and the Chaperone: Cultural Constructions of Identity and Heterosexual Politics among Adolescent Mexican American Women, 1920–1950." In *Delinquents and Debutantes: Twentieth-Century American Girls' Cultures,* ed. Sherrie A. Inness, 199–226. New York: New York University Press.

Schrum, Kelly. 2004. *Some Wore Bobby Sox: The Emergence of Teenage Girls' Culture, 1920–1940.* New York: Palgrave Macmillan.

Seiter, Ellen. 1993. "Children's Desires/Mothers' Dilemmas: The Social Contexts of Consumption." In *The Children's Culture Reader,* ed. Henry Jenkins, 297–317. New York: New York University.

Stearns, Peter. 2003. "Historical Perspectives on Twentieth-Century American Childhood." In *Beyond the Century of the Child: Cultural History and Developmental Psychology,* ed. William Koops and Michael Zuckerman, 96–111. Philadelphia: University of Pennsylvania Press.

Talbot, Margaret. 2001. "The New Counterculture." *Atlantic Monthly* (November): 136–43.

Wandersee, Winifred. 1991. "Families Face the Great Depression." In *American Families: A Research Guide and Historical Handbook,* ed. Joseph Hawes and Elizabeth Nybakken. Westport, CT: Greenwood Press.

White House Conference on Child Health and Protection. 1936. *The Young Child in the Home: A Survey of Three Thousand American Families.* New York: D. Appleton-Century Company.

Wolfenstein, Martha. 1955. "Fun Morality: An Analysis of Recent American Child-training Literature." In *Childhood in Contemporary Cultures,* ed. Margaret Mead and Martha Wolfenstein, 168–78. Chicago: University of Chicago Press.

Zelizer, Viviana. 1985. *Pricing the Priceless Child: The Changing Social Value of Children.* New York: Basic Books.

———. 2002. "Kids and Commerce." *Childhood* 9, no. 4: 375–96.

II Documents

5   Promoting the Child Consumer

Children's magazine publishers were among the very first to recognize and promote children as consumers. As magazines came to depend more on advertising revenues than subscription sales for their survival, publishers went to great lengths to woo prospective advertisers. At the start of the twentieth century, children's magazine publishers faced an uphill battle convincing businesses that children were worthy targets of their advertising dollars. *St. Nicholas* and *American Boy*, in particular, waged extended campaigns in the advertising trade press to promote the virtues of child consumers. The following six documents—all promotional advertisements by *St. Nicholas*, *American Boy*, and *Seventeen* magazines—illustrate how these magazines attempted to gain credibility as a profitable advertising medium. They provide a lens through which to examine changing constructions of childhood and changing understandings of the distribution of power and authority within the modern family. The distinctly gendered appeals of *American Boy*, a magazine for 9- to 19-year-old boys, and *Seventeen*, a magazine for teenage girls, also reveal how children's magazine publishers both shaped and exploited popular conceptions of masculinity and femininity.

1. "How Does This Service Fit Your Needs?" *Printers' Ink* 94 (January 20, 1916): 72.

How Does This Service Fit Your Needs?

This advertisement is directed to a certain food manufacturer (and his agent). It is *not* intended for Campbell, Swift, Libby, Kellogg, Quaker Oats, American Sugar, Walter Baker, National Biscuit, Beech-Nut, Genesee, Hills, Borden's, Post, Welch, Red Wing or Hungerford Smith because all of these are regular advertisers in St. Nicholas.

YOUR PROBLEM	OUR SERVICE
A—To make customers ask for your product by name instead of naming the general line.	A—For 16 years St. Nicholas has been educating its readers to "buy by name." It has now become their fixed habit.
B—To create active "consumer demand" instead of passive "consumer acceptance."	B—Youngsters have a way of their own of getting what they set their hearts on. There's nothing passive about *them!*
C—To counteract substitution, whether malicious or honest.	C—Children are not sophisticated. No one can make them believe that anything is "just as good" as the things advertised in their beloved magazine St. Nicholas.
D—To impress your package and trade-mark upon those who go to the stores.	D—Nine out of every ten St. Nicholas readers do much of the buying of your kind of goods for their parents—and they *study* St. Nicholas advertisements until they *know.*
E—To acquaint customers with *every* product in your line, and induce them to *buy* them all.	E—Young folks are impressionable and progressive. They respond readily and enthusiastically to an appeal about "Something good to eat—*try* it!"
F-G-H—To make *friends* who will be loyal for life; to sell the *best* people; to sell the *big* families.	F-G-H—St. Nicholas gives you a friendly introduction to young folks at the age (9 to 17) when they are forming life-long *habits;* its readers are the *cream* of the land; per family there are *three* children, father, mother, grandparents and servants.

OUR "SPECIAL COPY" DEPARTMENT is at YOUR SERVICE

ST. NICHOLAS
A Specific Magazine with a Definite Service

2. "Dictator to the Universe—the Boy," *Printers' Ink* 80 (September 5, 1912): 11.

Dictator to the Universe— the Boy

There never was one like him in the world before. That's what every parent thinks. Naturally in that home *boy* wants, *boy* opinions and *boy* knowledge *go*.

In every family the boy is the *acquisitive* member. With the divine optimism of youth he sees all the good things of life coming his way; he wants a share in the best of every- thing—and that share is usually a big one.

Every *boy home* is a home of enthusiasm, energy and genu- ine interest in the progress of the world. From the latest auto- mobile styles to the newest phonograph records; from baseball to army rifles—the boy knows what's going on and he sees that the rest of the family know it, too.

200,000 Boy Homes Reached by

The American Boy

Here are two hundred thousand families interested in *the* boy's magazine *because* the *boy* is the biggest thing in the world to them. Here are two hundred thousand *boy homes* where dozens of articles are going to be bought only because the boy wants them. Every American Boy home is a home of comfortable living, where money can be found to buy most of the things the boy sets his heart upon.

These boys average 15½ years of age. Their wants are almost a man's wants. And their knowledge stands behind most of the pur- chases in the home.

THE SPRAGUE PUBLISHING COMPANY

J. COTNER, JR., Secretary-Treasurer, DETROIT, MICH.
H. M. PORTER, Eastern Mgr., 1170 Broadway, NEW YORK

3. "When Slim Watson Talks Carburetors His Family Sits Up and Takes Notice," *American Boy* advertising proof sheet, 1926.

When Slim Watson talks carburetors his family sits up and takes notice

The young man at the left of the picture is Slim Watson, none other! He knows a pile about motor-cars and is letting Mother and Dad in on a big earful.

For some time, the head of the family (over there on the right) has been planning to trade in his old car. Like many car-owners, he's in the period of indecision as to which make to buy. Should he trade it in for the same make, an open car or a coupe, one of a different make? Pretty hard to make up his mind. Slim is convincing him that such-and-such a bus is the best buy . . . the one he really ought to have. It isn't the first time that Slim and his Dad have thrashed out the subject, either. Looks as though the youngest of the family were scoring a win at this session!

Slim is just one of the 500,000 up-and-coming near-men who read THE AMERICAN BOY and talk motor-car to their parents. These 500,000 enthusiasts are great boosters for the automobile that has won their respect and confidence. They're your equal in everything but years. Their man-sized opinions are heeded and usually followed by the man who pays the bills. Their wants are man-sized and they usually get what they want.

Enlist the powerful influence of this big army of rooters on your side. Tell them about your motor-car through the advertising columns of THE AMERICAN BOY. It's their favorite publication, and its say-so determines their buying habits. Copy received by January 10th will appear in March.

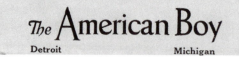

The **American Boy**

Detroit   Michigan

Box 200, N. W. Ayer and Sons Advertising Agency Records Collection, Archives Center, National Museum of American History, Smithsonian Institution. Reprinted with permission.

4. "When They Crack the Whip You Jump," *Printers' Ink* 137 (November 18, 1926): 7.

When they crack the whip you jump

Ask Sam and Andy Stevens what the well-dressed near-man will wear. They'll tell you. They have the latest dope on shawl collars, bat-wing ties, patent leathers and pompadours. If they don't like a thing—it's out.

And, believe it 'cause it's the truth, these chaps are just as much at home on a football field or a basketball floor as at a dance. They wear T-shirts, sweaters, golf hose, plus fours, shorts, longs, blazers —and they have to have 'em! Their shoes and hats and suits are man-sized. They eat like horses. Their appetites are man-sized as are their buying capacities. In short, they're a man's equal in everything but years.

THE AMERICAN BOY is read by 500,000 fellows like Sam and Andy, who average 15½ years of age, 115 pounds on the scales and 5 feet 4 inches tall in their stocking feet. They buy everything you sell to men. They hold man-sized opinions for or against a product. Win them to your side *now* while they are forming the buying habits of a lifetime.

It makes no difference what you make . . . tooth-paste, cameras, radios, automatic pencils, razors . . . these chaps form a big part of your market. Sell to them through the advertising columns of THE AMERICAN BOY, the publication they have made their own. Copy received by December 10th will appear in February.

The American Boy

Detroit   Michigan

5. "When Is a Girl Worth $11,690,499" (1948) *Seventeen Magazine* promotional advertisement. Estelle Ellis Collection, Archives Center, National Museum of American History, Smithsonian Institution. Reprinted with permission.

When is a girl worth $11,690,499?

...when 1738 advertisers spend just that much money in four years—to sell her their product and their name in the magazine she reads

...when advertisers in the cosmetic, toiletry, fashion, food and home product fields buy more than 3,500,000 lines of advertising in the magazine edited exclusively for her

...when 671 agencies tell their clients the magazine she reads and believes is a must on their advertising schedule

...when 1613 stores ran 2554 ads in one month tying in with the magazine she tucks under her arm when she goes shopping

...when manufacturers and retailers run special advertising campaigns to promote special products and special departments just for her— via the magazine she and her friends call their very own

...when the magazine she buys on the newsstands or subscribes to can show a 150% circulation gain—400,000 copies sold in September '44; 1,000,000 in September '48

...when the magazine devoted to her interests surveys her needs—sets up a research department, a consumer panel, a library of fifteen market studies to determine her powerful present, her promising future

...when the magazine she's devoted to can prove she's not a one and only—that there are 7,999,999 girls in America's homes just like her

...when she, her parents, her teachers and her friends can get together on one thing—their affection for, their belief in, their support of—

seventeen

—*the magazine that keeps pace with each new generation of teens*

6. Teena, A Girl with Influence (1947), *Seventeen Magazine* promotional advertisement. Estelle Ellis Collection, Archives Center, National Museum of American History, Smithsonian Institution. Reprinted with permission.

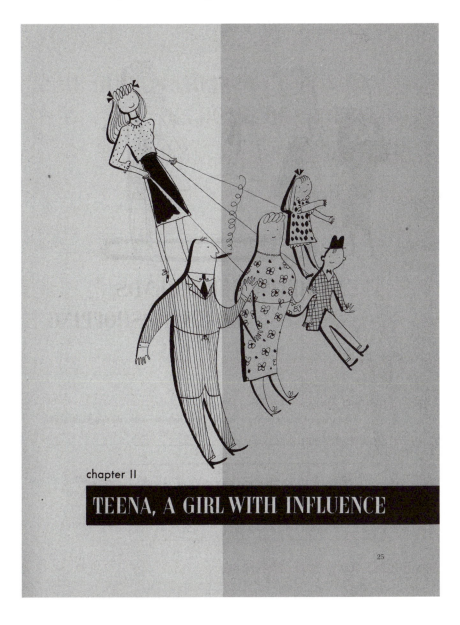

chapter II

TEENA, A GIRL WITH INFLUENCE

25

6   Courting Child Consumers

In the first two decades of the twentieth century commentary on juvenile advertising made barely a ripple in the advertising trade press. By the 1920s, however, articles explaining how to craft advertising campaigns that appealed to child consumers had become regular features in such journals as *Printers' Ink, Printers' Ink Monthly, Advertising and Selling,* and *Sales Management.* The documents in this section, all drawn from the advertising trade press, reveal how and why advertisers began to conceive of children as consumers who not only influenced family spending but were also purchasers in their own right. The first three documents explore kid psychology and highlight common advertising mistakes as well as surefire strategies to win juvenile good will. Horace Wade's 1920 article, "What Kind of Advertisements Do Boys Like?," is especially notable because the author was himself a 12-year-old boy, and a precocious one at that, having written a novel, acted in motion pictures, reported for the *New York World,* and worked as a copywriter for a department store. In the 1920s and 1930s, advertising authorities were especially enthusiastic about reaching boys, and the articles by Wade and S. C. Lambert suggest some reasons why that was the case.

Because children relied partly, and often entirely, on parents for their source of spending money, successful juvenile advertising campaigns had to strike a careful balance in appealing to kids without antagonizing parents. The final two documents reveal just how difficult that balancing act proved to be when advertisers took to the airwaves and began sponsoring children's radio programs in the 1930s. Although the trade press has periodically taken juvenile advertisers to task for overstepping the boundaries of good taste, we might wonder why advertisers have grown ever bolder in testing the limits of parental good will with each new media innovation, from radio and television to cable TV and the Internet. The excerpt from Cy Schneider's *Children's Television: The Art, the Business, and How It Works* (1989), reprinted in chapter 7, provides a partial answer.

7. S. C. Lambert, "Building a Business on Children's Good Will: A Firm That Makes Express Wagons Finds the Right Appeal in Selling Its Products to Boys," *Printers' Ink* 112 (July 29, 1920): 89–91.

To get anything out of this advertising story you must go back to your kid days—the days of the ol' swimmin' hole, the back lot where the "gang" held its baseball battles.

You must recall kid standards, kid ambitions and kid ideals. If you are one of the unfortunates to whom these things are but names, read no further, you are wasting your time, for though you may have mastered all the arts of prestige building, the wiles by which some men build up dealer co-operation, though you may know all there is to know about selling motor cars or overalls to millionaires, you can never be a success at putting over a product sold to boys of from ten to fifteen years of age, and that is what this story is about.

In a Middle West city, known principally as an important lumber centre, is a business which has been built up entirely on "Kid" good will. This good will was won through knowing boys—not the Little Lord Fauntleroy type,[1] but real honest-to-goodness back-lot boys who go to school, play and dream dreams, to say nothing of working at odd jobs once in a while when the chance offers to pick up a "couple of bits." The men who did this thing write nothing but advertising copy and letters, but they have the knowledge of kid psychology of the Tarkingtons and Mark Twains. That is their business—knowing how kids think and act.

They say that in this knowledge lies success or failure—that it is not enough simply to build something which fills the needs of a growing boy. He has to be "sold" and he cannot be "sold" except by someone who understands him. . . .

BOY PSYCHOLOGY THE GUIDE

. . . First of all, you want to get clearly into your head the fact that a boy is more or less a primitive creature, and from the beginning of time primitive races have formed themselves into tribes. If you were a real boy you belonged to a "gang." Not necessarily a tough gang—it may have sprung from a Sunday school class—but it was a gang nevertheless, and ruled by gang laws. Your gang had an informal leader. What made him so you cannot tell to this day. Sometimes it was physical prowess, but not always. As likely as not the leader of your gang was a skinny-legged kid with glasses, who when there was fighting to be done left it to one of his henchmen, but this informally chosen leader as a rule set the style for the gang. If he got a bicycle or a new variety of marbles you were not happy until you had the same thing. Don't forget this point, for it is almost the basis of this sled-selling campaign.

Another thing you must recall before we can get down to a proper under-standing of the business methods the company follows is the kid attitude toward "grown-ups." Think back and you will recall certain men whose front gates and porch chairs were perfectly safe on Hallowe'en. Why? Simply be-cause the owners were sort of honorary members of the gang, men who because of a friendly attitude were placed in a selected class by themselves. If your gang had encountered another gang disturbing their property it would have meant a battle.

As you think back from a mature viewpoint you will see that the secret lay in the fact that these men knew boys. They did not inflict themselves upon the gang, or aim at any "uplift," but when the baseball team needed new equipment they were always there with a quarter or a half a dollar. If the gang got into trouble, they would get a twinkle in their eyes and go to the front for you. Perhaps they would hand out a bag of candy once in a while, and when they did, they knew the right way to do it. Just a hint of the "here, little boy, is something nice for you" attitude and the gang would have been their enemies for life. Here is point No. 2 to remember.

Also, somewhere along between ten and fifteen years, there was a time when you began to take great pride in the fact that you could earn money. It made you feel like a man, and to be a man is one of the prides every real boy carries under his shirt. This is another worth-while thing to know in kid merchandising.

Now before we go any farther in the study of boy psychology, let me show you how the company uses the points I have mentioned. Take first of all the "gang spirit."

SEVERAL SALES ASSURED INSTEAD OF ONE

It does not seek to sell one boy a coaster; it follows the natural course and sells the gang, and this is the way it proceeds:

The company has formed a Coaster Club. Briefly, the scheme is this: If a boy will interest five other boys who own or will purchase express wagons, and form a club he will be formally made captain of his club. He receives free a nifty cap bearing the word "Captain" and each of the other boys re-ceives a club hat. They are also supplied with information on how to start the club, and told new ways to have fun and make money with their coast-ers. How this information is gathered will be explained later. The club idea is put across by advertising in boy papers and a few farm publications. There are seventeen publications on the list at present.

It has been found by experience that the "gang leader" is usually a careful reader of boy publications, and like any other good business man, he is on the lookout for new ideas which he can apply to his business. If they can sell him on the idea of forming a club the trick is turned, for he is pretty sure to sell the members of his gang. This may mean five or more sales instead of the one sale which might result if the copy simply aimed to sell the boy on the advantages of owning an express wagon himself.

Of course there is nothing about this plan which would put it across on its own merit. The trick lies in the boy appeal of the copy in which it is presented. Just as an example of the tone of this copy here is a paragraph taken from a circular selling the club idea:

"It's the boy who develops his genius for leadership that rises to be the bank president, the manager of the big business house, the college professor. Make your start as captain of the Coaster Club. It's an easy step from there to captain of the baseball team, manager of the football or basketball outfit, and similar chances to develop your qualities of leadership. It's a big thing to be the acknowledged leader in your crowd. Soon others consider you as a leader also, and you'll find yourself sought both socially and in business. But you must develop leadership first—there's no better way than by getting busy right now with the fellows and starting your local Coaster Club."

Note how this copy plays to kid ambition, the dreams that every real boy has in the back of his rattle head. It ties up the express wagon with the dream of being a bank president, a big executive, a professor, just a touch of respect for the boy who has won a place of gang leader, and stimulation to go on and make the most of his qualities for leadership. You will also note that this copy is entirely free from a patronizing tone—straight man-to-man stuff. All of the copy has the same ring, it is written in the same style as the man talks to boys whose front gate is safe on Hallowe'en.

SETTING THE BOYS TO WORK

Another thing the company is constantly striving for is to get in personal touch with the boys. It does this by contests. For instance, one successful contest was based on ways of making money. The advertising manager for the company told me that in this contest more than 2,000 letters were received, and you can imagine what a wealth of material they unearthed—uses for the coaster that did not come from the fagged brain of a copy-writer, but fresh and vital from the life of the boys themselves. For example, take these few uses picked at random from a list: Hauling water, hauling firewood, bringing in rocks for an oven, carrying papers, hauling sod, taking out ashes, bringing dirt for the flower bed, hitching up to your dog, making a train, collecting old papers to sell, delivering groceries. One boy told how he made $9.50 in two hours. He loaded up his coaster with old boxes and sold them to people waiting for a parade. Another fellow explained just how he "cleans up" hauling baggage from the boat at a summer resort. Another explained in detail how a fellow can handle a six mile newspaper route and not be late for school with the help of a coaster and how it netted him $117.

One thing which often stands in the way of boys getting express wagons is lack of money. The company is trying to get around this by the use of small banks. These banks are well made, pocket size, and will hold just about the price of a coaster. The boys are given the banks, told to put their money into them, and when the bank is so full it will hold no more, they take it to a dealer who has the key. Dealers report that this plan works.

So much for the way the boys are sold. Now for the dealer end of the campaign. The plan whereby the dealer is induced to stock is simply to show him how the coaster is sold to the boy. It has the same effect upon him as a big national advertising campaign would have, for that is what it is—a national advertising campaign to reach Boyville. He is shown that this particular brand of coaster is what the boys in his neighborhood want. If there is any doubt about it, the boys are very likely to tell him so themselves, for it has been found that the boy takes his advertising seriously and is inclined to scorn substitutes. In the finding of the right dealers the boys do a lot of the work themselves. They are induced to send in names of dealers in their localities, and the dealers they name are pretty likely to be the right ones, for they have a tendency to overlook any who do not "stand in" with the gang.

8. Horace A. Wade, "What Kind of Advertisements Do Boys Like?" *Printers' Ink Monthly* 2 (December 1920): 32, 99.

I think an awful lot of advertising and advertising men. If you don't believe it, ask the members of the New York Advertising Club, to whom I spoke some weeks ago, what I said about advertising. And I want to tell you this: It is harder to write an advertisement than a novel. I wrote my novel "In the Shadow of Great Peril" in less than a month, but—well, I couldn't write 171 pages of advertising in less than a century.

With a novel you can write just as long as the ink holds out, and if a character tries to argue with you, there's no law in book language to prevent him from being murdered. But you can't sit down and dispose of the things in an advertisement that way. You've got to make folks want a thing so bad that they'll hustle right out and buy it; but the minute you get to roving about, your readers will bang the magazine together and go off to a picture show.

Boys read advertisements a lot. But there are some advertisements which they don't read at all, and I'm going to tell you why I think they don't read them. Men who write these advertisements have forgotten what boys like.

They use words that boys don't understand. Boys are dreamers! There's hardly one of them who has not sometimes been a pirate with a black flag flying, or scalped a few Indians.

I remember, a short time since, that a bunch of us were reading a boys' magazine when we came upon a page of advertising. We were just passing by it when one of my chums fairly gasped, "Gosh, say, look at this, will you?" The headlines read: "How Would You Like to Meet Capt. Kidd?" and it went on to tell about two boys who had been camping in the woods of Wisconsin and had spied two robbers burying money at the foot of a tree. Both boys were armed with rifles and valiantly shouted "Hands up!" The robbers, taken by surprise, were marched back and handed over to the sheriff, and the money recovered. All because the boys had been wise enough to take along their rifles—rifles that never jammed or missed fire. Did it make us want rifles? Well, I guess *yes! Three of the boys bought them.*

Now, this is what I call a good advertisement. It made us all want rifles. If all the men who write advertisements for boys, or about things that are used for boys, will bring in something about boys' heroes it will catch a boy's eye much quicker. And it is ten to one that that boy will get *that* thing. It is strange to grown-ups, unless you remain young, what queer heroes boys choose. Outlaws like Capt. Kidd, Rob Roy, Jesse James and other blood-and-thunder fellows have a strange fascination for a boy. So do our national heroes—John Paul Jones, General Custer, Kit Carson, Davie Crockett, Daniel Boone—any man who has adventures.

Suppose you want to sell a bicycle, and you should put at the head of your advertisement this line: "What if Kit Carson had a Ranger?" and then have a picture showing a bunch of Indians coming toward Kit and a long road leading away to his back. Would a boy read that advertisement? Sure, and he'd have a bicycle to play "make believe" how he escaped being scalped by jumping on it and whizzing away out of danger.

Boys live in a "make believe" world, and when you come down off your high horse you can reach them every time.

I have often wondered why advertising men who write advertisements for a boy don't use fairy stories to catch his eye. He will fall for all the "Jack-the-Giant-Killer" stuff you can give him. I read a food advertisement all through once because it had a picture of Little Red Riding Hood with a basket on her arm and a wolf trotting along by her side. The advertisement, as I remember it, said something about not blaming the wolf because the ham in that basket was "Majestic," or something like that; but at any rate I wasn't satisfied till my mother bought it for me. And then how my mouth did water. . . .

And when your advertisement tells what boys dream it is going to make the boys want whatever you advertise.

And boys like pictures that make their toys look like practical things. If they look at an advertisement of a train they like to see the train running over a mountain or coming out of a tunnel. And if someone is telling about a chemical outfit boys want to think that when they use that outfit they are learning something. But they don't want to be told that they are being taught. No, they just want to feel that they are going to have lots of fun doing the things that they want to do when they grow up. . . .

Watch a boy read a newspaper and you'll get some fine ideas on what boys like. He'll read every line of a hold-up, but skip over an article about the high cost of living. He isn't concerned in what a thing costs—just so long as it can be used in making his dreams come true.

Now, Mr. Advertising Man, when you are writing for boys, write in their *own language.* Don't forget what I told you about using fairy stories and boy heroes in your advertisements. You'll get a boy every time, and whenever you get a boy he'll get his mother to buy what you make him want, or he will find a way to earn enough money to buy it.

9. "Children as Consumers and Persuaders: How Some Advertisers Are Selling to and Through the Great Juvenile Market," *Printers' Ink* 159 (June 9, 1932): 53–54, 61.

Though we grown-ups think we bring them up, the fact is that children hold sway over our manners, morals and money. They often influence buying decisions without even expressing a preference, so much are they in our minds. Just let them set their hearts on a thing, and they have or will eventually find an irresistible way of getting it.

Advertisers are fully cognizant of this last-mentioned trait. They know—sometimes to the sorrow of parents—that the juvenile brand of "acceptance and demand," created through copy addressed directly to children by a knowing member of the craft, rapidly becomes an alarming obsession. And parental resistance against the salesmanship of boy or girl is as the thinnest tissue before a roaring blow-torch.

The premium or prize for returning a certain number of labels, or disposing of a formidable case of soaps or perfumes, is a venerable method of enlisting the sales promotion aid of boys and girls. It works today just as well as it did in the days when many readers of this were out pulling doorbells with a mental picture of a coveted premium to buck up flagging courage.

A current example is the magazine advertising of Libby, McNeill & Libby offering every item of equipment in the official catalog to Girl Scouts who send in the required number of labels from Libby's evaporated milk cans. Since fifty labels are required for the collapsible drinking cup, it is obvious that an ambitious girl must look beyond the normal consumption of one family.

Other premiums are designed to promote individual purchases. Talon Slide Fastener copy tells boys of the newest "knickers and longies which open and close as fast as aviators' clothes," and offers free pictures of five famous fliers to every boy who sends price tag or size tag or the name of the Talon fastened knickers or longies he buys. . . .

It is undoubtedly true that no little of the demand of youngsters for Campbell soups may be traced to the cheerful Campbell Kids and their happy rhymes.

In its current advertising in juvenile publications Cocomalt is appealing to the natural pride of boys and girls in a robust physique, the product, so the copy infers, of its strength-building qualities. "Once frail . . . afraid . . . now school's champ boxer," is a typical headline for boys. . . .

Copy appealing to children is not necessarily confined to juvenile media, as witness the advertising of the Great Atlantic & Pacific Tea Company under the heading "A Word to Wise Children on the Care of Mothers." The copy told about a radio program on bringing up children. This put children where they rightfully belong as masters of household destiny, and probably few of the grown-up girls let it pass without an amused reading. . . .

There is growing use of juvenile clubs built around the consumption of a product, or patronage of theaters or stores. . . .

The Cream of Wheat Corporation advertised the "H.C.B. Club with a secret meaning," making a jolly game of the morning cereal for children who think it's akin to spinach. Free badges, commissions, official-looking certificates, gold stars and posters help along the game.

The difficulty with clubs is that they peter out quickly unless they are continually stimulated with new ideas. There are few club promoters who can keep up with the insistent demand of childhood for innovations.

10. Bernard A. Grimes, "Radio's Most Critical Audience: Children Are Easily, but Not Always Properly, Influenced by Advertisers' Programs," *Printers' Ink Monthly* 28 (June 1934): 23, 49.

Youth is radio's most critical audience.

Children's minds are easily influenced. But advertisers sponsoring juvenile radio programs go haywire in their strategy when they think of this influence in terms of just "dealing with kids." They make another mistake when they forget that parents are always within hearing distance of the radio.

Children are highly impressionable, and intensely loyal. They are quick to detect insincerity and to resent unfairness. Advertisers need a keen perception of these attributes, if they are to proceed intelligently in building programs of sound appeal.

The advertiser who appeals to children over the air must double-check if he would make sure he isn't building his program on dangerous ground.

He checks first to see if his program pulls with the juveniles. He checks again to see what parents think of his program and its influence on their children. A lot was learned about two years ago when blood and thunder programs evoked a wave of objection from teachers and parents.

Children do not understand fictional qualities. They take the characters of a story and invest them with realities. The difference between the real and the unreal is not strongly formed and what to the grown-ups is apparent as fictional exaggerations, to the child is something to be believed as seen or heard.

That is why the lurid, over-dramatized radio programs proved unpopular with the parents. Little Johnnie and sister would strain their ears to the last words of a children's radio thriller and then go to bed restless and alarmed over the ordeals of their radio hero. . . .

Contests are popular with youngsters. They are an outlet for enthusiasm and children, like their elders, are keen to get something for nothing or as near nothing as possible. Cost and values, however, are hazy factors to them and a gadget of slight cost may be more prized than an item of greater value.

As children become older they distinguish values more clearly but, regardless of age, every contest should bring something tangible to every entrant as an appreciation of his effort. The task set should never be too involved and, above all, it must concern something that will be constructive. A sure way to win resentment of the parents is to try to make the child work for the selfish interest of the advertiser.

A successful program at no point will conflict with the wishes of parents. It can be built on two appeals. One concerns what is good for the children. The other concerns what children like. It is no easy task to bring these two conflicting elements together but it can be done as some outstanding programs have demonstrated.

There should be a clear conception of the age group that the advertiser wants to reach. The ages from three to eight, roughly, constitute one group; eight to thirteen another, and the adolescents a third.

In every age group the advertiser can make himself a welcome ally of the parents; perhaps, by encouraging regularity in eating, or by setting forth examples of good character, or by stimulating an interest along constructive educational or creative lines.

Little girls will be interested in programs that interest little boys but the reverse, while it might hold a feminine audience, would find the little men paying no attention, should they be around long enough to pay any at all.

And you can't get away with just story-telling which, with rare exceptions, is ineffectual these days. There is so much drama on the air that children become sophisticates at an early age and they, too, want their stories acted out. Babe Ruth, for example, is a boys' hero but even the Babe has gone into dramatization of events, a mere telling of which, four years ago, would have sufficed. . . .

Advertisers have been prompt in recognizing radio as a means of addressing and entertaining the very young, thus making them an influence in consumer councils.

In many homes the little tots dictate some brand selections. They do this on the strength of the example set for them by a favorite fiction character of radio or at the request of a personality that has won their affection. This means that the form of entertainment and not the worth of a product has won their loyalty.

Parents realize this. Therefore, no advertiser should attempt to appeal to children if his product has not got the wholehearted support of health authorities. The welfare of children extends beyond the home and includes the vigilant eyes of teachers and the medical profession. Any glossing over of fundamental weaknesses in a product is bound to stir up trouble for the sponsor.

Broadcasting to young America is one activity in which an advertiser can ill afford to be shortsighted in policy. He must subordinate his business-building endeavor to genuine altruism. Let his selfish motives be revealed or overstressed, let him plug his product too much, let him try to get the parents' commodity dollar by chucking sonny under the chin, or wheedling little Betty into asking Mother to buy her something that Mother feels isn't good for her—and Mr. Advertiser will realize that he has hurt himself.

But, if he earnestly tries to help the parents, he will be rewarded with their good-will and possibly their patronage, and they will know this was what he has been after all the time.

11. Don Gridley, "Children and Radio: Best Juvenile Programs Are Not Those That Fray the Nerves and Irritate Parents," *Printers' Ink* 175 (April 9, 1936): 102, 104–9.

. . . It did not take long for advertisers to realize that radio itself was one of heaven's gifts to children. . . .

Advertisers who had played around with the idea of winning parent acceptance by creating juvenile demand began to find that properly planned radio programs bring in the inquiries by the bundle.

They soon made each inquiry mean a sale of the product. Little Jimmy was denied the inestimable privilege of owning a picture of his favorite radio character unless he forced mama to buy two packages of the product so that he could send in the two labels to the generous manufacturer who was offering the portrait.

The juvenile market assumed importance. The problem, then, was to build programs that would create a continuing interest upon the part of children.

Unimaginative advertisers, many of them reared upon a dime-novel diet, sought the quickest and easiest solution.

Into the ears of defenseless children were poured the moans and shrieks of dying men and women; the sharp, menacing rattle of the machine gun; the language of the gutter and all the other ingredients of the hair-raising thriller.

The children? Why, they loved it.

And why shouldn't they? A definite and exciting part of juvenile life has always been made up of playing pirates, detectives, cowboys, Indians, cops and robbers and all those other pleasant characters who make of life an adventure. . . .

Thousands upon thousands of packages of merchandise were sold because little Willie or little Annie raised so much cain around home that protesting parents were forced to buy the products. The parents didn't like the radio programs. But children and parents being what they are, returns kept piling in. . . .

The theory of advertising to children is that through the children a manufacturer gains the buying power of the parent. Potentially, of course, he gains the good-will of juveniles who some day will be purchasers themselves. To most advertisers, however, this is the secondary consideration. Primarily they are after the parent. . . .

One wonders, then, why in the name of common sense they insist upon programs that antagonize the parent and that they know antagonize the parent.

One of the phases of juvenile programs which has created the most antagonism among parents is the commercial.

On several juvenile programs the advertiser has baldly announced that the children cannot go on hearing their favorite character if they do not buy the product the character advertises. This is black-mail pure and simple and children and parents both resent it.

Yet advertisers continue to pound home their commercials with the threat that if the child doesn't buy the product he will be denied the privilege of listening to the program. In many homes children themselves have seen the essential unfairness of this idea with the result that they quite willingly have given up programs.

Another type of commercial that is bound to create antagonism is that which oversells. A short time ago one advertiser with an otherwise quite interesting children's program spoiled the effect of it by insisting in the commercial that the child use the product three times a day. The product was one of fair merit and no parent would have any particular objection to a child eating it occasionally. Eaten three times a day, however, it might be definitely harmful to the child's health. In addition, any child who ate the product three times a day for a week at the end of that time would be so sick of it that he would never want to see it again. And yet the advertiser continued in his commercial hammering home the idea that the product should be used three times a day, creating antagonism among children and parents and nullifying the effect of his advertising. . . .

Advertisers must realize that children resent the idea of the commercial. They want to be entertained and the commercial is an interruption of the entertainment. Therefore it must be carefully done.

Children are probably the bitterest critics of the sappy commercial. They are much less likely to be tolerant of this type of sales talk than are their parents.

The child's commercial should never force. The type of black-mail that threatens to discontinue the program if the children don't buy is bound to defeat itself. Children resent the unfairness and parents are antagonized.

So also must be avoided the commercial that tries to get children to use far more of the product than they would normally use.

Commercials that are short, well written will not be objectionable and will often have an appeal.

NOTES

1. Little Lord Fauntleroy, the title character in Francis Hodgson Burnett's widely read novel *Little Lord Fauntleroy* (1886), was an overprotected prissy, who dressed in lace-collared velvet suits and wore long curls.

7 Child Consumers, the Mass Media, and Mass Amusements

From the dime novels of the nineteenth century to the video games of the late twentieth century, the mass media and mass commercial recreations have been the focal point of a series of moral panics over children's consumption and the growth of an autonomous youth culture. Parents, moral reformers, child experts, and media watchdogs have frequently blamed such entertainments for corrupting children's innocence, promoting criminality and sexual promiscuity, and undermining parental authority. The intensity of public alarm, however, has rarely yielded unanimity of response. Those who condemned the effects of mass culture could still be poles apart on policy, with some recommending censorship and others calling for the construction of wholesome alternatives. Media producers might consent to more vigorous self-policing or reject reform altogether on the grounds that child consumers were neither as vulnerable nor as passive as critics asserted.

The documents in this section represent the viewpoints of a diverse array of reformers, critics, and defenders of children's media consumption. Anthony Comstock's 1891 exposé of the dime novel industry and Jane Addams's 1909 portrait of the youthful wage-earners seeking adventure in the modern industrial city both focus public attention on the problem of unsupervised working-class children and youth. Comstock's call for censorship and Addams's quest to uplift working-class recreation reflect their divergent assessments of who is most to blame for children's delinquent consumer practices. Writing in 1927, Wainwright Evans and Benjamin Lindsey, a prominent juvenile court judge, share Addams's sympathetic view of youthful rebellion but move beyond the Progressive reform tradition in urging greater acceptance of modern social mores. The next two documents—excerpts from Henry James Forman's *Our Movie Made Children,* a 1934 study based on interviews with 300 child moviegoers, and *Seduction of the Innocent,* a 1953 study of comic book readers conducted by the psychiatrist Frederic Wertham—detail the damaging effects of such media on children's psychological and moral development. In the final document, a selection from *Children's Television: The Art, the Business, and How It Works* (1989), Cy Schneider, a toy merchandiser and media executive who headed Nickelodeon in the 1980s, defends the practice of marketing toys and goods on children's television. In sharp contrast to Forman and Wertham, who stress children's gullibility and vulnerability to media messages, Schneider casts children as discerning and even resistant media consumers.

12. Anthony Comstock, "Vampire Literature," *North American Review* 153 (August 1891): 160–65.

. . . The first thing after an author has written a book of questionable character is to secure some reputable publisher or bookseller to handle and push it. The next step towards the realization of his desire for fame and gain is to have the book roundly attacked because of its lustful tendencies, by the daily and weekly papers and periodicals. The New York Society for the Suppression of Vice long ago learned that to attack a book or paper, and not carry through the prosecution to success in the courts, was to secure a quasi-indorsement by the courts and a large amount of free advertising for the offensive matter. Our plan has always been to discover the author and publisher, and secretly strike a blow at the fountain-head by seizing the publication and plates and arresting the publisher and author.

The care taken by the society in the preparation of cases may be illustrated by the results for the past three years. During 1888, of 103 cases brought to trial 101 were convicted. In 1889, out of 127 cases brought to trial 125 were convicted; while during 1890 we had 155 convictions out of 156 cases. This record speaks well for our district attorneys, as well as for the preparation of these cases. . . .

There is at present a strong competition among writers and publishers of cheap books and papers to see which one can excel the others in unclean stories.

The object and ambition of many writers seem to be to show how they can evade the law and yet publish stories of a suggestive and criminal character. The basest representatives of profligacy and unhallowed living are made the subjects for leading characters in many novels published at the present day. Many news-stands are no longer either safe or respectable places for children and youth to visit or purchase books at. Many of the publications are of such a character that they are sufficient when seen in the hands of any girl to blast her good name and reputation. A respectable person scarcely knows what novel to select from the numerous products offered by the newsdealers, and many books publicly offered for sale no decent person would be seen carrying in his or her hands upon a public conveyance.

There are two things of immense importance to be considered in this connection. The first is the class to be affected and the results of this kind of devil seed-sowing; the second, the kindred vices that are preying upon the youth of to-day.

As to the first, nearly one-third of the entire people of the United States are twenty-one years of age or under. This means that upwards of *twenty millions* of youth and children are in the plastic or receptive state, open to every insidious teacher, and subject to every bad influence—a period of life when character is forming and is most easily moulded.

Nor must we forget that the children of to-day are not only to be the men and women of to-morrow, but also the parents of a still more future generation. *This nation's highest interests to-day centre in these millions of youth and children.* Religion and morality are the only safe foundations for a nation's future prosperity and security. Any other foundations will crumble before the encroachments of vicious propensities and criminal avarice. By cursing the youth of to-day we heavily discount the prosperity of the future of this nation, and endanger the permanency of our national institutions. *These writers and publishers are conspirators against the nation's highest hopes for the future.*

Such authors may coin money from their publications; they may attain popular positions before the public; but as sure as the night follows the day, so sure must this nation's harvest from this seed-sowing of popularized nastiness be corrupt lives and blotches upon the face of society. These authors may evade the laws of the land, but they cannot evade the natural consequences that are sure to flow from the dissemination of their vile publications.

"Oh but," some author says, "my story always has a moral!" What does the boy care for a moral after his mind has been engrossed, his imagination fired, and his passions aroused by some florid description of the precincts of sin, or of the loose conduct of the vile principal characters? What boy or girl stops to read the moral of a sensational story of bloodshed, lust, or crime? . . .

Then, again, we have the "boy-and-girl story papers," the "nickel" and "dime novels," and so-called "monthly libraries" of cheap literature. Many of these are revealers of criminal secrets, instructors in the science of crime. Crime is glorified. The leading character in many of these stories is a criminal, who succeeds in winning a fortune for himself by setting at defiance the laws of the land. Morality and virtue are treated as things to be despised, while reckless living is made the means of rapid transit from poverty to affluence.

Better that our youth be taken by their parents into the sinks of iniquity and dens of vice, and their finer sensibilities shocked by the realities of crime, than that their fancies shall be taught fantastic scenes from these sensational and vivid descriptions of the purlieus of sin and shame. . . .

It was not long ago that, in Westchester County, three lads, crazed by these stories of crime, under a fourteen-year-old leader, presented a loaded revolver at the head of a gentleman upon the public street and demanded "your money or your life."

A few years ago we arrested a young man at Newburg, N.Y., who, hearing that the officers of the law were after him, had armed himself with a bowie knife. When asked what he had that for, he replied: "I heard you were after me, and so I fixed myself." The next day he and his young associate, after being locked up in a cell over night, confessed that they were victims of these "boy-and-girl" story papers. Both had been expelled from an institution of learning for insubordination and disorder.

A youth in one of our Western States, under fourteen years of age, was recently hung by a mob of citizens for having, in his mad craze to be famous like the boys in the stories he had been reading, shot three men.

A few months ago a lad about thirteen was arraigned in the Tombs Police Court, in New York, for shooting a boy about his own age. The evidence disclosed the fact that some boys had been gambling; that a dispute arose over a pencil, during which one of the boys told this young desperado that he "lied"; whereupon, after the manner of the hero of a story, the young gambler arose from his seat at the gaming-table, drew his revolver, saying, "Johnnie, that's got to be wiped out with blood," and shot his little companion down.

13. Jane Addams, *The Spirit of Youth and the City Streets* (New York: Macmillan, 1909), pp. 4–8, 67–69, 80–81, 117–19.

. . . The Greeks held their games so integral a part of religion and patriotism that they came to expect from their poets the highest utterances at the very moments when the sense of pleasure released the national life. In the medieval city the knights held their tourneys, the guilds their pageants, the people their dances . . . Only in the modern city have men concluded that it is no longer necessary for the municipality to provide for the insatiable desire for play. In so far as they have acted upon this conclusion, they have entered upon a most difficult and dangerous experiment; and this at the very moment when the city has become distinctly industrial, and daily labor is continually more monotonous and subdivided. We forget how new the modern city is, and how short the span of time in which we have assumed that we can eliminate public provision for recreation.

A further difficulty lies in the fact that this industrialism has gathered together multitudes of eager young creatures from all quarters of the earth as a labor supply for the countless factories and workshops, upon which the present industrial city is based. Never before in civilization have such numbers of young girls been suddenly released from the protection of the home and permitted to walk unattended upon city streets and to work under alien roofs; for the first time they are being prized more for their labor power than for their innocence, their tender beauty, their ephemeral gaiety. Society cares more for the products they manufacture than for their immemorial ability to reaffirm the charm of existence. Never before have such numbers of young boys earned money independently of the family life, and felt themselves free to spend it as they choose in the midst of vice deliberately disguised as pleasure.

This stupid experiment of organizing work and failing of to organize play has, of course, brought about a fine revenge. The love of pleasure will not be denied, and when it has turned into all sorts of malignant and vicious appetites, then we, the middle aged, grow quite distracted and resort to all sorts of restrictive measures. We even try to dam up the sweet fountain itself because we are affrighted by these neglected streams; but almost worse than the restrictive measures is our apparent belief that the city itself has no obligation in the matter, an assumption upon which the modern city turns over to commercialism practically all the provisions for public recreation.

Quite as one set of men has organized the young people into industrial enterprises in order to profit from their toil, so another set of men and also of women, I am sorry to say, have entered the neglected field of recreation and have organized enterprises which make profit out of this invincible love of pleasure.

In every city arise so-called "places"—"gin-palaces," they are called in fiction; in Chicago we euphemistically say merely "places,"—in which alcohol is dispensed, not to allay thirst, but, ostensibly to stimulate gaiety, it is sold really in order to empty pockets. Huge dance halls are opened to which hundreds of young people are attracted, many of whom stand wistfully outside a roped circle, for it requires five cents to procure within it for five minutes the sense of allurement and intoxication which is sold in lieu of innocent pleasure. . . . We see thousands of girls walking up and down the streets on a pleasant evening with no chance to catch a sight of pleasure even through a lighted window, save as these lurid places provide it. Apparently the modern city sees in these girls only two possibilities, both of them commercial: first, a chance to utilize by day their new and tender labor power in its factories and shops, and then another chance in the evening to extract from them their petty wages by pandering to their love of pleasure.

As these overworked girls stream along the street, the rest of us see only the self-conscious walk, the giggling speech, the preposterous clothing. And yet through the huge hat, with its wilderness of bedraggled feathers, the girl announces to the world that she is here. She demands attention to the fact of her existence, she states that she is ready to live, to take her place in the world. . . .

This desire for adventure . . . seizes girls. A group of girls ranging in age from twelve to seventeen was discovered in Chicago last June, two of whom were being trained by older women to open tills in small shops, to pick pockets, to remove handkerchiefs, furs and purses and to lift merchandise from the counters of department stores. All the articles stolen were at once taken to their teachers and the girls themselves received no remuneration, except occasional sprees to the theaters or other places of amusement. The girls gave no coherent reason for their actions beyond the statement that they liked the excitement and the fun of it. Doubtless to the thrill of danger was added the pleasure and interest of being daily in the shops and the glitter of "down town." The boys are more indifferent to this downtown life, and are apt to carry on their adventures on the docks, the railroad tracks or best of all upon the unoccupied prairie.

This inveterate demand of youth that life shall afford a large element of excitement is in a measure well founded. We know of course that it is necessary to accept excitement as an inevitable part of recreation, that the first step in recreation is "that excitement which stirs the worn or sleeping centers of a man's body and mind." It is only when it is followed by nothing else that it defeats its own end, that it uses up strength and does not create it. In the actual experience of these boys the excitement has demoralized them and led them into law-breaking. When, however, they seek legitimate pleasure, and say with great pride that they are "ready to pay for it," what they find is legal but scarcely more wholesome,—it is still merely excitement. "Looping the loop" amid shrieks of simulated terror or dancing in disorderly saloon halls, are perhaps the natural reactions to a day spent in noisy factories and in trolley cars whirling through the distracting streets, but the city which permits them to be the acme of pleasure and recreation to its young people, commits a grievous mistake.

May we not assume that this love for excitement, this desire for adventure, is basic, and will be evinced by each generation of city boys as a challenge to their elders? And yet those of us who live in Chicago are obliged to confess that last year there were arrested and brought into court fifteen thousand young people under the age of twenty, who had failed to keep even the common law of the land. Most of these young people had broken the law in their blundering efforts to find adventure and in response to the old impulse for self-expression. . . .

Out of my twenty years' experience at Hull-House I can recall all sorts of pilferings, petty larcenies, and even burglaries, due to that never ceasing effort on the part of boys to procure theater tickets. I can also recall indirect efforts toward the same end which are most pitiful. I remember the remorse of a young girl of fifteen who was brought into the Juvenile Court after a night spent weeping in the cellar of her home because she had stolen a mass of artificial flowers with which to trim a hat. She stated that she had taken the flowers because she was afraid of losing the attention of a young man whom she had heard say that "a girl has to be dressy if she expects to be seen." This young man was the only one who had ever taken her to the theater and if he failed her, she was sure that she would never go again, and she sobbed out incoherently that she "couldn't live at all without it." Apparently the blankness and grayness of life itself had been broken for her only by the portrayal of a different world.

One boy whom I had known from babyhood began to take money from his mother from the time he was seven years old, and after he was ten she regularly gave him money for the play Saturday evening. However, this Saturday performance, "starting him off like," he always went twice again on Sunday, procuring the money in all sorts of illicit ways. Practically all of his earnings after he was fourteen were spent in this way to satisfy the insatiable desire to know of the great adventures of the wide world which the more fortunate boy takes out in reading Homer and Stevenson. . . .

A Russian girl who went to work at an early age in a factory, pasting labels on mucilage bottles, was obliged to surrender all her wages to her father who, in return, gave her only the barest necessities of life. In a fit of revolt against the monotony of her work, and "that nasty sticky stiff," she stole from her father $300 which he had hidden away under the floor of his kitchen, and with this money she ran away for a spree, having first bought herself the most gorgeous clothing a local department store could supply. Of course, this preposterous beginning could have but one ending and the child was sent to the reform school to expiate not only her own sins but the sins of those who had failed to rescue her from a life of grinding monotony which her spirit could not brook.

"I know the judge thinks I am a bad girl," sobbed a poor little prisoner, put under bonds for threatening to kill her lover, "but I have only been bad for one week and before that I was good for six years. I worked every day in Blank's factory and took home all my wages to keep the kids in school. I met this fellow in a dance hall. I just had to go to dances sometimes after pushing down the lever of my machine with my right foot and using both my arms feeding it for ten hours a day—nobody knows how I felt some nights. I agreed to go away with this man for a week but when I was ready to go home he tried to drive me out on the street to earn money for him and, of course, I threatened to kill him—any decent girl would," she concluded, as unconscious of the irony of the reflection as she was of the connection between her lurid week and her monotonous years.

14. Judge Ben B. Lindsey and Wainwright Evans, *The Revolt of Modern Youth* (Seattle: University of Washington Press, 1927), pp. 157–63.

The boy who can grind the valves or adjust the carburetor of an automobile, or who can put together a radio set with a technical understanding of its complexities, has learned a way of thought and scientific respect for facts of which his father at his age was a stranger. Likewise, the Flapper who makes her own living, votes, holds her own in competition with men, refuses to let the corset makers put stays on her, and snaps her fingers at "styles" dictated by the makers of clothes, is capable of doing things her mother couldn't come within sight of.

And remember that they will both be grown up tomorrow, and bringing up their babies after their own notions, not ours.

I do not agree with the talk which is popular just now that this present younger generation is like all others and that Youth has always been thus. It is true that Youth has always been rebellious, and that it has always succumbed finally to conservatism. They had the "new woman" in the mid-Victorian period, and old-fashioned people wondered in alarm what the world was coming to.

But Youth couldn't get away with it then. It didn't have the economic independence. Now it has it. Machinery has made that possible. Once Youth paraded and shouted with a wooden gun; but today the weapon is loaded. Make no mistake about it; this revolt of Modern Youth is different; it is the first of its kind; and it possesses means for making its will effective.

The agencies of modern life have had so direct and powerful an effect even on us of the older generation that they have in many ways demoralized us. As for the effect on Youth, that has been perfectly resistless. But there is no point in blaming the new conditions, new laws, more force, more ignorance, more silence, fear, and other nonsense. We are trying to bring up by the standards of fifty years ago a generation that has never known what it was to lack a host of things which were unknown fifty years ago. Naturally the gap between ancient precept and modern practice is making trouble; particularly when we persuade ourselves that modern practice rather than ancient precept will have to yield the right of way. Why we should want it so I can't say, unless it be that we hate the effort of breaking new trails.

I have already named in a general way what these agencies of modern life are, but let's name the most evident of them over, just to make the issue clear. Some are good and some are not so good, but they all have to be in the reckoning. Those that immediately present themselves are the automobile, (and soon the aeroplane with the kids spooning in the clouds) the telephone, the motion picture, the radio, the jazz dance, jazz music, jazz booze, jazz journalism, "crime wave," the permanent wave, the permanent passing of the chaperone, the parking of the corset, the feminine invasion of the barber shop, growing and changing standards of living, rising wages, enough to eat and enough to wear in thousands of workingmen's homes where such abundance feels like a spree,—and so on. One could continue the list indefinitely. For instance, electrical appliances that make women something more than drudges in their homes; bath rooms, steam and hot-water heat that make the whole house usable all the year 'round, electric lights that enable people to read in the evening instead of sitting around till bedtime as they did with oil lamps. The list, you see, includes among other things physical comforts and speeding-up devices of all kinds; and the effect of it all is enormously stimulating. Most of the things I have named are direct and powerful inducements to freedom, well-being, leisure, and freedom of thought, speech, and action.

Of this great combination of influences, present-day Youth, with its present-day notions of conduct, is a result. What makes these agencies of modern life so often destructive and harmful is our insistence that they must blend with standards with which they have and can have nothing to do. Take the automobile, for instance, and the unchaperoned rides. You must take your choice. Either you must keep on with the chaperone—which is impossible —or you must prepare young people for the new convention by seeing to it, not only that they have a voluntary, informed, and responsible code of conduct, but also that they know all about Sex, and its place in the lives of men and women. So far we have refused to do this, on the ground that Sex is an unclean and shameful thing, rather than a sacred and lovely thing. If you, by implication, by silence, by innuendo, by concealment, by putting up veils, by talking in cryptic phrases, by winking, nodding, and looking significant, make it clear to children from their very infancy that Sex is essentially and fundamentally bad, what can you expect of them later? The most wicked thing in life, the uncleanest thing in life, turns out to be one of the most necessary and pleasant things in life. And so, convinced that they are doing wrong and yet determined to do it, they proceed to investigate Sex for themselves, with frequent disasters of a totally needless sort; and so the new freedom, instead of liberating them, destroys them.

Or perhaps you would insist on doing away with the automobiles. All right,—insist! Many silly people are doing it. It's a favorite indoor sport. . . .

Forty years ago John Smith took Sadie Brown driving behind old Dobbin. Dobbin ambled along, and John made love within the natural limitations prescribed by Dobbin's six miles an hour, that nearness to town and neighbors, and all that. Today John makes his date secretly. Today he sits at the wheel of a car that may be good for anything from two to eighty miles an hour. He can whisk Sadie far from all accustomed surroundings. There are road-houses; there are long stretches of road where the solitude is complete and easy to reach; there is every inducement under the moon to irresponsible conduct.

In a word, John and Sadie have money and freedom. Since that is so, protests and scoldings can but antagonize them. To handle them, approach them with as much tact as if they were adults, not to be coerced; You can't abolish the closed car, but you *can* abolish the closed mind and the shut mouth. . . .

It has been the fashion for some time now to hold the motion pictures responsible for the present changes. Well, they doubtless have had a lot to do with it. They have visualized in a dramatic way most of the activities of sex for youngsters who have never been given their bearings in any other way.

Here again, you can't suppress the movies, nor can you keep them from dealing constantly with love, as the most dramatic and universal thing in human life. Not even censorship can do it, though it tried hard enough.

If people's minds and hearts were right there would be no question about whether it is right to dance, go to movies, drive automobiles, smoke if they feel like it, and live completely, fully, fearlessly, and heartily—yet moderately —with all the zest and happiness possible. The way to make such freedom possible is not to suppress these things but rather to make the heart right through understanding. All that is needed to make the whole system work for righteousness is the internal restraints and codes of conduct which derive their power from within.

"There is nothing from without the man," said Jesus, "That going into him can defile him: But the things which proceed out of the man are those that defile him. . . . For from within, out of the heart of men, evil thoughts proceed, fornications, thefts, murders, adulteries, coveting, wickednesses, deceit, lasciviousness, an evil eye, railing, pride, foolishness: all these evil things proceed from within, and defile the man."

We, however, think we know better than that. We think we know that it is the things from without that defile people. We think the path must be made smooth for the feet of Youth; and the idea of teaching Youth to walk sure-footed on paths of natural roughness occurs to nobody. On this theory we suppress books; on this theory we talk of censoring even department-store windows and expurgating them of women's lingerie.—What I should like to know is the effect of all this on the angels; does it make them laugh or does it make them weep? It is, I should say, a first-rate measure of their sense of humor.

15. Henry James Forman, "The Path to Delinquency," in *Our Movie Made Children* (New York: Macmillan Company, 1934), 179–83.

. . . [T]he movies are a school, a system of education virtually unlimited, untrammeled and uncontrolled. It could be an immense and unprecedented instrument of civilization. Whenever what is called a good picture is produced, evidence is plentiful to show that those who see it, notably the young, are instantly affected by it. That type of picture, however, continues to be far too rare.

We used to smile at the goody-goody quality of what was called Sunday-school literature. Our pendulum has certainly swung far the other way when we reflect for a moment upon the evidence presented as to the contents of the volume of pictures daily emitted from Hollywood. When we recall that in 115 pictures presented to our 77,000,000 audience, as Dr. Dale found, 406 crimes are actually committed, and an additional forty-three attempted; that many of their characters are not only far from being models of human conduct, but are, many of them, highly objectionable in their occupations, in their goals, in their lives; that in thirty-five pictures fifty-four murders are committed, and in twelve pictures seventeen hold-ups successfully carried out—what can we possibly expect our young people to derive from all that?

If their minds, to use the old figure, are not precisely slates, but rather wax in their receptivity and fairly marble-like in their retention, as the writer must conclude from the Holaday and Thurstone studies, is it any wonder that the all too long procession of crimes, illicit enterprises, misdemeanors and techniques of delinquency presented in the movies should leave a certain deposit of impressions upon young minds? Yet constantly, in our ignorance, we have gone on exposing them to movie patterns of conduct and at the same time gone on wondering why the rising generation is restless, unruly, hard to control, and why crime waves are increasing in intensity. It is the present writer's hope that the very publication of these findings may contribute to better conditions.

We are all of us, it has been said, potential criminals, and the movies, some psycho-analysts believe, provide the spectator with opportunities for vicarious killing. It follows that the young, being more malleable, are likely to be more subject to influences than the adults. . . .

The question is, then, how much effect and what manner of effect do the motion pictures have in influencing tendencies toward delinquency? . . .

It would be absurd to say even now that Al Capone and his organization are products solely of the movies. Numerous forces of present-day civilization play constantly upon characters and tendencies of youth, of which the movies are doubtless one, and movies are what we are here considering. What do the movies contribute to an alarming condition? Through facility of seeing them is created a tolerance of criminal patterns and a ready stimulation to those either predisposed to delinquency and crime or to those whose environment is too heavily weighted against them. The seed is supplied all too lavishly to the fertile ground.

. . . Professor Blumer and Mr. Hauser endeavored to find out to what extent the usual run of boys and girls are made more tolerant of crime and criminality by the pictures dealing in those subjects. They found that high-school boys and girls often not only expressed sympathy for the criminal, but that a few drew the conclusion that mere hard, plodding work is not desirable. Sympathy for the criminal, it is the present writer's observation, often implicit in the plots of motion pictures, is naturally quite common among the young. To cite some of the cases listed by Blumer and Hauser, a sixteen-year-old girl writes:

"Movies have made me less critical of criminals when I consider that all are not as fortunate as we. Starvation has been the cause of more crime than anything else as I see it in the movies. As a result, I believe crime should be corrected instead of being punished for the latter encourages more crime." "Usually," says another, "crime pictures make me feel sorry for the criminals because the criminals probably do not get the right start."

"A lot of crime movies I have seen," declares a sixteen-year-old boy, "made me feel more favorable towards crime by depicting the criminal as a hero who dies protecting his best friend against the police, or some movies show them as a debonair gentleman who robs at will from the rich and spares the poor. I have thought I would like to be a Robin Hood." "Many times o'er," one lad poetically phrases it, "I have desired to become a crook—and my ideal is Rob Roy, Scotland's greatest honorable crook, with Robin Hood close behind him." Even young girls assert that motion pictures create desires in them to become "benevolent criminals." "I have always felt," announces a fifteen-year old miss, "that being a character like Robin Hood would be *the* life."

The Robin Hood model of criminal, or the "Alias Jimmy Valentine" type, appears as attractive to many youngsters. Now, all this does not mean that these young boys and girls have been definitely incited to crime by the pictures. It does show, however, how the sharp barriers between right and wrong, built up by other institutions and training, as in the home, the church and the school, are progressively eroded and undermined, and some young people are made more tolerant toward crime and the criminal. . . .

A number, on the other hand, declare that the movies showed them that crime does not pay and set them against it. Some are even vehement in protest that movies could not make them want to become criminals. Roughly, however, about one-fourth of all the high-school boys and girls who wrote on this subject indicated that motion pictures have made them on occasion more favorable to crime and criminals.

16. Frederic Wertham, *Seduction of the Innocent* (New York: Rinehart & Company, 1953), 93–103.

. . . The cultural background of millions of American children comes from the teaching of the home, the teaching of the school (and church), the teaching of the street and from crime comic books. For many children the last is the most exciting. It arouses their interest, their mental participation, their passions and their sympathies, but almost entirely in the wrong direction. The atmosphere of crime comic books is unparalleled in the history of children's literature of any time or any nation. It is a distillation of viciousness. The world of the comic book is the world of the strong, the ruthless, the bluffer, the shrewd deceiver, the torturer and the thief. All the emphasis is on exploits where somebody takes advantage of somebody else, violently, sexually or threateningly. It is no more the world of braves and squaws, but one of punks and molls. Force and violence in any conceivable form are romanticized. Constructive and creative forces in children are channeled by comic books into destructive avenues. Trust, loyalty, confidence, solidarity, sympathy, charity, compassion are ridiculed. Hostility and hate set the pace of almost every story. A natural scientist who had looked over comic books expressed this to me tersely, "In comic books life is worth nothing; there is no dignity of a human being."

Children seek a figure to emulate and follow. Crime comic books undermine this necessary ingredient of ethical development. They play up the good times had by those who do the wrong thing. Those who at the tail end of stories mete out punishment use the same violence and the same lingo as those whom they punish. Since everybody is selfish and force and violence are depicted as the most successful methods, the child is given a feeling of justification. They not only suggest the satisfaction of primitive impulses but supply the rationalization. In this soil children indulge in the stock fantasies supplied by the industry: murder, torture, burglary, threats, arson and rape. Into that area of the child's mind where right and wrong is evaluated, children incorporate such false standards that an ethical confusion results for which they are not to blame. They become emotionally handicapped and culturally underprivileged. And this affects their social balance.

Whatever may give a child some ethical orientation is dragged down to the crime-violence level. Inculcation of a distorted morality by endless repetition is not such an intangible factor if one studies its source in comic books and its effect in the lives of children. It is of course a question not of pious slogans like "Crime never pays" but of the emotional accents within the stories themselves.

In one comic an old man is killed during the hold-up of his jewelry store. He had not obeyed the order to back up against the wall quickly enough. After other crimes and murders the captured criminal says: "It was not right to kill him. . . . That man couldn't have obeyed me! . . . That old man was STONE DEAF!"

The moral principle is clear. If you hold up a man and he does not obey quickly enough because he is deaf, you are not supposed to shoot him. But if he is not deaf, shooting him is all right.

In one comic story called "Mother Knows Best," the mother advises her children: "I brought you kids up right—rub out those coppers like I taught you!"

One son answers: "Don't worry, ma! We'll give those flatfeet a bellyful of lead!"

Several boys have shown me this story. They themselves condemned and at the same time were fascinated by this anti-maternal story. . . .

What in a few words is the essential ethical teaching of crime comics for children? I find it well and accurately summarized in this brief quotation:

> It is not a question of right, but of winning. Close your heart against compassion. Brutality does it. The stronger is in the right. Greatest hardness. Follow your opponent till he is crushed.

These words were the instructions given on August 22, 1939, by a superman in his home in Berchtesgaden to his generals, to serve as guiding lines for the treatment of the population in the impending war on Poland. . . .

When I described how children suffer in their ethical development through the reading of comic books, the industry countered by pointing with pride to the "moral" lesson imprinted on many crime comics, that "crime does not pay." In the first place, this is not true. In comic books crime usually does pay, and pay very well, until the last picture or two. The crimes are glamorous; the end is dull. Frequently the ratio of "crime" to "does not pay" is as high as fifty to one. More important, the slogan "Crime does not pay" is not moral, but highly immoral. It is strange how responsible adults have accepted this slogan and refer to it on platforms, over the radio and in articles as admirable. Great harm has been done by teaching children that they should not play hookey, that they should not steal or lie, that they should not hit girls (as comic-book figures so often do)—*because it "doesn't pay"*! I have seen many children who were confused by this vicious crime-comic-book morality. The reason why one does not hit girls, even if comics have made it so attractive, is that it is cowardly and that it hurts them; the reason why one does not steal or break into stores is that that is not how one lives in a civilized community; that whether crime pays or does not pay, it is not what a decent person wants to do. *That* should be the lesson for children.

When I pointed out the hypocrisy of the "Crime does not pay" slogan and its bad effect on children, the industry accused me of "unfairness" in attacking their highest endeavors and introduced some more slogan morality. In one comic book are two pages by a police captain attacking me: "Don't let reformers kid you!" He is "shocked by what I read today about the people who condemn crime comics. These people are the menace." He goes on: "Children don't like to be kicked around by reformers who want to decide what's good for them to read." And he extols "the strong moral force" that comics exert on children.

Frequently I have been in the position of having to defend children who have received harsh judgments in courts and on psychiatric wards and equally harsh treatment in places of detention and reformatories. There is no better illustration of the state of affairs where we first victimize children and then put all the responsibility on them, the victims, than this same comic book. It has a story where two policemen are killed—and a real police captain pointing out what a "strong moral force" such a book is! . . .

The development of the superego, of conscience or, more simply, the sense of decency, takes place not only on the basis of identification with parents but also with successive parent-substitutes who are at the same time representatives and symbols of group demands and group responsibilities. In this sphere, comic books are most pernicious. They expose children's minds to an endless stream of prejudice-producing images. This influence, subtle and pervasive but easily demonstrable by clinical psychological methods, has not only directly affected the individual child, but also constitutes an important factor for the whole nation. It is currently fashionable to speak of "inter-group tensions," "group adjustments" and so on. The old term *race hatred* (or *race prejudice*) is more honest and more to the point. What we call "minorities" constitute the *majority* of mankind. The United States is spending at present millions of dollars to persuade the world on the air and by other propaganda means that race hatred is not an integral part of American life. At the same time, millions of American comic books are exported all over the world which give the impression that the United States is instilling race hatred in young children.

If I were to make the briefest summary of what children have told us about how different peoples are represented to them in the lore of crime comics, it would be that there are two kinds of people: on the one hand is the tall, blond, regular-featured man sometimes disguised as a superman (or superman disguised as a man) and the pretty young blonde girl with the super-breast. On the other hand are the inferior people: natives, primitives, savages, "ape men," Negroes, Jews, Indians, Italians, Slavs, Chinese and Japanese, immigrants of every description, people with irregular features, swarthy skins, physical deformities, Oriental features. In some crime comics the first class some-times wears some kind of superman uniform, while the second class is in mufti. The brunt of this imputed inferiority in whole groups of people is directed against colored people and "foreign born."

When the seeds of prejudice against others first appear in a child, or when he first becomes aware of belonging to a group against which there is prejudice, depends on many diverse factors: family, education, community, social stratum. From my studies, the second apparently appears later. But in general both feelings appear much earlier than is commonly supposed. A four-year-old can imbibe prejudice from comic books, and six- or seven-year-olds are quite articulate about it. Sometimes their feeling of dislike for a group ("They are bad." "They are vicious." "They are criminals." "They are dirty." "You can't trust them.") is derived from crime comic books. In other cases, distorted stereotypes acquired at home, on the street, in school, are given new nourishment and perpetuation by comic-book reading. These conclusions are based entirely on *what the children themselves say.*

The pictures of these "inferior" types as criminals, gangsters, rapers, suitable victims for slaughter by either the lawless or the law, have made an indelible impression on children's minds. There can be no doubt about the correctness of this conclusion. For example, when a child is shown a comic book that he has not read and is asked to pick out the bad man, he will unhesitatingly pick out types according to the stereotyped conceptions of race prejudice, and tell you the reason for his choice. "Is he an American?" "No!"

Attacks by older children on younger ones, inspired or fortified by the race prejudice shown in comic books, are getting more frequent. I have seen such cases (which do not always come to the attention of the authorities) with victims belonging to various minorities. For the victims, this is frequently a serious traumatic emotional episode. Some juvenile gangs make it a practice to beat dark-skinned children, and they do it with comic-book brutality. So comic books provide both the methods and the vilification of the victims.

17. Cy Schneider, "How to Communicate with Children on Television," in *Children's Television: The Art, the Business, and How It Works* (Lincolnwood, IL: NTC Business Books, 1987), 83–87.

Children aged two to 11 are exposed on average to 20,000 commercials a year. That's somewhere between 150 and 200 hours of pure commercial messages—either in 30-second or 60-second doses.

Most of those messages are about cereals, toys, non-carbonated beverages, snacks, candy, and chewing gum. The manufacturers of these products and others primarily consumed by children invest more than $500 million a year trying to tell children about the virtues of their particular brands. Children are being courted and cultivated for their buying power.

Generally, there is not a great deal of differentiation between brands within a given category. Since most products within a given category tend to be very much alike in their purpose, look, flavor, texture, and use, advertisers try to make their products more appealing or different by adding a fun element, often borrowing interest from some other reference within the child's culture. Eventually, children begin to see through this technique. The sheer accumulation of television commercials makes children cynical.

THEY DON'T BELIEVE EVERYTHING THEY'RE TOLD ON TELEVISION

Younger children, aged five to six, tend to be greater believers of commercial messages, but these children rely more on parental decisions anyhow; however, by the time a child is 11 or 12 he or she has decided much of the advertising he or she sees is a sham. The drop in attention span is considerable—so is interest in children's television. The middle group, children seven to nine, like commercials more and pay more attention. They are also heavier watchers of television.

It isn't easy to communicate with children in any of the age groups. It's certainly not as easy as television's critics would have you believe. Adults look at children's television commercials through their own eyes, intelligence, and experience and suppose that children are so innocent and gullible that they will swallow the whole proposition before them. This is hardly the case. Ask any articulate child some questions in-depth about almost any given commercial. You'll be surprised at the reservations and the distrust.

That children are a special audience is true. But the social, educational, and parental caretakers of children are the ones who perceive children as helpless, without understanding that children are perceiving images differently than adults. This attitude of protectionism is rooted in the 19th Century, when children were regarded as property that belonged to parents. All legal, philosophical, and religious precedents sustained this perception of children. Children were, and still are, seen as miniature adults. They are looked upon as empty receptacles that must be filled up with adult ideas and values. What isn't realized is that while these miniature adults are in their first 12 to 15 years of growth, they are usually out of step on an adult staircase.

Children must be viewed as the world's largest minority group. They have their own language, their own level of understanding, and their own view of the adult world. The words and pictures that communicate to adults do not necessarily communicate the same things to children. These different levels, needs, and rights must be respected and nurtured.

CHILDREN ARE NOT ONE MARKET

Children under 12 are not one market; they are three or four segmented markets. Children in these markets are constantly developing and within a 12-year period they progress from infancy to almost the independency of adulthood.

Over this time there is a constant need by the child to change his feelings of weakness and helplessness into competence with people and things. The child strives to reverse his feelings of being small, weak, and incompetent to becoming capable, knowledgeable, and victorious over the challenge of living.

As children pass through their early stages, their rate of mental growth is enormous. A few years makes for very dramatic differences. A five-year old and a 12-year old have less in common than a 20-year old and a 40-year old.

The Preschooler

The one- to five-year olds can't read and rely more on parental decisions. These children are highly stimulated by television and can watch it for hours at a time. They do not take in whole messages, only parts. They are not yet capable of putting the parts together and only retain fragments of any particular message. Their comprehension increases when the visual part of the message is very clearly defined. They also react better to passive, quiet television programming that is organized in short bursts. The attention span of this group is short; they simply cannot follow a long story.

The Six to Nines

The six- to nine-year olds are the most fad conscious. They are the real fans of children's television and make or break the Saturday morning shows or the shows in late afternoon syndication. They are the heaviest watchers of television, the kids who love cartoon shows, the sitcoms, and adventures.

A child coming out of the toddler, preschool, and kindergarten stage is suddenly aware that he or she is no longer a child, but a boy or a girl. Sexual identity has suddenly become an important issue.

Children of this age are most intrigued by speed, power, skill, and beauty. The stories they understand and relate to best are those of the hero and winner. The hero performs a deed, kills an ogre, defeats the bad guys, outwits the villain, or marries the princess or prince.

This group also starts to become involved with friends. The things their friends do, eat, wear, play with, and talk about become a paramount factor in their lives. Peer and fad influence are terribly important.

Certain attitudes and activities come into play:

- Boys are not yet interested in the opposite sex but girls are using male-female relationships as part of their play fantasy.
- Skills such as building, painting, or doing have become part of their lives.
- Possessing and collecting are important. This is the age for the beginning stamp collector and the collector/trader of baseball cards.
- This is the time when learning how things work begins to emerge. There is a fascination with flashlights, radios, and consumer electronics of all sorts.

In short, this is the phase where a child learns to be a consumer of products beyond those he eats and drinks.

The Preteen

The 10- to 12-year olds are a subculture unto themselves. They have their own mannerisms, argot, and point of view. Essentially, they begin to imitate the teenager. They regard themselves as much older than the eight-year-old. At this age:

- Fantasies are expressed through real people rather than animals or fairy princesses or superheroes.

- Their appearance and behavior start to become more adult-like. So does their speech.

- They want to be in vogue with teenage fads and fashions.

- Horizons start to turn away from the home. Special bonds develop with their peers. There is a secret sharing of problems and a kind of "double life" begins to form, the one they experience at home and the one they have with their friends.

- Parental influence on dress, hairstyles, and footwear as well as other values begins to diminish.

- Other adult figures enter their lives as heroes—usually from the sports or entertainment world.

- The desire to learn becomes more closely associated with the payoff of a better future.

- They are more interested in winning prizes or contests.

With differences as dramatic as all of the aforementioned, how is it possible to talk to all of them the same way at the same time?

It simply isn't.

As a parent, can you get through to your kids? Visualize the job of the professional communicator who is trying to get through to millions at the same time. Is it any wonder that children's programs and/or commercials appear so simpleminded. The communicator, without a sharp focus on which group he or she is addressing, risks going over the heads of the younger ones or appearing dumb to the older ones. In commercials, where brevity is essential, omissions of certain details appear deliberately dishonest and the inclusion of too many details is both awkward and confusing to the younger part of the group. I am convinced that any critic of children's commercials should try to write one. They would develop a greater understanding of the problem. It is a difficult and perplexing art at best.

8   Advertising in the Public Schools

Advertising in the public schools has a long and controversial history. By the 1920s, advertisers were supplying teachers with a wide array of charts, maps, pamphlets, and other teaching aids built around branded goods. These supplemental educational materials or SEMs, as they are called today, joined advertisers and public schools in a marriage of convenience: advertisers supplied cash-strapped schools with much-needed teaching materials and schools in turn provided advertisers what the mass media could not always deliver: a captive audience. The documents in this section address the pros and cons of school advertising from the vantage point of an advertising authority, John Allen Murphy, and two social scientists, Dewey Palmer and Frederick Schlink, who figured prominently in the burgeoning consumer movement of the 1930s. The two documents offer sharply contrasting assessments of advertising's role in American life and public education, and present different visions of the kind of consumer education that public schools ought to provide.

Criticism of advertising in the public schools has continued to mount since the mid-1930s. In fact, media watchdogs and consumer activists have created Web sites that catalog and publicize the exploitative and manipulative impact of in-school marketing. Three such Web sites worth exploring are http://commercialalert.org/issues/education, http://commercialfree childhood.org, and http://www.obligation.org.

18. John Allen Murphy, "How Advertisers Are Getting Schools to Use Their Literature: The Demand from Teachers for Charts, Maps, Product Geographies and Special Text Books Is Greater Than the Supply," *Advertising and Selling* 8 (April 6, 1927): 23–24, 86–88.

A recent editorial in a New York newspaper complained of the growing practice of "exploiting" pupils for the benefit of commercial enterprises. In many parts of the country business men are getting school children to do part of their selling. They arrange contests between schools or classes, offering prizes to the side that sells the most; or, they ask students to write essays in behalf of their product, cause, or store and award cash prizes to the winners.

The conclusion of the editorial was that business men have no right to introduce such practices into our schools; a sentiment with which I am absolutely in accord. Business should not be allowed to divert our school facilities to its own selfish purposes.

But the same editorial refers critically to another custom that is coming into wide use in both private and public schools—the tooth brush drill, the daily soap-and-water check-up, the balanced diet chart sponsored by commercial organizations. I am not in sympathy with the newspaper's criticism of that kind of school work. Dozens of our leading advertisers are cooperating with the schools and the teachers of the nation in supplying educational "helps" of that character. After investigating the subject for several weeks, I am prepared to say that there is no activity in which advertisers engage that is more appreciated and more productive of results than this school work. All of it is beneficial; some of it has done a great deal of good. Not only are the manufacturers satisfied with what they have accomplished but, what is more important, both parents and teachers are also delighted with it.

Teachers appreciate this help from manufacturers because if it were not supplied by them, the chances are that it would not come from any other source. In a class-room many "helps" are needed which the school board does not furnish and the teacher cannot afford to buy with her own money: maps, charts, hygienic instruction books, pictures, commodity geographies, and numerous other teaching devices. . . .

Nearly every manufacturer receives an occasional request from a teacher asking for literature about his product that could be used in classrooms. Most manufacturers answer these requests by sending out their regular literature. That is a mistake. Teachers will not, as a rule, use literature that is prepared for the general consumer, because it too obviously stresses an advertising viewpoint. . . .

The companies who have been most successful in getting their literature used in schools prepare special material for this purpose. There is for example, a book published by the Palmolive Company called "A Day in the Palmolive Factory." While this book mentions the name of the company and its products throughout the text, it is by no means an advertising publication. Its purpose is, primarily, to tell the reader something of the history of soap, what the ingredients of Palmolive Soap are, and just how Palmolive Soap is made. . . .

The thing that surprises most manufacturers is the ease with which specially designed school literature can be distributed. When an advertiser first enters this field, he usually makes the mistake of not being prepared for the avalanche of requests that he is likely to receive. Many advertisers have told me that the school teachers of this country are avaricious for industrial educational material. . . .

Lever Brothers, makers of Lifebuoy Soap . . . ran two full page advertisements in an educational publication, offering wash-up charts and sample cakes of soap. As a result of those two advertisements 39,000 teachers responded. They requested 1,560,000 charts and the same number of sample cakes of Lifebuoy. In the communities from which these inquiries came, the company wrote to its dealers and "prospects" explaining its campaign on the schools. As a result approximately 2000 new accounts were opened.

This campaign also demonstrates how a manufacturer can work with school children to overcome a prejudice which may exist against his product. Because of the presence of carbolic acid in Lifebuoy Soap many persons are prejudiced against its odor; so Lever Brothers decided to acquaint school children with the soap and to get them into the habit of using it before they had a chance to form a prejudice.

The school campaign accordingly centered around the wash-up chart; an interesting method of getting children to acquire habits of daily bathing. On the chart there is a place for the teacher to mark each child's credit, and on its reverse there is a talk to mothers, to make sure that the message will go into the home. . . .

Most of the manufacturers who are conducting campaigns to school children are in one way or another delivering a health message; for in the last few years a tremendous change has come into the average school curriculum. Education no longer revolves around the three "R's." Educators now admit that it is more important to build good character and strong physique than it is merely to teach such basic subjects as reading, writing and arithmetic. Advertisers have contributed almost as much to this change in education as have the educators themselves. Colgate & Company have been working in this field for seventeen years. It is largely due to the efforts of that company that the use of the tooth brush has become a daily habit, particularly among the school-attending generation in this country.

The California Fruit Growers Exchange, the Cream of Wheat Company, the Pro-phy-lac-tic Brush Co., the Borden Company, the Shredded Wheat Company, the Postum Cereal Company, the Kellogg Company, Sealright Company, Inc., and the Royal Baking Powder Company are a few of the many advertisers who have been contributing to these changes in the average curriculum. . . .

The Cream of Wheat Company uses a card on one side of which is a message addressed to the mother in which the child tells her what she learned at school about playing a breakfast game. This is signed both by pupil and teacher. On the reverse side of the card is a space in which the mother can indicate that her child has eaten a hot cereal for breakfast three times a week for four weeks. At the end of that period the mother signs the card and returns it to the teacher.

Maltop, Inc., manufacturers of Toddy, employs an athlete who does a number of physical culture stunts. The entertainment he offers is furnished free to schools. This man gives a talk in which he says that he owes his own fine physical condition to eating such helpful products as Toddy.

19. Dewey H. Palmer and Frederick J. Schlink, "Education and the Consumer," *Annals of the American Academy of Political and Social Science* 193 (May 1934): 188–97.

The idea that a healthy, wise, and a working consumer—the person who eats the food, wears the clothes, and uses the appliances produced by modern industry—is an indispensable unit in our industrial-commercial complex has not entered the minds of educators and is only now being sensed by a very few of the more advanced and realistic thinkers among the economists. Students are, of course, consumers and for the most part play no other role in the economic order; yet educators have never, if one may judge by their activities and the products of their labors, had any concept of the student other than as a person who must at some future date take his or her place in society as a producer, or, if unlucky, as a cog in a producers' or distributors' mechanized commercial world.

EDUCATION FOR BUSINESS SUCCESS

Consistent with such views, and as an incentive to students to get more education, the schools have constantly held up the goal of an independent enterpriser's or successful employer's life as the crowning end and achievement of learning. . . .

[T]he majority of the courses offered in arithmetic, accounting, and sales management, and some courses in economics and engineering, only train increasing numbers of individuals as processors, advertisers, and sellers of goods and securities, who will desire and take in private and personal profits as great as the market will bear. The young person who cannot select tooth powder intelligently or even know whether it serves any useful function whatever, who cannot refrain from urging his parents to purchase the latest model radio or pseudo-streamlined car (80 mile per hour on the straightaway!) is taught either directly or by implication to look forward to the time when he may be a successful department store owner, division manager of sales, a real estate or insurance personage, a contact man for the power trust, or a chief executive engineer in some great telephone or electrical company.

Only a few years ago, much ado was made about the need to offer practical trade courses in the elementary and high schools. The skills which such work developed were all to the good, but here again the emphasis was placed on increasing one's money-making ability as a worker, or more often one's usefulness to an employer, and not at all on developing consumer skills that would tend to increase the purchase value of the worker's dollar after it was earned. Manual training schools have taught boys how to make unneeded candlesticks, taborets, and hammered copper letter openers, but none of them has ever so much as mentioned the satisfaction and savings resulting from compounding supplies of daily need that would otherwise have to be bought—shoe dressing, writing ink, or floor and automobile polish. The least one might expect from a woodwork shop course would be a careful study of woods and finishes and the construction of different kinds of furniture, to enable a person to recognize and avoid shoddy materials and cheap construction, and, when the time to set up a home arrived, to purchase their opposite as nearly as the pocket-book should permit.

ADVERTISING IN THE SCHOOLS

The public schools, particularly the elementary and high schools, have been fertile ground for the insinuation and dissemination of advertising and sales propaganda for all kinds of branded goods. . . .

Teachers of home economics are especially to blame for the huge amounts of so-called free advertising material that are going into the schools. Look through the advertising section of any issue of such publications as the *Journal of Home Economics* and *Practical Home Economics*, and note the free material offered there for the slight trouble of clipping an advertisement or sending a few cents. Teachers admit using a great amount of such material, and if any doubts arise in their minds as to the possible effect on the consuming habits of their pupils, they simply recall that they themselves have been told to use such "enrichment material" freely, by professors of their art in teachers' colleges and state universities. . . .

It will be a sorry day for business if publicly owned enterprises ever go on a cost accounting basis, as so many business men urge. Free premiums to school children would not be so profitable if the advertiser had to carry his share of the school system overhead by direct payments instead of by the inexpensive but seemingly generous little acts which now serve the purpose, *sans* cost accounting! . . .

If consumers had received the practical technical training necessary to enable them to judge the qualities of complex goods, they could never have been persuaded to endure the businesslike pressures that are responsible for maintaining present widespread consumer ignorance, now practically a vested right of the automobile, radio, and tooth-paste manufacturers.

For instance, if science teaching were real and geared to the social and economic order, no high school boy would ever naively assume, after taking the required number of hours in general science and physics, that octane selectors, free-wheeling, and streamlining (as sold), are real or fundamental developments in the perfection of motor cars, or that "Interstation Tuning Silencer," "Filterizer," or "Duo-Diode-Triode Detector" represents the last word or words in the technical improvement of the radio.

COMMERCIAL BIAS IN GRADE SCHOOLS

What of "progressive education"? Must it not give consideration to the consumer's problems through its special and boasted program of socialized education? It has not yet done so, and may never do so to any significant extent. No doubt much can be said for the increased activity and interest resulting from the child's participation in projects built around adult activities. But these planned activities or projects are directed by adults, and many of them show the noteworthy commercial bias which has so thoroughly permeated the older parts of the education system. A few such projects or teaching units for the lower grades, published by the Bureau of Publications of Teachers College, Columbia University, are listed here:

"Banking"—in which to answer correctly a completion test, the child must affirm that a checking account provides a *safe* place to put money; also that banks have *better* means of protection against robberies than we have in our homes (which might be true if one had never read a Detroit or New York newspaper, and did not consider the inside operations and the outside business relationships of bank presidents and directors.)

"Saving"—in which emphasis is placed up the supposed security of banking and investing money.

"The Grocery Store"—wherein the activity centers around operating an "A. and P. Store" (why not Reuben White, General Merchandise; must even the university advertise the national chains?) with little containers labeled Fairy, Ivory, Chipso, Lux, and so forth.

"A Fair and a Study of Milk"—in which the teacher "hoped that attitudes of appreciation of the food value of milk, and an appreciation of those who made it possible for us to have milk and milk products were built." Who is to provide us with an appreciation of the values of potatoes and eggs and ripe tomatoes and homemade soup, which being less tightly organized in a trade sense, do not fare quite so well in the educational program? Milk, on account of the wealth and power of the dairy firms and their close tie to medical and public health services, has always fared especially well at the hands of the school system and of nutrition teachers.

"Shoes"—which concerns the manufacture of shoes but contains no critical discussion of their quality, durability, or cost of manufacture, and only the briefest and most indefinite suggestion that shoes should fit properly.

Others of the same series of lesson units are "The Radio Enters the Classroom," "The Story of Lighting," and "How the Fishing Industry Helps to Satisfy the Needs of Man"—none containing the obviously needed critical analysis of industry's relation to the consumer, and all frankly enamored of our aimless and planless and profit-bent industrial growth. . . .

The colleges and universities are doing no more, and possibly less, than the elementary schools and the high schools to dispel the ignorance and gullibility that surround the purchase of even the most simple and daily used articles of clothing and food. What do the brightest students in the departments of electrical and mechanical engineering know about the relative merits or demerits, let us say, of various brands of electric irons, oil burners, gasoline, or building materials? What one can tell you the proper oil for a clock or a phonograph, or why lead is good for paint out of doors, and very bad for floors? Not one. Many, however, will, after college, become masterful sales exponents of the superlative features of the appliances sold by the great electric companies with which they have accepted jobs, or will, as sales engineers, give free "technical" advice to all and sundry on matters of vital moment to livelihood and health. . . .

[W]e find the curriculums of universities and colleges (not trade schools, where the work would be more at home) loaded down with courses in business: business economics, corporate finance, salesmanship, marketing, business psychology, business English—even foreign business correspondence for sales executives.

Most of such courses have no place in a rational program of general public education; that is, consumer education. They must be eliminated entirely if students are to leave school with any clear-cut notion about the position they must take in the rapidly rising conflict between consumers vainly seeking for goods of reasonable quality and durability at minimal prices, and producers driving successfully for a larger and larger share of the depressed and dwindling social income.

EDUCATION FOR CONSUMPTIVE ENDS

The era of expanding production is rapidly drawing to a close. Here and there new business ventures will rise to prominence and then subside, only because our present economic system cannot support the waste that goes into costly and planless speculation. At the moment there is a rising tide of interest and a growing murmur of dissatisfaction at the hopeless position into which the ultimate consumer has been forced by ruthless drives of competitive salesmanship and planless production and marketing.

One need hardly expect that the public schools of themselves will take up the cudgels in the consumer's behalf, but, as in similar social revolutions, consumers themselves will in time force consideration of their rights in public education. When that day arrives, science classes will find that testing electric toasters, vacuum cleaners, can openers, household rubber, leather, and paper articles, and analyzing soap, cosmetics, shoe pastes, prepared flours, and baking powders is an integral part of their work. . . .

In the home, stamp collecting, the accumulation of glass and ivory trinkets on the mantelpiece, and new forms of bridge will give way to small work benches and chemistry laboratories where tooth powder, ink, and floor polish are compounded and made to replace inferior and costly commercial products, and where commercial products are analyzed and made to give an accounting of themselves, both technically and economically. . . .

Teachers of economics must become familiar, at least in a broad sense, with the technical nature of consumers' goods and with the doctrine of value as measured in terms both of production and of cost of production rather than in terms of what products will bring either on the so-called free market or on the price-controlled market set up by the seller with the aid of price-fixing or "stabilizing" agreements or of quasi-monopolies due to advertising pressure.

9 Thrift Education and School Savings Banks

In the late-nineteenth and early-twentieth centuries moral reformers, educators, and thrift advocates introduced a new institution—the school savings bank—to control children's spending and encourage the practice of regular saving. Originating in the mid-1880s, school savings bank programs were gradually integrated into elementary and secondary schools located predominantly in the East Coast, West Coast, and Midwest. By the 1920s, schoolteachers routinely turned over a half hour of lesson time each week to allow students to deposit money into their school savings account.

As the following documents demonstrate, parents, teachers, and children ranked both among school savings banks' most enthusiastic supporters and most vigorous detractors. In the first two documents, Andrew Price and Russell Curtis Grimshaw set forth the case for school savings banks and explain why advocates of thrift education envisioned school banking as an instrument of moral reform. The next three documents explore school savings banks from the perspectives of a student, a parent, and teacher, each revealing the merits and flaws of school savings banks that their chief proponents either overlooked or failed to consider. In his autobiographical account of growing up poor in St. Louis during the late 1920s and 1930s, Anthony Hotchner recalls the great hopes he invested in school banking and the bitter disappointment it ultimately delivered. Chester Crowell, an upper-middle-class New Jersey father, presents a humorous yet pointed critique of school savings banks in a 1930 article for the *American Mercury*, while Olive T. Jones, a schoolteacher and president of the National Education Association, illuminates both the logistical and pedagogical limitations of thrift education in her speech at the 1924 National Conference on Thrift Education, held in Washington, D.C. All these documents reveal the crucial role of class in shaping how parents and children used money, measured its value, and experienced school savings banks.

Document 25, the interior pages of a 1947 pamphlet produced by the Farmers and Mechanics Savings Bank in Minneapolis, Minnesota, highlights the greater emphasis many school savings bank programs placed on wise spending and consumption-driven saving after World War II. Instead of prizing saving as a virtue in itself, thrift education increasingly stressed the value of saving for some definite end.

20. Andrew Price, "Teaching Thrift as a Branch of Public Instruction," *Education* 37 (October 1916): 116–21.

Many schemes have been evolved for elevating the masses, but they have utterly failed in their purpose unless there has been a previous development of character and mind which were capable of wisely using the opportunities thus made available. As a result, when we are confronted with an industrial or moral problem we turn to education as essential to its solution, for education is a ladder for industrial reform and illiteracy is an insurmountable impediment. Without education there is no progress, and without progress there is no advance in civilization. . . .

In the actual operation of the School Savings Bank, in which the children take the greater part, many things are impressed upon their receptive minds. It gives them practical business experience and correct information concerning the general financial systems of their country, which many would not otherwise receive. Great importance attaches to this fact, for the average girl or woman has little or no knowledge concerning these matters, and in her hands often lies the success or failure of a household. By her waste in the home, she can destroy it; or, by her frugality, learned while in school, she can be the medium to a higher and better plane of living. Moreover, the plan teaches all the pupils, system, something which every instructor tries in many unsuccessful ways to impart to the children under his care. In the teaching of Arithmetic, Interest, Bookkeeping, Banking, and in fact all commercial and economic subjects, the School Savings Bank is of inestimable aid, for it gives the child an idea of these, in terms with which he is perfectly familiar. . . .

Another feature of school banks is the children's accounts not only often instruct their parents about Savings Banks, but are the means of getting them to open accounts in local institutions. In some cases where the parents have been too proud to deposit their small savings, they have had their child act as their agent in so doing. . . .

Statistics prove a large percentage of the scholars save with some good object. And here let me state that this very fact proves that the system does not tend to develop a spirit of "parsimony and jealousy" among the children. Instances are many where savings accumulated by children have been a great help to families in time of sickness, or when the head of the family has been thrown out of work, says F. R. Hathaway, formerly Superintendent of the Grand Rapids, Michigan, Public Schools, or as J. K. Gotwals, formerly Superintendent of Norristown, Pennsylvania, Public Schools, says, "money that might have been foolishly spent has been used for family support in times of need." If the system does no more than teach the habit of restraining "present indulgence" for "future advantage" it is well worth while.

Most successful charitable organizations and reform agencies are based on the principle that man must be made to help himself by "exercising his inherent power and by husbanding his own resources." The hunger for immediate satisfaction and the clamor of impulsive desires is universal. It is only when the individual is able to look into the future and see what it has in store for him, to realize the pain and deprivations and the accompanying weakening of power that results from wanton waste, that he is able to muster sufficient force to check his spendthrift inclinations. In aiding children of such tendencies the School Savings Bank plays an important role. It does not rely upon precept; but rather on indoctrinating by drill into the child, the habit of thrift, which once formed is "the possessor's second nature."

When thrift is taught in the schools it is taken into almost every home. This resulting widespread frugality reduces pauperism and the attendant expense necessary to keep this class. The desire to save among the boys has a tendency to cause them to give up the use of cigarettes and all forms of tobacco. In communities where School Savings Banks are in vogue many places supported by slot machines have been compelled to close their doors for lack of patronage. The same spirit tends to prevent pool playing and gambling. The system works a powerful influence in checking the growth of all evil habits. It builds character. According to Mr. E. H. Spein, "another proof of the good accomplished is the fact that the transient candy and confectionery stands that unusually did business near some of our schools have nearly all quit on account of lack of patronage." Mr. F. S. Weaver, Superintendent of the Schools of Hartford, Connecticut, gives the following account of a School Savings Bank in a certain district of that city, to-wit:— "This bank was formed, not primarily as a Savings Bank, but to prevent children from spending money at the nearby candy stores in the morning and getting into bad shape during the forenoon from too little breakfast and too much sweets. It has been very successful." Many similar instances have occurred throughout the country. The Worlds National Woman's Christian Temperance Union after careful investigation of the system, "took up its work as a department and are aiding in its extension, because they saw its value as a 'temperance force'."

21. Russell Curtis Grimshaw, "Is the School Bank Worthwhile?" *Educational Review* 73 (March 1927): 161–67.

. . . For the most part the benefits of the school savings bank are obvious. There is danger, however, in accepting this statement too readily, for we are apt to dismiss the whole matter from our thoughts, ere we have scarcely probed beneath the surface for returns not altogether apparent.

The "rainy-day" idea is old. We have heard much of "saving for a rainy day," of "making hay while the sun shines," and of "setting aside something for to-morrow." The age of these platitudes should not invalidate their present worth, but it should, rather, strengthen their force with all its weight of years.

A pathetic incident comes to mind. A twelve-year-old boy had been a regular depositor in a school savings bank for a period of three years or more. In that time he had saved the immense sum of forty dollars. I say immense, because to him it represented months of hard work and sacrifice. Then followed a period of lean days and weeks. His father through sickness and unemployment could not provide for the family of six children. One day the boy applied at the school bank, and with a solemn pride, that was his alone, asked to withdraw his money. It was the custom of the teacher in charge to inquire the reason for all drafts. Then it was that he heard this story. The boy saw the family through its difficulty. Since the father's recovery the good man has been able to replace his son's savings, a small amount at a time. The boy has to his credit now almost as much as he had before. What a lesson in thrift that was to an American boy. What a moral was brought home to that family. . . .

However great the benefits of the rainy-day attitude may be, I believe that the school bank offers a second return of far greater value to the life of a community or a nation. The school bank gives training in good habits —habits of thrift, habits of sacrificing the immediate pleasure for the ultimate good, habits of guarding against vain squandering, habits of avoiding the rush of the pleasure-mad. That the school bank does this cannot be denied. These same habits of intelligent conservation persist through life and enrich the welfare of all. Who are the bone and the sinew of the American nation today? They are the throng of hard-working independent homeowners that have toiled and saved and who now make up a prominent part of our citizenry.

The school bank has still another social value. In all banking systems, where much of the work is done by pupils themselves, the qualities of reliability and honesty are deeply embedded into the character of the several employees. To be able to handle the money of others without feeling the tempter's urge is certainly a trait worth bringing out. If the school bank can effect this in the case of a dozen or more pupils each term, then it has performed a valuable service. This is one of the reasons why I stand in favor of banking systems operated by pupils rather than by outside agencies. . . .

There is still another benefit from the school savings bank which we must not overlook. It is this. After a child has started on his way to a substantial bank account, he acquires a sense of ownership and a sense of value. There is only one way to realize the full meaning of ownership, and that is to own something; there is only one way to appreciate the value of anything, and that is to measure it in terms of the sacrifice it cost. How unfortunate is the child in the orphanage, who wears the clothes of the institution and plays with the toys of the group. He holds no property of his own. Property rights and ownership mean nothing to him. He cannot evaluate, because he can make no comparison. I have taken this extreme case to show how important are these conceptions often taken for granted, the sense of ownership and the sense of value. The school bank brings out these qualities to the fullest. Bolshevism cannot live in a community where each one owns something. I believe that the school bank is a most formidable foe to all Bolshevistic forces.

22. Chester T. Crowell, "Bank Day," *American Mercury* 20 (May 1930): 87–93.

Tuesday is bank day in our local school and every pupil is expected to bring a coin for deposit with his teacher. The size of the coin makes little difference, but great stress is laid upon keeping each class record perfect. Perfect means that every child has made a deposit every Tuesday. If anyone fails he is pointedly made to understand that he has injured his entire class, and not only his class, but also the whole school. . . .

I remember when this great work was inaugurated, some four or five years ago. It caused quite a stir in our household. About five or six minutes before school time each Tuesday morning one of the children would suddenly shout "Bank day!" in a tone that implied "Oh, my God!" Immediately afterward I would hear, upstairs in my bedroom, what a poet once referred to as the patter of little feet. (But he was mistaken on that point: Mrs. Crowell and I refer to such occasions as a stampede by the thundering herd.) Purses and vest pockets would be hunted down and rifled, and if their contents failed to meet the demand the maid would be held up. Often it was necessary for one member of the family to do a Paul Revere to the drug-store with a dollar bill and then hasten on to school and distribute the change to his panting brothers and sisters who waited in the doorway, caught between the Scylla of tardiness and the Charybdis of a mortal sin against the school banking record.

I regarded all this as silly but not serious and dismissed it from my mind until one day I listened to the complaint of a woman neighbor whose little boy had been stood in the corner for failing to bring his bank money. She told me that she had no money that day, not even a penny, and that her son was too proud to make public acknowledgment of this fact. He had therefore pleaded guilty, eager to take the blame upon his own shoulders and save the family pride. But the teacher had been obsessed with the great importance of the class record and, anxious to save it, had sent him home to get a coin. Naturally, financial conditions had not changed there in half an hour, so he had to return and again take the blame on himself. That was just a little too much, so the teacher stood him in the corner. She felt that she had gone as far as she could with this youngster; it was bad enough for him to have forgotten bank day in the first place but to fail her even after she allowed him to return home placed him beyond mercy. He took his medicine, but the class record, even so, was ruined. . . .

Every possible advantage of the system would still remain if banking were optional instead of compulsory. I tried to explain that it was outrageously unjust to punish a child, no matter how mildly, for any remissness beyond his control. And I also explained that the children, out of a most commendable pride, would never inform the teachers when the failure actually was beyond their control. In short, I argued that banking had no proper place in the public schools if it were made a device for whooping up "school spirit" and school pride. I maintained that it ought to be absolutely optional, and preferably even casual.

These were quite friendly discussions and the school authorities tried honestly to understand what I was talking about, but it was all quite foreign to their customary way of thinking. Most of these people, I found, were and are just about old enough to have been permanently impressed by certain activities and points of view current during the War to End War. The idea that the individual has any inalienable rights is not part of their thinking. They can see no reason why a child shouldn't rise in the classroom and say that there was no money in the house on Tuesday morning, or not enough to spare a coin for banking. The idea of privacy seems to be strange to them. A new conception of compulsion comes into their minds, for even after all the facts were stated they did not see that the situation involved it. . . .

They were out to Do Good—with a teeth-gritting determination that made it impossible for them to remember the rights of others. . . .

Such obstinate persistence, and such loyalty on the part of the school authorities to this nuisance of enforced banking may reasonably raise a question as to whether there is any profit in it for the teachers. I hasten to say that there is none; only a fearfully burdensome mass of bookkeeping.

Even the local banks which hold these tiny deposits suffer a loss by carrying them because the bookkeeping costs so far outweigh the profit. The only cash return goes to the organization which sells the little bank-books for the children. That organization collects a percentage of the deposits from the banks holding them. The local banks pay this percentage and take a loss on their deposits because they are persuaded that the system is good advertising and excellent propaganda for savings accounts. But even the bankers are sold primarily on the point that they are performing a public service. They, too, are out to Do Good. They are Teaching Thrift.

On that point I have been much amused by the reactions of the children. Ours receive weekly allowances, but they do not think it would be fair to deposit part of that money. As they see it, the school banking system levies a tax, which is part of the cost of their education and therefore properly chargeable to paterfamilias. Their own money is for their own use. Some time ago I remarked to Cathleen that she had thirty dollars in the bank. She thought I was joking. Money, to her, is something in hand; if not in hand, it doesn't count. And that is typical of the results of this great educational effort. . . .

Terrific pressure is constantly exerted upon them [public schools] to undertake and discharge the most amazing good works, only remotely related to education. For example, Miss Cathleen comes home from school carrying a little card on which her mother is expected to write a report stating that she has been fed a hot cereal for breakfast. And just to keep the record straight her mother is also required to state the name of that cereal. I have heard dietitians discuss the feeding of the young and I gathered from their remarks that there is a great deal more to it than just a hot cereal for breakfast. Why, I wondered, do they enter upon this one item, to the woeful neglect of so many other phases of the science?

While wondering I picked up the card and examined it to see what else might be mentioned. At the top I found a delightful and appetite-provoking picture, in full colors, of a dish of cereal. Nor was I left in doubt as to what cereal that beautifully tinted art work represented. It was Cream of Wheat. Now, I may be utterly wrong, and cynical, but from that moment I ceased to wonder about the heavy emphasis on just one item of the child's diet. I reached the conclusion that someone had harnessed up the public school system to help him sell breakfast food. But I was sure, of course, that the fundamental purpose was Service. These people are out to Do Good. I don't know what would happen to Cathleen if she reported "No cereal." I haven't tried to find out. Mrs. Crowell wrote on the card the names of all the other patent breakfast foods we could think of. At least we can do that and stay out of the hoosegow.

I can't help wondering where all this tom-foolery will finally lead the public schools. Beyond doubt they are rapidly becoming a sort of adjunct to the police department, and in their loftier, academic services a delousing plant for the offspring of immigrants.

23. Olive M. Jones, "Wise Spending As A Teacher Sees It," *Report of the Conference on Thrift Education*, June 27–28, 1924, in Washington, D.C. (National Education Association and National Council of Education).

. . . The subject I have chosen today is "Wise Spending as a Teacher Sees It," and I have had a special reason for selecting that subject. I thought that if I spoke from that point of view I might call to the attention of those of you who are not in the actual classroom work of schools some of the difficulties confronting teachers in regard to this subject; and maybe some of you would learn the reason that occasionally teachers do not welcome the introduction of thrift education, as possibly it would seem that they ought to.

Thrift not hoarding—The fact is that there is just as much thrift required for wise spending as for saving money. There is just as much thrift involved in teaching people how to use the money they save as in teaching them to put it into banks; more thrift, really, than there is in inculcating the idea that saving is hoarding. Therein was one of the first difficulties among the teachers. They objected to teaching the individual to hoard, and the first introduction of thrift education that come to us as teachers was the idea of saving or hoarding money. We objected to it very strenuously because we felt that was not the main question in which the children needed instruction.

The saturation point—. . . [W]e teachers have reached the saturation point in the inclusion in the curriculum of things to teach. Unless something is dropped from the course of study, so that the teacher is relieved, or unless the school day and the school year are lengthened, and the objections to that are just as strong from the point of view of the parent and the child as from the point of view of the teacher, we can consider no further additions. . . .

Over-emphasis on saving—A second reason why at first I was not interested in thrift, was the over-emphasis on mere saving, and the competition which existed in regard to amounts saved. My teaching life has been spent among a people whose racial inheritance and conditions of living imposed upon them by people in other lands has brought them to a place where they don't need any great urging to get money. What they need is rather understanding in the wise use of money. Consequently when our school savings banks were introduced with the idea of competition among the children as to the amount that they had saved, we teachers of children of the type of which I am speaking, objected very strongly. We did not want them to feel that competition. Besides that, we had only just begun to see the evil in that kind of competition in athletics, and now, after we had resolved to get out of the field of athletics, we were introducing competition into the field of thrift education.

Delinquent boys—Nineteen of the years that I am speaking of have been spent in work among delinquent boys. The most common fault among boys who come under that category probably is stealing. Consequently again we hesitated, because here we were introducing something that was going to make those children desire to get money, and money would provide a temptation toward additional stealing, beyond that which they had.

I am reminded, as I speak of those boys, of an incident that happened among them one day, which indicates that they needed very little urging in the matter of getting money, or of appreciation of the value of money. The superintendent came in one day, and desiring to be very local in the problem that he gave to them in arithmetic, he said to the class that he was examining: "Two push cart dealers bought brooms at twenty-five cents a dozen. One sold them at two for a quarter, and one sold them at twenty-five cents apiece. Which dealer made the more money and how much?" Before he had the question out, the boys had their hands up to give him the answer. He was startled. "You can take your pencils and paper to work out that problem. You can't do it in your minds," he said. The boys shook their heads and kept their hands up; so he called on one boy for the answer, which was, "The man that sold them two for a quarter; the other fellow didn't sell any." Boys of this kind don't have to be taught the value of money and how much they can do with it, and how far it will go.

Saving to use money—But on the day that I am speaking of, Mr. MacDowell came in and talked to those boys, and the very same boys about whom I have just told the story were in the group. He said very little indeed to them about putting money in the bank. He did talk to them about using their money so that it would produce the greatest amount of good for themselves now and in the future, and for those who might be dependent upon them. It was a clear exposition of the difference between *saving to get money and saving to use money.* And that sentence contains the point of view of the teacher—to teach children to save money, not with the aim of getting but with the aim of using, as the wise point of view of thrift for us to give to the children that come under our care. . . .

A changed viewpoint—I referred a moment ago to the question of stealing and now I want to speak of the difference in the effect upon that question that this changed point of view about saving and thrift education brought about. Of the 200 boys that come to our school, probably 40 of them are thieves, usually pickpockets. They have a point of view in regard to it that the majority of us do not understand. To the average boy who picks pockets it is a legitimate business. He needs money; he knows where there is money to get, and he makes a business of going out to get it. That is the whole story as those boys see it, and when you get their confidence so that they are willing to talk to you, they will tell it to you in almost the same words that I have told it to you now.

It is the most common thing to have a boy who has got into trouble by picking pockets say to his teachers, "Well, I had to have the money." He believes there is a legitimate connection between the need and the act.

Just as soon as the saving in the school bank and the thrift education was undertaken by the teachers from the new point of view, the boys began to see the relationship between stealing and property rights. That was an unexpected result, but it happened, and consequently we encouraged those boys that we knew had the temptation to steal to become immediately contributors to the school bank. We didn't always know and were not always quite sure whether or not the money that they put into the school bank was honestly obtained in the beginning, but sooner or later we found with everyone of them that the mere fact that he had a certain amount of money that he was saving for a definite purpose, as soon as he became conscious of the fact that he had that, and realized that it was his property, he learned a respect for the rights of property in everybody else. Many a boy has been induced to give up the practice of stealing just for this reason. . . .

New York slums—The section of the city where we are located is an exceedingly poor one. It is the slum district of New York, and the people who are there are terribly poor; and naturally the children that we get represent the poorest of the poor. The most constant problem with them is rent, and that drove us into a consideration of this whole question of thrift education, wise saving and wise spending in relation to the rent. We have talked with the children about it, and have gotten them to bring their parents to school, and we have talked it over with the parents. It is shocking to realize the relationship that actually exists between the rent that people pay and the whole amount of their income. It is absolutely disproportionate—absolutely. They pay rent according to the kind of place that they make up their minds to want to live in, the number of rooms that they feel they must have, and numerous other questions that come up for consideration. They fail absolutely to consider it in relation to food or to health or to possible emergencies and accidents that may arise. Therefore, in the instruction about thrift and in relation to the saving of the children, we have used the question of rent as one of the ways of reaching these children, and one of the ways of teaching real thrift to the parents. Incidentally I might say that a good many of us had to take the lesson to heart ourselves, because when we made an investigation into the subject and got together some statistics and inquired as to the budget making of family incomes, we found that many of us were far exceeding the proportion of income that should go to rent.

24. A. E. Hotchner, *King of the Hill* (New York: Harper & Row, 1972), 85–86.

When school started that fall, I took all the money out of my pirate box and I put it in the Students' Savings Bank, where I already had $4.23 I had saved from before. The St. Louis schools had this savings system where they gave you a savings book with your name on it, and every Friday you could give your teacher anything from a penny on up and she marked it in your book. They paid you interest, but the big thing was that nobody could get at that money but you. The school promised you that. For me that was very important, because all summer my father had been taking my money, always asking to "borrow" a dollar for gasoline or carfare, but naturally he never paid any of it back. Once I put it in the bank, I didn't have it to "lend" to him any more.

I was a very saving type and I guess I'd still have had that money to buy my graduation things if it hadn't been for what happened to the Students' Savings Bank. Our teacher came in one morning and read us a bulletin from the principal, Mr. Herbert P. Stellwagon. It was his sad duty to tell us, he said, that the St. Louis Bank & Trust Co., which is where the Students' Savings Bank kept its money, had run out of money and gone out of business, and that all of the students' money was lost.

Mr. Hoover, who was President then, was always on the radio telling everyone that the bankers and the businessmen were going to save the country, and how we should trust them, so that night I wrote him a letter, President Herbert Hoover, The White House, and I told him about the way the bankers had cleaned out us kids and asked him to help us get our money back. I told him how I had worked so darn hard all summer for that money and how my father and mother didn't have jobs and would he please get that money back from the bankers for me. He never even answered my letter. That's when I started to hate Herbert Hoover. I never called him President after that.

25. "'Hold It!' You Belong in this Picture" (Minneapolis, MN: Farmers and Mechanics Savings Bank, 1947). Courtesy of Hagley Museum and Library.

1. FLAT BROKE most of the time . . . that was me. I never saved a cent out of my allowance or the money I earned . . . I couldn't afford the worthwhile things I wanted . . . until one day I got *smart* . . .

2. LOOK WHAT DEVELOPED! I started putting away money regularly in my School Savings Account. Now I've got my own new camera, equipment, and money to spare, besides!

3. THE MOWER THE MERRIER! And the more I save, the easier it seems. I figure that a lot of the things I want and need I ought to be able to buy for myself . . . and I'm doing it with my own savings.

4. A GOOD SLICE of my birthday and Christmas money goes into the bank, too. You can't beat that swell feeling of having your own dough in your own bank account to spend as you choose.

5. FUN MONEY? Sure . . . I keep out cash for eats and shows and dates . . . but I never miss a School Savings deposit, because that money will help pay for college and clothes and vacations.

6. GET THE PICTURE? Regular deposits in your School Savings Account won't break you . . . and they can add up to a real chunk of money! Easy, too . . . and the smartest way to save you ever tried!

Acct. No..
(Leave this space blank)

SCHOOL SAVINGS BANK SIGNATURE CARD

I hereby make application to open an account with the School Savings Department of the Farmers & Mechanics Savings Bank, under its rules and regulations.

My Signature ....

My Home Address ....

Name of My {Parent or / Guardian} ....

High School ....Grade..........of Birth | Month | Day | Year |

Date..First Deposit $....................

8-804 25M 2-52

HOW TO START A SCHOOL SAVINGS ACCOUNT

1. FILL OUT ABOVE CARD, enclose it with money for first deposit in regular Deposit Envelope. Hand to High School Cashier of your School Savings Bank.

2. YOUR NEW PASS BOOK will be delivered to you on next school day. Seal Pass Book in Deposit Envelope with money for each future deposit.

3. DEPOSITS are sent to Farmers & Mechanics Savings Bank where they earn regular interest and are insured by the Federal Deposit Insurance Corp.

4. WITHDRAWALS or extra deposits can be made any time at the bank during business hours. Be sure to bring your School Savings Pass Book with you!

10 Parenting and Parent-Child Relationships in the Consumer Household

Children's expanding roles as consumers in the twentieth century accompanied and informed transformations in parenting practices and childrearing advice. As parents granted children greater autonomy and a greater say in family decisions, children also began to assert their independence in consumer spending. Paradoxically, child experts in the 1920s and 1930s endorsed more egalitarian parent-child relationships and gentler, even veiled, assertions of parental authority as a way to regain some measure of parental control. The democratization of family life, especially within the middle class, was thus both a cause and a consequence of children's growing consumer freedoms.

The documents in this section explore how parents, children, and childrearing experts attempted to revise and reaffirm the proper balance between children's autonomy and parental control in the face of children's stepped-up consumer demands. In the first document, Sidonie Gruenberg, who served as president of the Child Study Association and wrote numerous articles for *Parents' Magazine* in the 1920s and 1930s, assesses the merits of allowances as a means to teach children the value of money and habits of financial discipline. The next document, an article entitled "'Selling' Food to Children," appeared in *Mother's Own Book*, a compendium of childrearing advice published in 1928. As the metaphor of selling suggests, much childrearing advice of the era urged parents to master the arts of persuasion—psychological techniques that could be as useful in compelling children to eat their spinach as they could be in compelling children to spend within limits.

The third and fourth documents, excerpts from *Middletown*, Robert and Helen Lynd's famous 1929 sociological study of Muncie, Indiana, illuminates the historical transformations—in family life, the economy, and youth culture —that made many parents receptive to such childrearing advice. It also suggests why at least some children may not have responded to the new parenting techniques, either as experts predicted they would or as parents would have liked. The final document, "One Girl's Family," appeared in *Scholastic Magazine*'s "Boy Dates Girl" column by Gay Head, a tremendously popular teen advice writer. Written at the tail end of the Great Depression, Gay Head's column on morals and manners endorsed family democracy while urging teens to adopt a spirit of compromise and sacrifice in managing limited family finances. All the documents address a central question in the history of twentieth-century childhood: did the turn to greater permissiveness work more to enhance parental control or to expand children's consumer freedoms?

Advice on how to raise responsible and respectable consumers has continued to multiply. In the past decade, dozens of books, with titles like *Money Doesn't Grow on Trees: A Parents' Guide to Raising Financially Responsible Children*, *Raising Money Smart Kids: What They Need to Know about Money and How to Tell Them*, and *Allowance Magic: Turn Your Kids into Money Wizards*, have advocated allowances and other forms of money training for kids. Readers who wish to assess just how much or just how little such advice has changed since the early twentieth century might visit www.kidsmoney. org, which provides access to articles and related Web sites on children and financial literacy.

26. Sidonie Gruenberg, "Children and Money," *Federation for Child Study Bulletin* 1 (January 1924): 1–3.

In his Children's Story-Sermons, the Rev. Dr. Hugh T. Kerr tells the following story: "One morning when Bradley came down to breakfast, he put on his mother's plate a little piece of paper neatly folded. His mother opened it. She could hardly believe it, but this is what Bradley had written:

Mother owes Bradley

For running errands $0.25
For being good 10
For taking music lessons 15
Extras 05
Total $0.55

"His mother smiled, but did not say anything, and when lunch time came she placed the bill on Bradley's plate with fifty-five cents. Bradley's eyes fairly danced when he saw the money and thought his business ability had been quickly rewarded, but with the money there was another little bill, which read like this:

Bradley owes mother

For being good . . . $0.00
For nursing him through his long illness with scarlet fever . . . $0.00
For clothes, shoes, gloves, and playthings $0.00
For all his meals and his beautiful room $0.00
Total that Bradley owes mother . . . $0.00

"Tears came into Bradley's eyes, and he put his arms around his mother's neck, put his little hand with the fifty-five cents in hers, and said, 'Take all the money back, mamma, and let me love you and do things for you.'"

The homes of this country are full of Bradleys who know nothing of rights and duties as related to money. And how should they know, never having learned? Among the children of the poor there usually develops rather early in life a keen appreciation of the value of money. Whatever money there is is quickly spent, and comes to represent pretty definitely the necessities and the luxuries of life. A dime means a loaf of bread and a nickel means a stick of candy. Money is hard to get and good to have; and without it we have privation and misery. On the other hand, in the homes of the well-to-do and in the country, where comparatively little cash is handled the opportunities to become acquainted with the sources and properties of money are comparatively narrow. Here people somehow have what they need, and no special effort or hardship is associated with getting these things. What is wanted is "ordered," and the children know nothing about the cost. Whatever money they may wish for the trifles that they buy themselves can usually be had for the asking.

Money plays so important a role in modern life, that we are apt to take it for granted without thinking especially of teaching children what they should understand of the matter. Children should learn these things definitely and practically, beginning as soon as they are old enough to appreciate relative values. A child can begin by buying things for the household when he is able to distinguish the coins and count up the amounts. The age for this will, of course, vary with different children. It is, however, only through experience in buying that a person can ever attain to judgment in buying. The sense of values comes from familiarity with many values in terms of a common denominator. The methods by which people come to be possessed of money, and the relation of service to payment, should enter the child's experience as soon as he can understand these things.

An eight-year-old boy, tired after the strenuous exertions of the day, was disinclined to put away the toys and blocks. But there was no compromise; mother insisted and the task was soon accomplished. He came back to mother and said, "Now they're all put away, Mother. Give me a nickel."

"A nickel?" asked the mother, not perceiving the relevancy of the last remark. "Why should I give you a nickel?"

"For putting away those things; that's work; I don't want to be a slave," came the answer.

This suggested a possible misunderstanding, and mother asked rather than declared, "You don't know what a slave is, Clarence!"

"Oh, yes, I do," persisted the boy. "A slave is like the colored people in the South who used to be made to work without getting paid."

That was near enough to the truth for the immediate purpose and Clarence's mother had to stop fencing. She closed right in. People get paid for doing work for others, she explained, only where they cannot get any other return for their service. But people do not get paid for doing their duty. We all have to do things for each other; else we could not get along together. Indeed, we could not get along at all, for children are quite helpless at first, and if things were not done for them they would soon perish. Clarence understood that. He had seen the kittens dependent upon the mother cat for food. He shuddered at the thought of baby sister being left to her own resources. And parents do not expect pay for what they do; there is no one to pay them and they are not working for pay. They love their children and so they do all they can for them.

The explanation was entirely satisfactory to Clarence, except at one point. He did not see how he was going to get any money, if not in payment for the things he could do—and he had already discovered that he needed money. When a child reaches the point at which he has the germ of appreciation for money, he certainly should have an opportunity to get it, if that can possibly be arranged. And if the family has the means, there are two ways in which this can be arranged.

A child may be given a small regular allowance for his own use. Through this he may learn the joy of immediate indulgence of trifling whims; or he may learn to expend his resources with discrimination; or he may learn the advantages of deferring expenditure for more favorable purchasing. The child's claim to such an allowance can be justified to his mind on exactly the same ground as his claim to food and clothing and other material and immaterial wealth shared in the home. He gets these things not as a reward of merit; but through his status as a dependent member of a household.

For the reason that the allowance is a part of the routine income of the child, by virtue of his membership in the home community, it should never be used as an instrument of "discipline." If the allowance can be justified at all, it should be increased only in recognition of larger needs, and it should be diminished only when retrenchment is necessary for the family as a whole, or when changing conditions indicate reduced needs for the child. Thus, older children may legitimately expect to receive larger allowances than the younger ones.

The regular receipt of the allowance may be made contingent upon a child's maintaining a satisfactory level of conduct, or on his manifesting a spirit of cooperation in the home. But this arrangement must not permit us to make specific misconduct an occasion for deducting from the allowance. When Agnes failed to return from a visit to a friend at a sufficiently early hour, her mother said nothing; but at the end of the week she took off ten cents from the allowance. In this the mother was entirely in the wrong, for in the first place the money allowance of the child should be on exactly the same basis as the other privileges which he enjoys as a member of the family, and not be singled out as a club for penalizing delinquencies. In the second place, by using it in this way the mother at once reduces the responsibilities of the child to a cash basis. Agnes can calculate next time whether staying out later is worth the ten cents that it costs. This attitude also opens up the whole field of the child's conduct to petty bickerings and bargainings about the number of cents to be paid for each "good" deed, or the number of cents to be deducted for each "bad" deed.

In addition to an allowance, children should have opportunities to earn extra amounts of money. It is the money earned that gives them the necessary inner experience without which one is never able to translate money values into terms of effort and exertion and sacrifice. Money that comes without effort may teach the child to spend wisely, or to save; but it can never teach him the human cost of the things that he uses from day to day. It is perhaps at this point more than anywhere else that the children of the well-to-do fail to become acquainted with the life problems of the mass of the people. They come to feel the value of money in terms of what it can buy, but not in terms of what it costs.

In many a household it becomes necessary for a number of the daily tasks to be performed by the children. If these tasks are looked upon as duties, if they represent definitely the children's share of the upkeep of the establishment, they should not be paid for. Nevertheless, it would be proper to agree upon a scale of payment for doing many of the necessary chores. But in that case, the child should have the option of not doing the assigned work when he feels that it is not worth his while. Otherwise the payment for work is merely a pretext for compelling the child to do work. At the same time, the child should not be free to perform his tasks some days, and leave them out at will. If he makes up his mind that he can use his time to better advantage, he may abandon the arrangement entirely, but he must not use the opportunity to earn money as a convenience entirely detached from the responsibility of regularity or uniformity.

Many parents see in the plan of paying children for work, the danger that whenever a child is asked to do something, he may make it the occasion for exacting payment. This danger is more apparent than real. On the contrary, should such occasions arise, they should be utilized as the most favorable opportunities for explaining to the children that there are some things for which we pay, and others which we do for each other without getting any pay. Of course, parents should be clear in their own minds as to what their standards are in these matters.

The amounts paid to a child can not, of course, be accurately gauged to the value of his services. But they should neither be excessive nor too low.

When children come to have money with which to buy things for themselves, we are usually tempted not only to guide them, but to regulate them. Now while guidance is a good thing, too much regulation is likely to defeat its own ends. It is so easy to spend money foolishly; and we wish to save the children from folly. But it is only by spending money both foolishly and wisely that the child can ever learn to know the difference. It is only by having experience with both kinds of spending that he can come to choose intelligently. It is more important, in his early years, to teach the child how to spend his money than to make sure that he has spent it well. He will have more to spend later on, and the lessons will be worth more than the advantage of the early protection against unwise purchases. Caution and advice are to be given, of course; but like many other good things, they should be given in moderation.

Even in the matter of learning to save, it is better to begin by spending. By spending trifling amounts as fast as they are obtained, children come to realize the limitations of a penny or two. By occasionally omitting an expenditure and thus acquiring the power to purchase more satisfying objects, the child may acquire sufficient ability to project himself into the future for the purpose of saving for more and more valuable things. There is no virtue in saving that comes from putting the pennies in the bank through force of a habit formed under the compulsion of penalties imposed arbitrarily from without. The child should learn to save through the experience of advantage gained by making sacrifices in the present for a prospective return in the future.

In households that do not manifest through their activities and conversation the methods by which the family income is obtained, children should be explicitly informed on the subject. It is not only embarrassing to the child to display his ignorance when comparing notes with other children, but it is a necessary part of his understanding of the world to know just how people obtain the precious tokens by means of which they secure all their necessities and extras.

27. "'Selling Food to Children," *Mother's Own Book* (New York: The Parents' Publishing Association, Inc., 1928), 59–64.

There is no doubt about it, the competition which exists between the corner store and the home for the patronage of the youthful public is just about putting the average parent out of business. Perhaps you have noticed that the demand for spinach tends to fall off despite constant appeals. As for oatmeal, your young customers don't drop in for a dish of it more than once a month.

And while good old-fashioned, wholesome foods are wasting on the shelves of the home shop, the crowd of boys and girls at the corner store grows larger and more enthusiastic each day. Soda water can't be squirted fast enough. There is a constant pop, and clink, and gurgle of busy pop bottles. And the candy which was once sold in tiny bags is now carried away in cartons like so many sacks of flour.

It almost seems as though, what with the chain stores and national advertising against them, the only step left for the parents of the country is to form a merger and get some system into their business.

Getting down to business, let us imagine that you, the parent, are the unsuccessful salesman, while your adolescent child, who is really not a child but a brilliant young man or woman, is the disinterested customer. You have already made several suggestions regarding a valuable dish of spinach you have for sale, but each time your approaches have been turned down. You have even gone so far as to tell your customer that if he or she does not eat his or her spinach, he or she will not grow up to be a healthy boy or girl. (We hope you haven't really said that. If you have, you might just as well stop reading this right now, for not even I can save you.) Or perhaps you have approached your rather stubborn customer with the proposition that if he or she will eat the beautiful spinach, you may be willing to pay as much as five or even ten cents.

How can parents expect to do business with such underselling going on? How can you hope to conduct a successful enterprise by *paying* your customers to patronize your goods?

And just what would you think of a chap who would offer you a "valuable" piece of real estate (not necessarily in Florida), and also agree to pay you to take it off his hands?

The moment you gave your child the ten cents, the spinach lost value. It became a sticky, unpleasant job, only worth ten cents a helping. And as you handed the dime over, your customer raced out of the door and down the street back to the corner store, the very concern with which you are trying to compete.

Or perhaps you are one of those parents who believe in discipline, who *demands* that your customer "remain at the table until every bit of that spinach is eaten." As a rule this method will work and the spinach is usually disposed of. But I can't help wondering just what memories will hang around the transaction. In the child's mind hasn't the spinach become a thing which has kept him from doing something that was much more important, and won't he unconsciously avoid it the next time it is offered?

Perhaps you know the answer.

EXAMINE THE PRODUCT—NOT THE CHILD

But let's not be too pessimistic. Let us suppose you have approached your child simply as a good friend and great admirer and still failed. Usually the first impulse, when he refuses to eat, is to have him examined. Have you ever considered examining not the child, but the product?

Perhaps the article you are trying to sell is neither attractive nor appetizing. Is it made irresistible to your public, so to speak? Remember, your competitors are flooding the market with highly colored sweets and bright colored pop bottles. About the only one of the wholesome foods that can naturally take the attention of the eye from a candy case is bright colored fruit. And even then I have seen more than one green grapefruit or rusty apple passed across the table to a child without an appetite, like so much bad change.

Does your product appeal to the eye and to the taste of your customer?

If it does, and he still refuses to clip the coupon and sign on the dotted line, look over your sales force. Are both of you parents attractive, popular salesmen, who use your own products?

Don't tell me. I know the answer.

The next important phase of your campaign is the publicity. If you doubt my word, step into the corner store and see the placards and stickers which advertise what Babe Ruth, Valentino, Red Grange, Mary Pickford, Jackie Coogan, and the rest of that famous crowd have to say about the sweets for sale in the place. When the product isn't named directly after one of these idols, it is christened with a catch phrase snatched from the great American adolescent vocabulary.

FOOD PUBLICITY THAT APPEALS

How about the spinach you are trying to sell your customer? Is it presented as highly endorsed by popular heroes? If it isn't, you aren't much of a salesman.

Try this out on your adolescent some time: "One reason Red Grange is always in the pink of condition is because he eats green vegetables."

I'll admit it isn't very clever, but it's better than that one I once heard, which ran: "For heaven's sake, eat your spinach!"

Why not name a few dishes after these heroes? Why not "Babe Ruth's Home Plate" or "Mary Pickford's Beauty Compound"? And incidentally you might let it be known that there is a rumor to the effect that both Babe Ruth and Mary Pickford are very fussy and demand that they have their spinach at least three times a week. If your customer should ask how you know, you can safely say that you read it in a newspaper, which, so far as it goes, is true.

I'll admit that this method sounds rather childish. But no more so than the one employed by a million-dollar railroad of calling its crack train "The Broadway Limited," and allowing the rumor to be broadcast that only millionaires ever travel on it. Just as you do, I like the idea and am quite willing to pay nine dollars extra for such a name, and the opportunity to pretend that all the passengers on board, including myself, are millionaires.

The next step toward interesting your customer in the spinach is your first sales talk, which at the least will be exciting.

Do you really know your child?

Your conversation with this temperamental person must be carefully studied, just as a salesman studies you at least indirectly before he ever calls on you. Remember, your child is no more interested in your club, or business, and the things you like to talk about, than you are in his crowd and the chatter regarding it. But, my friend, you are the salesman. It is your *business* to be interested in all that concerns your customer.

HOW TO APPLY CHILD PSYCHOLOGY

Again, if you doubt my word, slip around to the corner store. I refer to the one where the boys and girls can be found in the greatest number. The clerk, although he never studied the subject, is probably a genius at child psychology. If anything, he is no doubt inclined to be a bit childlike himself. He knows the latest slang, the latest jokes. He knows the kind of people children like and so accordingly takes them as his friends, too. He knows baseball, basketball, football, hockey. And he *listens* to the children from morning to night.

That's why the boys and girls trade there. This big, good-natured fellow, with the wrinkled face, is one of the gang. And so you, too, must adapt yourself to the life of your child, if you hope to win his or her interest and confidence. You must know the adolescent language backward. And, worst of all, you must even laugh at your customer's stories. All good salesmen do. If I am trying to sell a painting to an aristocratic old gentleman, I naturally choose a different style of approach, and talk in another language, from that which I would choose were I trying to convince a mill hand that a certain pair of dollar-fifty overalls is a bargain.

But while you talk to your customer in the adolescent tongue, I warn you to be subtle about it. Let your boy convince himself. Your work is simply to set his mind working and he will do the rest, if any sale at all is going to be made.

GETTING CHILDREN TO LIKE SPINACH

I have heard so many parents, genuinely anxious over the health of their children, explode: "Now I've told you nearly seven times to eat your spinach. I don't want to hear another word out of you. Just keep still and eat it or you'll be even punier than you are."

Supposing the clever fellow who sold you your vacuum cleaner had forced his way into your home and announced in a most unpleasant voice: "I've asked you seven times to buy this cleaner. Now don't argue with me any more. Just keep your mouth shut and buy it or your house will look even dirtier than it does!"

Ever think of your child as a perfectly normal, intelligent human being who responds to flattery and every other form of salesmanship just as you do?

One reason you bought that vacuum cleaner, although you may not want to believe it, is because the salesman slipped in one or two rather charming remarks about the appearance of your home. And he naively assured you that any one with as much pride and taste as you have would fully appreciate the benefits of his vacuum cleaner. And after that one you just had to listen to everything he said.

When that agent rang your bell he knew very well you wouldn't want to buy his cleaner. He knew you would make it a point to immediately think up some mighty good reasons for not wanting it. But rather than answer those arguments himself, he let you do it. Yes he did. He first invited you to pour out all the arguments you had as to why you shouldn't buy. After that you were at his mercy. He then proceeded to show you, in a delightfully subtle way, what a marvelous instrument the vacuum cleaner is. He was ready to listen to anything you wanted to talk about. As long as you talked, your door was open. Gradually, by indirect suggestions, he made you rather wish you owned one of the things. He encouraged you to talk about the machine. And, without your knowing it, he helped you yourself to evade every one of your original arguments.

Parents, be patient with your children. Try not to be too eager. As worried as you may be regarding your child's health, be just as indifferent outwardly as possible. You two parents, of course, may enjoy the spinach to your heart's content. Speak about how fresh it tastes. Notice how it melts in the mouth. Somehow the spinach never seemed to taste quite as good as it does this evening. That touch of melted butter is what does it. That slice of yellow egg against the green. . . .

But none of this directly to the child. So much as even a shift of the eyes toward this suspicious customer may upset your entire campaign.

And so it goes. It makes no difference whether you are selling a vacuum cleaner, a dish of spinach, or a bath, the job can easily be done if a real desire is finally created. It may take much careful advance work before your customer even nibbles at the spinach. Perhaps during the entire campaign absolutely no signs of interest will be shown. But if your spinach is tempting, if your publicity is good, and if your sales talk is both appealing and in the language of your customer, then trade will pick up and your hard-earned profits will begin to pour in.

Of course, some innocent parent may try the idea out, and just before closing the contract will let it be known that there is a whole kettle of spinach out in the kitchen which must be eaten so that it won't go to waste. If your customer doesn't dash away after that one, it's only because he's too weak.

No, good friend, we haven't a kettleful going to waste. On the contrary, we have a limited amount. In fact, what you see in the dish before you is all that there is in stock. Even that has been practically promised to somebody else. I'm sorry, because this evening it is unusually delicious.

Must I be so trite as to remind you that when the supply goes down, the demand shoots up.

Of course boys and girls will always love sweets. I like them myself. But we can save the home from bankruptcy and put it on a better paying basis. We can create a desire for the things our children should eat.

And instead of our letting them feel that they are doing us a privilege when they trade with us, we can put such a price on our goods that it will be a privilege when we allow them to patronize our offerings.

28. Robert S. Lynd and Helen Merrell Lynd, "Child-rearing," in *Middletown: A Study in American Culture* (New York: Harcourt, Brace, and World, 1929), 140–48.

The declining dominance of the home and early sophistication of the young bring still another difficulty to Middletown parents in the increased awkwardness of the status of the child, particularly the boy, as he nears adulthood. Socially, children of both groups are entering earlier into paired associations with members of the other sex under a formalized social system that makes many of the demands for independence of action upon them that it does upon self-supporting adults. Sexually, their awareness of their maturity is augmented by the maturity of their social rituals and by multiplied channels of diffusion, such as the movies and popular magazines. But meanwhile, economically they are obliged by the state to be largely dependent upon their parents until sixteen, the age at which they may leave school, and actually the rapidly spreading popular custom of prolonged schooling tends to make them dependent from two to six years more. The economic tensions inherent in this situation are intensified by the fact that, as in the case of their parents, more of their lives than in any previous generation must surmount intermediate pecuniary hurdles before they can be lived. Expenses for lunches purchased in the high school cafeteria, for movies and athletic games, as well as for the elaborate social life—with its demands for club dues, fees for formal dances and banquets, taxis, and variety and expense of dress—mean that children of all classes carry money earlier and carry more of it than did their parents when they were young. Thirty-seven per cent. of the 348 high school boys and 29 per cent. of the

382 girls answering the question checked "spending money" as a source of disagreement between them and their parents.

"One local youth sighs for the return of the good old days when one could sit on the davenport at home with one's 'best girl' and be perfectly contented," says a local paper. "You can't have a date nowadays," he says, "without making a big hole in a five-dollar bill."

And again, "The coal dealer and the gas men may fear the coming of summer—but florists aren't much worried over the fact that spring flowers will soon be seen growing in every front yard. 'It don't mean anything,' says one local florist. 'The days have gone by when a young man may pick a bouquet of flowers from his own yard and take them to his best girl. Nowadays she demands a dozen roses or a corsage bouquet in a box bearing the name of the best florist.'"

"There are still some youths," says another note, "who believe that a girl is overjoyed when they take her into a soda fountain after they have been to a moving picture show. That is what one calls 'the height of being old-fashioned.' Nowadays one has to have a six-cylindered seven-passenger sedan to take her joy-riding in, and one must patronize the most expensive shows and take her to the most exclusive restaurants to cap the evening off."

If such statements represent journalese hyperbole, they nevertheless reflect a powerful trend affecting the young of every economic level. A wide variety in the kinds of adjustment different families are attempting to effect in regard to these new demands for money appears in the answers of 386 boys and 454 girls, high school sophomores, juniors, and seniors, to a question on the source of their spending money: 3 per cent. of the boys and 11 per cent. of the girls receive all their spending money in the form of an allowance; 15 per cent. of the boys and 53 per cent. of the girls are dependent for all their spending money upon asking their parents for it or upon gifts; 37 per cent. of the boys and 9 per cent. of the girls earn all their spending money.[19] It is perhaps significant that, while over three-fourths of these Middletown boys are thus learning habits of independence as regards money matters by earning and managing at least a part of their money, over half of the girls are busily acquiring the habits of money dependence that characterize Middletown wives by being entirely dependent upon their parents for their spending money without even a regular allowance.[20] At no point is parental influence more sharply challenged than by these junior-adults, so mature in their demands and wholly or partially dependent upon their parents economically but not easily submitting to their authority.

A natural reaction to these various encroachments upon parental dominance and shifts in the status of children is the vigorous reassertion of established standards. And in Middletown the traditional view that the dependence of the child carries with it the right and duty of the parents to enforce "discipline" and "obedience" still prevails.

"Study the lives of our great men. Their mothers were true home-makers who neither spared their prayers nor the rod and spoiled the child," says a paper read before one of the federated women's clubs in 1924. "It is the men and women who have been taught obedience from the cradle, who have been taught self-control and to submit to authority and to do things because they are right who are successful and happy in this world."

A prominent banker and a prominent physician agreed in a dinner-table discussion that there must be once in every child's life a brisk passage at arms that "will teach them where authority lies in the family. You have to teach them to respect parental authority. Once you've done this you can go ahead and get on the best possible relations with them." "My little grand-child has been visiting me," said a teacher in a Sunday School class in a leading church, "and he's a very bad little boy; he's so full of pep and energy that he doesn't do what I want him to do at all." "I am going to bring my little girl up just as strict as I can," said one perplexed working class mother; "then if she does go bad I won't feel that I haven't done my duty."

And yet not only are parents finding it increasingly difficult to secure adherence to established group sanctions, but the sanctions themselves are changing; many parents are becoming puzzled and unsure as to what they would hold their children to if they could. As one anxious business class mother said:

"You see other people being more lenient and you think perhaps that it is the best way, but you are afraid to do anything very different from what your mother did for fear you may leave out something essential or do something wrong. I would give anything to know what is wisest, but I don't know what to do."

As a possible index of the conscious emphases of Middletown mothers in training their children as well as of the points at which this generation is departing from the ways of its parents, the mothers interviewed were asked to score a list of fifteen habits according to their emphases upon them in training their children, and each was asked to give additional ratings of the same list as her own home training led her to believe her mother would have rated it thirty years ago when she was a child.[21] To the mothers of the last generation, according to both groups, "strict obedience" and "loyalty to the church" were first in importance as things to be emphasized.[22] The working class mothers of the present generation still regard them as pre-eminent, but with closer competitors for first place. In the ratings of the group of business class mothers of the present generation, however, "strict obedience" is equaled and "loyalty to the church" is surpassed by both "in-dependence" and "frankness." "Strict obedience does not accomplish any-thing at all," said one business class mother, marking it an emphatic zero. And another commented: "I am afraid that the things I really have em-phasized are obedience, loyalty to the church, and getting good grades in school; those are the things easiest to dwell on and the things one naturally emphasizes through force of habit. But what I really believe in is the slower but surer sort of training that stresses concentration, independence, and tolerance."

A more democratic system of relationships with frank exchange of ideas is growing up in many homes: "My mother was a splendid mother in many ways, but I could not be that kind of mother now. I have to be a pal and listen to my children's ideas," said one of these mothers who marked obedience zero for herself and "A" for her mother. One worker's wife commented, "Obedience may be all right for younger children, but, now, take my boy in high school, if we tried to jerk him up like we used to be he'd just leave home." And another, "We are trying to make our boy feel that he is entitled to his own opinion; we treat him as one of us and listen to his ideas." The value that the children apparently place upon this policy is indicated by the fact that "respecting children's opinions" is rated by 369 high school boys and 415 high school girls second only to "spending time with children" as a quality desirable in a father; this trait was rated fourth and fifth in importance respectively by these boys and girls as a quality desirable in a mother.[23] The different ratings for father and mother in this regard may reflect the fact that, although the father is less immediately concerned with the daily details of child-rearing, it is he who puts the family's "foot down" periodically. . . .

Despite the difficulty of holding children to established sanctions and the shifting of the sanctions themselves, not all of the currents in the community are set in the direction of widening the gap between parents and children. It is the mother who has the chief responsibility in child-rearing, and many Middletown mothers, particularly among the business class, are devoting a part of their increasing leisure to their children. Such comments as the following represent many of the business class wives interviewed:

"I accommodate my entire life to my little girl. She takes three music lessons a week and I practice with her forty minutes a day. I help her with her school work and go to dancing school with her."

"My mother never stepped inside the school building as far as I can remember, but now there are never ten days that go by without my either visiting the children's school or getting in touch with their teacher. I have given up church work and club work since the children came. I always like to be here when they come home from school so that I can keep in touch with their games and their friends. Any extra time goes into reading books on nutrition and character building."

"Every one asks us how we've been able to bring our children up so well. I certainly have a harder job than my mother did; everything today tends to weaken the parents' influence. But we do it by spending time with our children. I've always been a pal with my daughter, and my husband spends a lot of time with the boy. We all go to basketball games together and to the State Fair in the summer."

"We used to belong to the Country Club but resigned from that when the children came, and bought a car instead. That is some-thing we can all enjoy together."[28]

At the opposite pole from the most-leisured mothers of the business group are a considerable group of the working class wives for whom the pressure of outside work or of housework never done prevents the giving of much time and thought to the day-by-day lives of their children:

"I would like to play with the children more than I do, but I'm too tired to do it even when I have the time," was one comment. "I just can't get up any energy. My man is so tired when he comes home from work that he just lies down and rests and never plays with the children."

Another woman replied blankly to question after question about her eight children and their future, "I ain't ever give it a thought."

Certain others, less hard-pressed, give to the rearing of their children scarcely less time and consideration than do the most conscientious of the business class mothers:

One foreman's wife, wrapped up in her only child of eight, spends over an hour practicing with him each day at the piano, goes with him twice a week to his music lessons, works in the garden with him, and visits school once a month.

"I just can't afford to grow old," said another wife. "I have a boy of fifteen in high school and another of thirteen. I put on roller skates with the boys and pass a football with them. In the evenings we play cards and on Sundays we go to ball games. My mother back East thinks it's scandalous, but I tell her I don't think anything very bad can happen to boys when they're there with their father and mother."

NOTES

19. In addition 9 per cent. of the boys and 5 per cent. of the girls both earn money and have an allowance; 31 per cent. of the boys and 17 per cent. of the girls supplement earnings in some other way than by an allowance; 5 per cent. of the boys and 5 per cent. of the girls supplement allowances in some other way than by earnings.

20. As one senior girl put it, "Some of us don't want an allowance; you can get more without one."

21. See Table XIV. The list consisted of fifteen habits observed to be stressed in greater or less degree in Middletown in the training of children: frankness; desire to make a name in the world; concentration; social-mindedness (defined as "a sense of personal responsibility for those less fortunate"); strict obedience; appreciation of art, music, and poetry; economy in money matters; loyalty to the church; knowl-edge of sex hygiene; tolerance (defined as "respect for opinions opposed to one's own"); curiosity; patriotism; good manners; independence (defined as "ability to think and act for oneself"); getting very good grades in school. The lists were given to the women and they first marked the habits which they themselves regard as most important, rating the three most important "A," the five next most important

"B," any of third-rate importance "C," and any which they regarded as unnecessary or undesirable zero. They then set down in another column what they thought, in the light of their own home training, their mothers' ratings would have been. This procedure is, of course, precarious. It represents verbalizations only, but every effort was made to check up on a woman's memories of her own training and to secure careful consideration.

22. See Chs. XX and XXII regarding shifting religious emphases.

23. See Table XV.

28. The amount of time actually devoted to their children, even by mothers of the business class, should not be over-estimated. Clubs, bridge, golf, and other leisure-time outlets make heavy inroads upon women's time. One woman spoke of having played eighteen holes of golf on three afternoons during the preceding week with a mother of three children. Sand piles and other devices are provided at the Country Club where the children of members may be parked. The small daughter of one member said with evident bitterness, "I hate the Country Club because Mother is out there all the time." More than one mother who spoke of devoting most of her time to her children considered herself exceptional.

A very rough check of the time spent by mothers of the two groups with their children is afforded by the following summaries of their estimates. Of the forty business class mothers, none reported no time at all spent by her on a usual day with her children, two spend less than an hour a day, nineteen spend more than an hour a day but less than sixteen hours a week, nineteen spend sixteen or more hours a week. Of the eighty-five working class mothers answering this question, seven said they spend no time, thirteen less than one hour a day, twenty-six at least one hour a day and less than sixteen hours a week; thirty-nine spend sixteen hours or more a week. Sunday time was added to time spent on week days and the total divided by seven to secure these daily averages. Meal times were not included in these totals. Answers of women of both groups on the amount of time their mothers spent with them would suggest a trend in the direction of more time spent with children today, but these data are too rough to carry much weight.

29. Robert S. Lynd and Helen Merrell Lynd, "Food, Clothing, and Housework," in *Middletown: A Study in American Culture* (New York: Harcourt, Brace, and World, 1929), 162–64.

The early sophistication of the young includes the custom of wearing expensive clothing; as in other social rituals, entrance to high school appears to be the dividing line. The cotton stockings and high black shoes of 1890 are no longer tolerated.[13] The wife of a working man with a total family income of $1,638, said as a matter of course, "No girl can wear cotton stockings to high school. Even in winter my children wear silk stockings with lisle or imitations underneath." Similarly, the invariable dark flannel waists and wool skirts of the nineties, with a silk waist for "dress up," have given way before an insistence upon a varied repertory in everything from sweaters to matching hose. As one business class mother said, "The dresses girls wear to school now used to be considered party dresses. My daughter would consider herself terribly abused if she had to wear the same dress to school two successive days." Another business class mother said that she started her thirteen-year-old daughter to high school wearing fine gingham dresses and lisle hose, thinking her very suitably dressed. "Mother, I am just an object of mercy!" wailed the child after a few days at school, and her mother, like many others, provided silk dresses and silk stockings rather than have her marked as peculiar.

The taboos of this intermediate generation on plain dress are the effective taboos of their elders: the males stay away. Girls fight with clothes in competition for a mate as truly as the Indians of the Northwest coast fight with the potlatch for social prestige. Since one of the chief criteria for eligibility for membership in the exclusive girls' clubs is the ability to attract boys, a plainly dressed girl feels the double force of this taboo by failing to receive a "bid" which she might otherwise get. "We have to have boys for the Christmas dances, so we take in the girls who can bring the boys," explained a senior member of the most exclusive high school girls' club. A girl who had just been asked in her junior year to join this club said, "I've known these girls always, but I've never been asked to join before; it's just clothes and money that make the difference. Mother has let me spend more money on clothes this last year." A fifteen-year-old son, wise in the ways of his world, protested to his mother because his sister of fourteen in the eighth grade wore lisle stockings to school: "Well, if you don't let her wear silk ones next term when she goes to high school," was his final retort, "none of the boys will like her or have anything to do with her." "I never thought I would dress *my* daughter this way, but it's a concession I had to make for her happiness," is a remark heard over and over again; in many cases "happiness" is frankly accepted as meaning popularity. Summer and winter the contest keeps up. "I want to get my daughter of fifteen off to a summer camp," insisted one harried mother. "I dread summer particularly because so many youngsters spend all their time worrying about the proper way to dress."

Daughters of families of the working class do what they can to keep up with the procession, and if they fall too far behind, frequently leave school. A working class mother of five children, with a family income of $1,363, complains that her oldest daughters of eleven and twelve are "so stuck up I can't sew for them any more," and despite poor health, she has tried to get any kind of work outside her home, "so as to hire their sewing done." In discussing the question of their children's leaving school, many workers' wives said:

"She stopped because she was too proud to go to school unless she could have clothes like the others"; or "Most of my time goes into sewing for my daughter. She's sixteen and I do want her to keep on until she graduates from high school and she wants to too, but she won't go unless she has what she considers proper clothes."

NOTE

13. A Middletown woman of the working class who thirty-five years ago bought three pairs of cotton stockings for herself or for a daughter and made them last a whole year may today sacrifice durability and pay thirty-five cents, eighty cents, a dollar or more, for meretricious silk hose. Only 1,570,000 pounds of artificial silk was produced in the United States in 1913. In 1923 the country produced 33,500,000 pounds, though not all of this was for domestic consumption.

30. Gay Head, "Boy Dates Girl: One Girl's Family," *Scholastic Magazine* 37 (November 25, 1940): 39–40.

Jinks took one mouthful and then put down her spoon. "Why, what's the matter, dear?" Mrs. Ferris asked anxiously. "Don't you like the soup? It has lima beans in it."

"Oh, the soup's all right, I guess, but how can anybody eat surrounded by these—these cannibals?" She eyed her two brothers across the table. "Just listen to them—sloop-gulp, sloop-gulp, sloop-gulp. . . ."

"Oh, re-lax, *re-lax*, Duchess!" said Bud, taking another gulp, louder than ever, just to infuriate her, which it did.

"Ugh! Such manners! And look at Nonie." Jinks turned to her ten-year-old sister next. "She sits at the table like a Parkerhouse roll!"

"Shoot the gravy to me, Davey!" Bud said, helping himself to mashed potatoes. Dave obliged by sliding the bowl of gravy down the table so that it slopped over on the table cloth. Jinks scowled.

"Mother, I see the price of meat has . . ." Mr. Ferris looked up from the evening paper and, for the first time, saw the overhanging clouds. "What's the matter Jinks?"

"Nothing . . . only why can't we have things like other people?" Jinks burst out.

"Like *what* other people?" Mr. Ferris asked.

"Well, like the Merritts . . . or the Gilpins, for instance. At Betty's they have real napkins—not paper ones, like ours—and they have flowers . . . and a maid who passes things instead of dumping everything on the table. . . ."

"I like it dumped." Bud speared a piece of bread halfway down the table from him. "Then you can reach what you want."

"See there, just like savages!" Jinks cried. "Betty's brother eats like a gentleman, and he holds Mrs. Gilpin's chair for her when she sits down to dinner and, what's more, he doesn't hang around when Betty has dates! She has the whole living room to herself without any family cluttering up the place!"

"Oh, cut the primadonna stuff," Bud said in disgust. "You know you practically ran us all out of the living room last night—even before Dad had a
chance to hear the nine o'clock news!"

"Oh, you can talk," Jinks blazed back, "because you're a boy and you
never want the living room at nights. You're always out with E. Z. Pickens or
Shoo Warren—that glob!"

"You lay off my friends." Bud shook his fork at her. "The Warrens may not
have flowers or . . . or finger bowls, but, by George, they have something
to say that's worth listening to! They discuss things. Every night they pick
out some subject of current interest to be discussed the next night at dinner, and each member of the family digs up something to tell about it. Boy,
they're what I call a real family! And the Warren girls respect their brothers, instead of low-rating them. Why, Shoo told me in their Family Council
they decide whether or not certain public dances are all right for the girls
to attend, or which one should buy a new coat that year . . . things like
that!"

"Why don't we have one of those—a Family Council?" Asked Dave.

"Sounds good to me," Mr. Ferris commented dryly. "In fact, I'd be *delighted* for you kids to try to balance the budget for a while."

"Now, Charles, don't get wrought up over finances," Mom warned. "I
think a Family Council would be fine, but not until *after* dinner."

"Me too," Jinks said, patting her Mother's hand. "And, about the napkins and stuff, Mom, I was just kidding. . . . But I do think the boys eat like
cannibals and I do wish I had some place to have dates," she added with a
woeful sigh.

An hour later the Ferris Family Council convened. At first, it gave every
indication of developing into another free-for-all, but when Mr. Ferris asked
for attention so that he could present the budget, they listened carefully.
He explained just what the family income was, how much was spent on *food,
shelter, clothing, health, education* and *recreation.* Bud and Jinks both said they
thought the amount spent on *shelter* was way too much.

"Perhaps you're right," Mom nodded, "but remember that *shelter* includes
all household expenses. If there weren't so much laundry to send out, we
could afford your 'real napkins', Jinks, but I simply can't undertake doing
it here. . . ."

"What if you had two helpers . . . Nonie and me?" Jinks asked: "We could
get up early Monday mornings and wash, then iron after school."

"I can iron like . . . everything," Nonie added enthusiastically.

"That might work. At least, we three could do everything except the heavy
towels and bed linen but . . ." Mom shook her head, ". . . ironing would take
all afternoon, and who'd get dinner?"

"Why, Dave and I," Bud spoke up. "We shook a mean skillet at 'Y' camp
this summer and nobody died of indigestion."

"Well, one night a week, I think the family could put up with your 'skillet-
shaking,'" Mrs. Ferris smiled.

"Good," said Dave. "Oh, and, Dad, I'd like to make you a proposition on the repair bills. If I do all the odd jobs, like mending that hole in the roof, could I have the money saved to spend on . . . a few new clothes, instead of always wearing Bud's old stuff?"

"Look, Dad, I could save enough on repairs and general upkeep of the car to—to pay for the gas I'd use, say, a couple of nights a week," Bud suggested.

"Anything you boys save me, you are welcomed to—in clothes or mileage," Mr. Ferris agreed.

"Oh, boy!" Dave could see himself in a new blue double-breasted suit.

"Thanks, Dad," Bud said, "and I think I've got an idea for you, Jinks. Why don't you take the dining room for dates—fix it up with that old sofa from the upstairs hall, move the vic and all the games and stuff in there. I'll make a ping-pong table to fit over the dining room table, if you like."

"Why, Bud!" Jinks exclaimed. "That's wonderful! Could I, Mom?"

Mrs. Ferris nodded.

"And incidentally, Mom, I was going to volunteer to stay at home on Thursday nights, so that you and Dad could go to the movies—or something."

"The movies?" Mrs. Ferris was all smiles. "Why, we might even step out dancing. . . . That is, if some of you kids would brush me up a bit on the new steps."

"That's for me," Jinks cried. "Crank up the vic, Dave . . . oh, and put on *Beat Me Daddy!*"

"Wha-at? What's that?" Mr. Ferris said in a startled voice. "Oh . . . oh, the record. I see."

III Bibliography

11 Childhood, Youth, and Consumer Culture

CHILDREN AND CONSUMER CULTURE IN HISTORICAL PERSPECTIVE

Alexander, Victoria A. 1994. "The Image of Children in Magazine Advertisements from 1905–1990." *Communication Research* 21, no. 6: 742–65.

Benson, Susan Porter. 1998. "Gender, Generation, and Consumption in the United States: Working-Class Families in the Interwar Period." In *Getting and Spending: European and American Consumer Societies in the Twentieth Century,* ed. Susan Strasser, Charles McGovern, and Matthias Jundt, 223–40. Washington, DC: German Historical Institute, and New York: Cambridge University Press.

Cook, Daniel Thomas. 2004. *The Commodification of Childhood: The Children's Wear Industry and the Rise of the Child-Consumer, 1917–1962.* Durham, NC: Duke University Press.

Cross, Gary. 1997. *Kids' Stuff: Toys and the Changing World of American Childhood.* Cambridge: Harvard University Press.

———. 2004. *The Cute and the Cool: Wondrous Innocence and Modern American Children's Culture.* New York: Oxford University Press.

Formanek-Brunell, Miriam. 1993. *Made to Play House: Dolls and the Commercialization of American Girlhood, 1830–1930.* New Haven: Yale University Press.

Jacobson, Lisa. 2004. *Raising Consumers: Children and the American Mass Market in the Early Twentieth Century.* New York: Columbia University Press.

James, Allison. 1998. "Confections, Concoctions, and Conceptions." In *The Children's Culture Reader,* ed. Henry Jenkins, 394–405. New York: New York University Press.

Kline, Stephen. 1993. *Out of the Garden: Toys, TV, and Children's Culture in the Age of Marketing.* London: Verso.

Kincheloe, Joe L. 2002. "The Complex Politics of McDonald's and the New Childhood: Colonizing Kidworld." In *Kidworld: Childhood Studies, Global Perspectives and Education,* ed. Gaile S. Cannella and Joe L. Kincheloe, 75–122. New York: Peter Lang.

Leach, William. 1993. "Child-World in the Promised Land." In *The Mythmaking Frame of Mind: Social Imagination & American Culture,* ed. James Gilbert, et al., 209–38. Belmont, CA: Wadsworth Publishing Company.

———. 1993. *Land of Desire: Merchants, Power, and the Rise of a New American Culture.* New York: Pantheon Books.

Lynd, Robert S. and Helen M. Lynd. 1929. *Middletown: A Study in American Culture.* New York: Harcourt, Brace, and World.

———. 1937. *Middletown in Transition: A Study in Cultural Conflicts.* New York: Harcourt, Brace, and World.

Matt, Susan. 2002. "Children's Envy and the Emergence of the Modern Consumer Ethic, 1890–1930." *Journal of Social History* 36: 283–302.

Moehling, Carolyn. 2005. "'She Has Suddenly Become Powerful': Youth Employment and Household Decision Making in the Early Twentieth Century." *Journal of Economic History* (June): 413–37.

Paris, Leslie. 2008. *Children's Nature: The Rise of the American Summer Camp.* New York: New York University Press.

Plumb, J. H. 1982. "The New World of Children." In *The Birth of a Consumer Society: The Commercialization of Eighteenth-Century England,* ed. Neil Kendrick et al., 286–315. Bloomington: Indiana University Press.

Seiter, Ellen. 1993. *Sold Separately: Parents & Children in Consumer Culture.* New Brunswick, NJ: Rutgers University Press.

———. 1998. "Children's Desires/Mother's Dilemmas: The Social Contexts of Consumption." In *The Children's Culture Reader,* ed. Henry Jenkins, 297–317. New York: New York University Press.

Stearns, Peter. 2003. "Historical Perspectives on Twentieth-Century American Childhood." In *Beyond the Century of the Child: Cultural History and Developmental Psychology,* ed. William Koops and Michael Zuckerman, 96–111. Philadelphia: University of Pennsylvania Press.

Zelizer, Viviana A. 2002. "Kids and Commerce." *Childhood* 9, no. 4: 375–96.

TEENAGERS AND YOUTH CULTURE IN HISTORICAL PERSPECTIVE

Alexander, Ruth M. 1995. *The "Girl Problem": Female Sexual Delinquency in New York, 1900–1930.* Ithaca: Cornell University Press.

Austin, Joe. 2001. *Taking the Train: How Graffiti Art Became an Urban Crisis in New York City.* New York: Columbia University Press.

Austin, Joe, and Michael Nevin Willard, eds. 1998. *Generations of Youth: Youth Cultures and History in Twentieth-Century America.* New York: New York University Press.

Bailey, Beth. 1988. *From Front Porch to Back Seat: Courtship in Twentieth-Century America.* Baltimore: Johns Hopkins University Press.

Best, Amy. 2000. *Prom Night: Youth, Schools, and Popular Culture.* New York: Routledge.

Breines, Wini. 1992. *Young, White, and Miserable: Growing Up Female in the Fifties.* Boston: Beacon.

Brumberg, Joan Jacobs. 1997. *The Body Project: An Intimate History of American Girls.* New York: Vintage Books.

Daniel, Pete. 2000. *Lost Revolutions: The South in the 1950s.* Chapel Hill: University of North Carolina Press for Smithsonian National Museum of American History, Washington, DC.

Devlin, Rachel. 2005. *Relative Intimacy: Fathers, Adolescent Daughters, and Postwar American Culture.* Chapel Hill: University of North Carolina Press.

Douglas, Susan. 1994. *Where the Girls Are: Growing Up Female with the Mass Media.* New York: Times Books.

Enstad, Nan. 1999. *Ladies of Labor, Girls of Adventure: Working Women, Popular Culture, and Labor Politics at the Turn of the Twentieth Century.* New York: Columbia University Press.

Ewen, Elizabeth. 1985. *Immigrant Women in the Land of Dollars: Life and Culture on the Lower East Side, 1890–1925.* New York: Monthly Review Press.

Fass, Paula. 1977. *The Damned and the Beautiful: American Youth in the 1920s.* New York: Oxford University Press.

Gaines, Donna. 1998. *Teenage Wasteland: Suburbia's Dead End Kids.* Chicago: University of Chicago Press.

Gilbert, James. 1986. *A Cycle of Outrage: America's Reaction to the Juvenile Delinquent in the 1950s.* New York: Oxford University Press.

Graebner, William. 1990. *Coming of Age in Buffalo: Youth and Authority in the Postwar Era.* Philadelphia: Temple University Press.

Hine, Thomas. 1999. *The Rise and Fall of the American Teenager.* New York: Bard.

Inness, Sherrie A., ed. 1998. *Delinquents and Debutantes: Twentieth-Century American Girls' Cultures.* New York: New York University Press.

Kelley, Robin D. G. 1994. *Race Rebels: Culture, Politics, and the Black Working Class.* New York: Maxwell Macmillan International.

Kett, Joseph. 1977. *Rites of Passage: Adolescence in America, 1790 to the Present.* New York: Basic Books.

Lipsitz, George. 1998. "The Hip Hop Hearings: Censorship, Social Memory, and Intergenerational Tensions Among African-Americans." In *Generations of Youth: Youth Cultures and History in Twentieth-Century America,* ed. Joe Austin and Michael Willard, 395–411. New York: New York University Press.

Macías, Anthony. 2004. "Bringing Music to the People: Race, Urban Culture, and Municipal Politics in Postwar Los Angeles." *American Quarterly* 56: 693–717.

Males, Mike A. 1996. *Scapegoat Generation: America's War on Adolescents.* Monroe, ME: Common Courage Press.

———. 1999. *Framing Youth: Ten Myths about the Next Generation.* Monroe, ME: Common Courage Press.

May, Kirse Granat. 2002. *Golden State, Golden Youth: The California Image in Popular Culture, 1955–1966.* Chapel Hill: University of North Carolina Press.

Milner, Jr., Murray. 2004. *Freaks, Geeks, and Cool Kids: American Teenagers, Schools, and the Culture of Consumption.* New York: Routledge.

Modell, John. 1989. *Into One's Own: From Youth to Adulthood in the United States, 1920–1975.* Berkeley: University of California Press.

Odem, Mary E. 1995. *Delinquent Daughters: Protecting and Policing Adolescent Female Sexuality in the United States, 1885–1920.* Chapel Hill: University of North Carolina Press.

Pagán, Eduardo Obregón. 2003. *Murder at the Sleepy Lagoon: Zoot Suits, Race, and Riot in Wartime L.A.* Chapel Hill: The University of North Carolina Press.

Palladino, Grace. 1996. *Teenagers: An American History.* New York: Basic Books.

Peiss, Kathy. 1986. *Cheap Amusements: Working Women and Leisure in Turn-of-the-Century New York.* Philadelphia: Temple University Press.

Pipher, Mary. 1994. *Reviving Ophelia: Saving the Selves of Adolescent Girls.* New York: Putnam Books.

Quart, Alissa. 2002. *Branded: The Buying and Selling of American Teenagers.* New York: Perseus.

Ruiz, Vicki. 1998. "The Flapper and the Chaperone: Cultural Constructions of Identity and Heterosexual Politics among Adolescent Mexican American Women, 1920–1950." In *Delinquents and Debutantes: Twentieth-Century American Girls' Cultures,* ed. Sherrie Inness, 199–226. New York: New York University Press.

Scheider, Eric C. 1999. *Vampires, Dragons, and Egyptian Kings: Youth Gangs in Postwar New York.* Princeton, NJ: Princeton University Press.

Schlossman, Steven L. 1977. *Love and the American Delinquent: The Theory and Practice of "Progressive" Juvenile Justice, 1825–1920.* Chicago: University of Chicago Press.

Schrum, Kelly. 1998. "'Teena Means Business': Teenage Girls' Culture and *Seventeen Magazine,* 1944–1950. In *Delinquents and Debutantes: Twentieth-Century American Girls' Cultures,* ed. Sherrie Inness, 134–63. New York: New York University Press.

———. 2004. *Some Wore Bobby Sox: The Emergence of Teenage Girls' Culture, 1920–1940.* New York: Palgrave Macmillan.

Stamp, Shelley. 2000. *Movie-Struck Girls: Women and Motion Picture Culture after the Nickelodeon.* Princeton, NJ: Princeton University Press.

CHILD CONSUMERS AND THE MASS MEDIA

Adler, Richard, et al. 1980. *The Effects of Television Advertising on Children.* Lexington, MA: Lexington Books.

Avery, Gillian. 1994. *Behold the Child: American Children and Their Books, 1621–1922.* Baltimore: Johns Hopkins University Press.

Beisel, Nicola Kay. 1997. *Imperiled Innocents: Anthony Comstock and Family Reproduction in Victorian America.* Princeton, NJ: Princeton University Press.

Brown, Jane D., Jean R. Steele, and Kim Walsh-Childers, eds. 2002. *Sexual Teens, Sexual Media: Investigating Media's Influence on Adolescent Sexuality.* Mahwah, NJ: Lawrence Erlbaum Associates.

Cantor, Joanne. 1998. *"Mommy I'm Scared:" How TV and Movies Frighten Children and What We Can Do to Protect Them.* San Diego: Harvest.

deCordova, Richard. 1990. "Ethnography and Exhibition: The Child Audience, the Hays Office and Saturday Matinees," *Camera Obscura* 23: 90–107.

———. 1994. "The Mickey in Macy's Window: Childhood, Consumerism, and Disney Animation." In *Disney Discourse: Producing the Magic Kingdom,* ed. Eric Smoodin, 203–13. New York: Routledge.

Doherty, Thomas Patrick. 1988. *Teenagers and Teenpics: The Juvenilization of American Movies in the 1950s.* Boston: Unwin Hyman.

Fox, Roy. 1996. *Harvesting Minds: How TV Commercials Control Kids.* Westport, CT: Praeger.

Hendershot, Heather, 1998. *Saturday Morning Censors: Television Regulation before the V-Chip.* Durham, NC: Duke University Press.

———. ed. 2004. *Nickelodeon Nation: The History, Politics, and Economics of America's Only TV Channel for Kids.* New York: New York University Press.

Jenkins, Henry, ed. 1998. *The Children's Culture Reader.* New York: New York University.

Johnson, Deirdre. 1993. *Edward Stratemeyer and the Stratemeyer Syndicate.* New York: Maxwell Macmillan International.

Jones, Gerard. 2002. *Killing Monsters: Why Children NEED Fantasy, Super-Heroes, and Make-Believe Violence.* New York: Basic Books.

Jowett, Garth S., Ian C. Jarvie, and Kathryn H. Fuller, eds. 1996. *Children and the Movies: Media Influence and the Payne Fund Controversy.* Cambridge: Cambridge University Press.

Kinder, Marsha. 1999. "Ranging With Power on the Fox Kids Network: Or, Where on Earth is Children's Educational Television?" In *Kids' Media Culture,* ed. Marsha Kinder, 177–203. Durham, NC: Duke University Press.

Levin, Diane, E. 1998. *Remote Control Childhood? Combating the Hazards of Media Culture.* Washington, DC: National Association for the Education of Young Children.

MacLeod, Anne Scott. 1994. *American Childhood: Essays on Children's Literature of the Nineteenth and Twentieth Centuries.* Athens, GA: University of George Press.

Maltby, Richard. 1995. "The Production Code and the Hays Office." In *Grand Design: Hollywood as a Modern Business Enterprise, 1930–1939,* ed. Tino Balio, 37–72. Berkeley: University of California Press.

Montgomery, Kathryn C. 1989. *Target: Prime Time, Advocacy Groups and the Struggle over Entertainment Television.* New York: Oxford University Press.

Morrow, Robert W. 2006. *Sesame Street and the Reform of Children's Television.* Baltimore: The Johns Hopkins University Press.

Murray, Gail S. 1998. *American Children's Literature and the Construction of Childhood.* New York: Twayne Publishers.

Nasaw, David. 1992. "Children and Commercial Culture: Moving Pictures in the Early Twentieth Century." In *Small Worlds: Children and Adolescents in American, 1850–1950,* ed. Elliott West and Paula Petrik, 14–25. Lawrence: University of Kansas Press.

Nyberg, Amy Kiste. 1998. *Seal of Approval: The History of the Comics Code.* Jackson: University Press of Mississippi.

Parker, Alison M. 1997. *Purifying America: Women, Cultural Reform, and Pro-Censorship Activism, 1873–1933.* Chicago: University of Illinois Press.

Ravitch, Dianne, and Joseph Viteritti, eds. 2003. *Kid Stuff: Marketing Sex and Violence to America's Children.* Baltimore: John Hopkins University Press.

Sammond, Nicholas. 2005. *Babes in Tomorrow Land: Walt Disney and the Making of the American Child, 1930–1960.* Durham, NC: Duke University Press.

Seiter, Ellen. 1993. *Sold Separately: Children and Parents in Consumer Culture.* New Brunswick, NJ: Rutgers University Press.

Spigel, Lynn. 1992. *Make Room for TV: Television and the Family Ideal in Postwar America.* Chicago: University of Chicago Press.

———. 1998. "Seducing the Innocent: Childhood and Television in Postwar America." In *The Children's Culture Reader*, ed. Henry Jenkins, 110–35. New York: New York University.

Sternheimer, Karen. 2003. *It's Not the Media: The Truth About Pop Culture's Influence on Children*. Boulder, CO: Westview Press.

Watts, Steven. 1997. *The Magic Kingdom: Walt Disney and the American Way of Life*. Columbia: University of Missouri Press.

West, Mark I. 1998. *Children, Culture, and Controversy*. Hamden, CT: Archon Books.

Wright, Bradford W. 2001. *Comic Book Nation: The Transformation of Youth Culture in America*. Baltimore: Johns Hopkins University Press.

CHILD CONSUMERS AND PUBLIC SCHOOLS

Boyles, Deron. 2000. *American Education and Corporations: The Free Market Goes to School*. Reading, PA: Addison-Wesley.

Consumers Union. 1995. *Captive Kids: Commercial Pressures on Kids at School*. Yonkers, NY: Consumers Union Education Services. Available at: www.consunion.org/other/captivekids/evaluations.htm.

Molnar, Alex. 1996. *Giving Kids the Business: The Commercialization of America's Schools*. Boulder, CO: Westview Press.

———. 2005. *School Commercialism: From Democratic Ideal to Market Commodity*. New York: Routledge.

Spring, Joel. 2003. *Educating the Consumer-Citizen: A History of the Marriage of Schools, Advertising, and Media*. Mahwah, NJ: Lawrence Erlbaum Associates, Inc.

Tucker, David M. 1991. *The Decline of Thrift in America: Our Cultural Shift from Saving to Spending*. New York: Praeger.

CONSUMER CULTURE AND LATE TWENTIETH-CENTURY CHILDHOOD

Aird, Enola G. "Advertising and Marketing to Children in the United States." In *Rethinking Childhood*, ed. Peter Pufall and Richard Unsworth, 141–53. New Brunswick, NJ: Rutgers University Press, 2004.

Bogart, Leo. 2005. *Over the Edge: How the Pursuit of Youth by Marketers and the Media Has Changed American Culture*. Chicago: Ivan R. Dee.

Center for Media Education. 1996. *Web of Deception: Threats to Children from Online Marketing*. Washington, DC: Center for Media Education.

Chin, Elizabeth. 2001. *Purchasing Power: Black Kids and American Consumer Culture*. Minneapolis: University of Minnesota Press.

Del Vecchio, Gene. 1997. *Creating Ever-Cool: A Marketer's Guide to a Kid's Heart*. Gretna, LA: Pelican Publishing Company.

Frank, Thomas. 1997. *The Conquest of Cool: Business Culture, Counterculture, and the Rise of Hip Consumerism*. Chicago: The University of Chicago Press.

Giroux, Henry A. 2000. *Stealing Innocence: Corporate Culture's War on Children*. New York: Palgrave.

Gruber, Selina, and Jon Berry. 1993. *Marketing to and Through Kids*. New York: McGraw-Hill.

Gunter, Barrie, and Adrian Furnham. 1998. *Children and Television*. 2nd ed. London: Routledge.

Jordan, Amy, and Emily Woodward. 2003. *Parents' Use of the B-Chip to Supervise Children's Television Use.* Philadelphia: Annenberg Public Policy Center, University of Pennsylvania.

Lamb, Sharon, and Ly Mikel Brown. 2006. *Packaging Girlhood: Rescuing Our Daughters form Marketers' Schemes.* New York: St. Martin's Press.

Linn, Susan. 2004. *Consuming Kids: The Hostile Takeover of Childhood.* New York: The New Press.

McNeal, James U. 1992. *Kids as Customers: A Handbook of Marketing to Children.* New York: Lexington Books.

————. 1999. *The Kids Market: Myths and Realities.* Ithaca, NY: Paramount Market Publishing.

————. 2007. *On Becoming a Consumer: Development of Consumer Behavior Patterns in Childhood.* Burlington, MA: Butterworth-Heinemann.

Merchants of Cool. 2001. PBS Frontline Documentary. Directed by Barak Goldman.

Nader, Ralph. 1996. *Children First: A Parent's Guide to Fighting Corporate Predators.* Washington, DC: Children First.

Nightingale, Carl. 1993. *On the Edge.* New York: Basic Books.

Orenstein, Peggy. 2006. "What's Wrong with Cinderella?" *New York Times Magazine* (December 24): section 6, p. 34.

Postman, Neil. 1982. *The Disappearance of Childhood.* New York: Delacorte Press.

Schor, Juliet. 2004. *Born to Buy: The Commercialized Child and the New Consumer Culture.* New York: Scribner.

Siegel, David L., Timothy J. Coffey, and Gregory Livingston. 2004. *The Great Tween Buying Machine: Capturing Your Share of the Multi-Billion-Dollar Tween Market.* Chicago: Dearborn Trade Publishing, A Kaplan Professional Company.

Steinberg, Shirley R., and Joe L. Kincheloe, eds. 1998. *Kinderculture: The Corporate Construction of Childhood.* Boulder, CO: Westview Press.

Taylor, Betsy. 2003. *What Kids Really Want That Money Can't Buy: Tips for Parenting in a Commercial World.* New York: Warner Books.

12 Consumer Culture: General Works

ROOTS OF CONSUMER SOCIETY

Agnew, Jean-Christophe. 1988. *Worlds Apart: The Market and the Theater in Anglo-American Thought, 1550–1750.* New York: Cambridge University Press.

Bushman, Richard L. 1992. *The Refinement of America: Persons, Houses, Cities.* New York: Knopf.

Grier, Katherine C. 1988. *Culture and Comfort: People, Parlors, and Upholstery, 1850–1930.* Rochester, NY: Strong Museum.

Horowitz, Daniel. 1985. *The Morality of Spending: Attitudes toward the Consumer Society in American, 1875–1940.* Baltimore: The Johns Hopkins University Press.

McKendrick, Neil, John Brewer, and J. H. Plumb, eds. 1982. *The Birth of Consumer Society: The Commercialization of Eighteenth-Century England.* London: Europa Publications.

Sekora, John. 1977. *Luxury: The Concept in Western Thought, Eden to Smollett.* Baltimore: The Johns Hopkins University Press.

Shammas, Carole. 1990. *The Preindustrial Consumer in England and America.* Oxford: Clarendon Press.

THE FLOWERING OF CONSUMER CULTURE, 1880–1945

Abelson, Elaine. 1989. *When Ladies Go A-Thieving: Middle-Class Shoplifters in the Victorian Department Store.* New York: Oxford University Press.

Banner, Lois. 1983. *American Beauty.* Chicago: The University of Chicago Press.

Benson, Susan Porter. 1986. *Counter Cultures: Saleswomen, Managers, and Customers in American Department Stores, 1890–1940.* Urbana, IL: University of Illinois Press.

Blaszczyk, Regina. 2000. *Imagining Consumers: Design and Innovation from Wedgwood to Corning.* Baltimore: The Johns Hopkins University Press.

Breazeale, Kenon. 1994. "In Spite of Women: *Esquire Magazine* and the Construction of the Male Consumer." *Signs* 20: 1–22.

Calder, Lendol. 1999. *Financing the American Dream: A Cultural History of Consumer Credit.* Princeton, NJ: Princeton University Press.

Campbell, Colin. 1987. *The Romantic Ethic and the Spirit of Modern Consumerism.* Oxford: Blackwell.

Cohen, Lizabeth. 1986. *Making a New Deal: Industrial Workers in Chicago, 1919–1939.* New York: Cambridge University Press.

Cross, Gary. 1993. *Time and Money: The Making of Consumer Culture.* New York: Routledge.

Curtis, Susan. 1991. *A Consuming Faith: The Social Gospel and Modern American Culture.* Baltimore: The Johns Hopkins University Press.

de Grazia, Victoria, with Ellen Furlough, eds. 1996. *The Sex of Things: Gender and Consumption in Historical Perspective.* Berkeley: University of California Press.

Donohoe, Kathleen. 2003. *Freedom from Want: American Liberalism and the Idea of the Consumer.* Baltimore: Johns Hopkins University Press.

Enstad, Nan. 1999. *Ladies of Labor, Girls of Adventure: Working Women, Popular Culture, and Labor Politics at the Turn of the Twentieth Century.* New York: Columbia University Press.

Ewen, Elizabeth. 1985. *Immigrant Women in the Land of Dollars: Life and Culture on the Lower East Side, 1890–1925.* New York: Monthly Review Press.

Ewen, Stuart. 1976. *Captains of Consciousness: Advertising and the Social Roots of the Consumer Culture.* New York: McGraw-Hill Book Company.

———. 1996. *PR!: A Social History of Spin.* New York: Basic Books.

Fields, Jill. 2007. *An Intimate Affair: Women, Lingerie, and Sexuality.* Berkeley: University of California Press.

Finnegan, Margaret. 1999. *Selling Suffrage: Consumer Culture and Votes for Women.* New York: Columbia University Press.

Fox, Richard Wightman, and T. J. Jackson Lears, eds. 1983. *The Culture of Consumption: Critical Essays in American History, 1880–1980.* New York: Pantheon Books.

Frank, Dana. 1994. *Purchasing Power: Consumer Organizing, Gender, and the Seattle Labor Movement, 1919–1929.* New York: Cambridge University Press.

Garvey, Ellen. 1996. *The Adman in the Parlor: Magazines and the Gendering of Consumer Culture, 1880s to 1910s.* New York: Oxford University Press.

Glickman, Lawrence. 1997. *A Living Wage: American Workers and the Making of Consumer Society.* Ithaca, NY: Cornell University Press.

Gudis, Catherine. 2004. *Buyways: Billboards, Automobiles, and the American Landscape.* New York: Routledge.

Heinz, Andrew. 1990. *Adapting to Abundance: Jewish Immigrants, Mass Consumption and the Search for American Identity.* New York: Columbia University Press.

Horowitz, Roger, and Arwen Mohun, eds. 1998. *His and Hers: Gender, Consumption, and Technology.* Charlottesville: University Press of Virginia.

Horowitz, Roger, and Philip Scranton, eds. 2001. *Beauty and Business: Commerce, Gender, and Culture.* New York: Routledge.

Jacobs, Meg. 2005. *Pocketbook Politics: Economic Citizenship in Twentieth-Century America.* Princeton, NJ: Princeton University Press.

Jacobson, Lisa. 2004. *Raising Consumers: Children and the American Mass Market.* New York: Columbia University Press.

Johnston, Patricia. 1997. *Real Fantasies: Edward Steichen's Advertising Photography.* Berkeley: University of California Press.

Laird, Pamela. 1998. *Advertising Progress: American Business and the Rise of Consumer Marketing.* Baltimore: Johns Hopkins University Press.

Leach, William. 1984. "Transformations in a Culture of Consumption: Women and Department Stores, 1890–1925," *Journal of American History* 71: 319–42.

———. 1993. *Land of Desire: Merchants, Power, and the Rise of a New American Culture.* New York: Pantheon Books.

———. 1993. "Child-World in the Promised Land." In *The Mythmaking Frame of Mind: Social Imagination and American Culture,* ed. James Gilbert, et al, 209–38. Belmont, CA: Wadsworth Pub. Co.

Lears, Jackson. 1983. "From Salvation to Self-Realization: Advertising and the Therapeutic Roots of the Consumer Culture, 1880–1930." In *The Culture of Consumption: Critical Essays in American History, 1880–1980,* ed. Richard Wightman Fox and T. J. Jackson Lears, 1–38. New York: Pantheon Books.

———. 1994. *Fables of Abundance: A Cultural History of Advertising in America.* New York: Basic Books.

Levine, Lawrence. 1993. "American Culture and the Great Depression." In *The Unpredictable Past: Explorations in American Cultural History,* 221–23. New York: Oxford University Press.

Lynd, Robert S., and Helen M. Lynd. 1929. *Middletown: A Study in American Culture.* New York: Harcourt, Brace, and World.

———. 1937. *Middletown in Transition: A Study in Cultural Conflicts.* New York: Harcourt, Brace, and World.

Manring, M. M. 1998. *Slave in a Box: The Strange Career of Aunt Jemima.* Charlottesville: University Press of Virginia.

Marchand, Roland. 1985. *Advertising the American Dream: Making Way for Modernity, 1920–1940.* Berkeley: University of California Press.

———. 1998. *Creating the Corporate Soul: The Rise of Public Relations and Corporate Imagery in American Big Business.* Berkeley: University of California Press.

Matt, Susan J. 2002. *Keeping Up with the Joneses: Envy in American Consumer Society, 1890–1930.* Philadelphia: University of Philadelphia Press.

McGovern, Charles. 2006. *Sold American: Consumption and Citizenship, 1890–1945.* Chapel Hill: University of North Carolina Press.

Moskowitz, Marina. 2004. *Standard of Living: The Measure of the Middle Class in Modern America.* Baltimore: Johns Hopkins University Press.

Ohmann, Richard. 1996. *Selling Culture: Magazines, Markets, and Class at the Turn of the Century.* New York: Verso.

Peiss, Kathy. 1998. *Hope in a Jar: The Making of America's Beauty Culture.* New York: Metropolitan Books.

Pleck, Elizabeth. 2000. *Celebrating the Family: Ethnicity, Consumer Culture, and Family Rituals.* Cambridge, MA: Harvard University Press.

Register, Woody. 2001. *The Kid of Coney Island: Fred Thompson and the Rise of American Amusements.* New York: Oxford University Press.

Rosenzweig, Roy. 1983. *Eight Hours for What We Will: Work and Leisure in an Industrial City, 1870–1920.* New York: Cambridge University Press.

Sanchez, George. 1993. *Becoming Mexican American: Ethnicity, Culture and Identity in Chicano Los Angeles, 1900–1945.* New York: Oxford University Press.

Scanlon, Jennifer. 1995. *Inarticulate Longings: The Ladies' Home Journal, Gender, and the Promise of Consumer Culture.* New York: Routledge.

Scharff, Virginia. 1991. *Taking the Wheel: Women and the Coming of the Motor Age.* New York: Free Press.

Schmidt, Leigh Eric. 1995. *Consumer Rites: The Buying and Selling of American Holidays.* Princeton, NJ: Princeton University Press.

Schudson, Michael. 1984. *Advertising, The Uneasy Persuasion: Its Dubious Impact on American Society.* New York: Basic Books.

Stamp, Shelley. 2000. *Movie-Struck Girls: Women and Motion Picture Culture after the Nickelodeon.* Princeton, NJ: Princeton University Press.

Strasser, Susan. 1989. *Satisfaction Guaranteed: The Making of the American Mass Market.* New York: Pantheon Books.

Susman, Warren. 1984. "'Personality' and the Making of Twentieth-Century Culture." In *Culture as History: The Transformation of American Society in the Twentieth Century,* 271–85. New York: Pantheon Books.

Tedlow, Richard. 1990. *New and Improved: The Story of Mass Marketing in America.* New York: Basic Books.

Tucker, David M. 1991. *The Decline of Thrift in America: Our Cultural Shift from Saving to Spending.* New York: Praeger.

Zelizer, Viviana. 1994. *The Social Meaning of Money: Pin Money, Paychecks, Poor Relief, and Other Currencies.* New York: Basic Books.

A CONSUMERS' REPUBLIC, WORLD WAR II–PRESENT

Belasco, Warren. 1993. *Appetite for Change: How the Counterculture Took on the Food Industry.* Ithaca, NY: Cornell University Press.

Bentley, Amy. 1998. *Eating for Victory: Food Rationing and the Politics of Domesticity.* Urbana: University of Illinois Press.

Chin, Elizabeth. 2001. *Purchasing Power: Black Kids and American Consumer Culture.* Minneapolis: University of Minnesota Press.

Cohen, Lizabeth. 2003. *A Consumers' Republic: The Politics of Mass Consumption in Postwar America.* New York: Alfred A. Knopf.

Cowan, Tyler. 1998. *In Praise of Commercial Culture.* Cambridge, MA: Harvard University Press.

Cross, Gary. 2000. *An All-Consuming Century: Why Commercialism Won in Modern America.* New York: Columbia University Press.

Erhenreich, Barbara. 1983. *The Hearts of Men: American Dreams and the Flight from Commitment.* Garden City, NY: Anchor Press.

Frank, Dana. 1999. *Buy American: The Untold Story of Economic Nationalism.* Boston, MA: Beacon Press.

Frank, Thomas. 1997. *The Conquest of Cool: Business Culture, Counterculture, and the Rise of Hip Consumerism.* Chicago: The University of Chicago Press.

Ingraham, Chrys. 1999. *White Weddings: Romancing Heterosexuality in Popular Culture.* New York: Routledge.

Jacobs, Meg. 2005. *Pocketbook Politics: Economic Citizenship in Twentieth-Century America.* Princeton, NJ: Princeton University Press.

Kelley, Robin D. G. 1994. *Race Rebels: Culture, Politics, and the Black Working Class.* New York: Free Press.

Lasch, Christopher. 1979. *The Culture of Narcissism: American Life in an Age of Diminishing Expectations.* New York: Warner Books.

Lipsitz, George. 1990. *Time Passages: Collective Memory and American Popular Culture.* Minneapolis: University of Minnesota Press.

May, Elaine Tyler. 1988. *Homeward Bound: American Families in the Cold War Era.* New York: Basic Books.

Otnes, Cele C., and Elizabeth Pleck. 2003. *Cinderella Dreams: The Allure of the Lavish Wedding.* Berkeley: University of California Press.

Radway, Janice. 1984. *Reading the Romance: Women, Patriarchy, and Popular Literature.* Chapel Hill: University of North Carolina Press.

Spigel, Lynn. 1992. *Make Room for TV: Television and the Family Ideal in Postwar America.* Chicago: University of Chicago Press.

Twitchell, James. 1996. *Adcult USA: The Triumph of Advertising in American Culture.* New York: Columbia University Press.

Weems, Robert E.. 1998. *Desegregating the Dollar: African American Consumerism in the Twentieth Century.* New York: New York University Press.

Westbrook, Robert. 1993. "Fighting for the American Family: Private Interests and Political Obligation in World War II." In *The Power of Culture: Critical Essays in American History,* ed. Richard Fox and T. J. Jackson Lears, 195–221. Chicago: University of Chicago Press.

Whiting, Cecile. 1997. *A Taste for Pop: Pop Art, Gender, and Consumer Culture.* New York: Cambridge University Press.

EDITED COLLECTIONS, READERS, AND THEORETICAL WORKS

Appadurai, Arjun. 1986. *The Social Life of Things: Commodities in Cultural Perspective.* New York: Cambridge University Press.

Bronner, Simon, ed. 1989. *Consuming Visions: Accumulation and Display of Goods in America, 1880–1920.* New York: Norton.

Butsch, Richard, ed. 1990. *For Fun and Profit: The Transformation of Leisure into Consumption.* Philadelphia: Temple University Press.

de Grazia, Victoria, with Ellen Furlough, eds. 1996. *The Sex of Things: Gender and Consumption in Historical Perspective.* Berkeley: University of California Press.

Douglas, Mary, and Baron Isherwood. 1979. *The World of Goods: Toward an Anthropology of Consumption.* New York: Basic Books.

Featherstone, Mike. 1982. "The Body in Consumer Culture," *Theory, Culture and Society* 1: 18–33.

Fox, Richard Wightman, and T. J. Jackson Lears, eds. 1983. *The Culture of Consumption: Critical Essays in American History, 1880–1980.* New York: Pantheon Books.

Horkheimer, Max, and Theodor Adorno. 1972. "The Culture Industry: Enlightenment as Mass Deception." In *Dialectic of Enlightenment.* Translated by John Cumming, 120–67. New York: Continuum Pub. Co.

Glickman, Lawrence B., ed. 1999. *Consumer Society in American History: A Reader.* Ithaca, NY: Cornell University Press.

McCracken, Grant. 1988. *Culture and Consumption: New Approaches to the Symbolic Character of Consumer Goods and Activities.* Bloomington: Indiana University Press.

Scanlon, Jennifer, ed. 2000. *The Gender and Consumer Culture Reader.* New York: New York University Press.

Schor, Juliet B., and Douglas B. Holt, eds. 2000. *The Consumer Society Reader.* New York: New Press.

Strasser, Susan, ed. 2003. *Commodifying Everything: Relationships of the Market.* New York: Routledge.

Strasser, Susan, Charles McGovern, and Mathias Judt, eds. 1998. *Getting and Spending: European and American Consumer Societies in the Twentieth Century.* New York: Cambridge University Press.

13 History of Childhood, Childrearing, and the Family: General Works, 1870–2000

HISTORY OF CHILDHOOD: GENERAL WORKS

Ariès, Philippe. 1962. *Centuries of Childhood: A Social History of Family Life.* Translated by Robert Baldick. New York: Knopf.

Berrol, Selma Cantor. 1995. *Growing Up American: Immigrant Children in America, Then and Now.* New York: Twayne.

Calvert, Karin. 1992. *Children in the House: The Material Culture of Early Childhood, 1600–1900.* Boston: Northeastern University Press.

Cavallo, Dominick. 1981. *Muscles and Morals: Organized Playgrounds and Urban Reform, 1880–1920.* Philadelphia: University of Pennsylvania Press.

Chudacoff, Howard P. 1989. *How Old Are You? Age Consciousness in American Culture.* Princeton, NJ: Princeton University Press.

Clement, Priscilla Ferguson. 1997. *Growing Pains: Children in the Industrial Age, 1850–1890.* New York: Twayne.

Colman, Penny. 2000. *Girls: A History of Growing Up Female in America.* New York: Scholastic.

Demos, John. 1986. *Past, Present, and Personal: The Family and the Life Course in American History.* New York: Oxford University Press.

Elder, Glen. 1974. *Children of the Depression: Social Change in Life Experience.* Chicago: University of Chicago Press.

Elkind, David. 1981. *The Hurried Child Growing Up Too Fast Too Soon.* Reading, MA: Addison-Wesley.

Fass, Paula. 1997. *Kidnapped: Child Abduction in America.* New York: Oxford University Press.

Fass, Paula S., and Mary Ann Mason, eds. 2000. *Childhood in America.* New York: New York University Press.

Graff, Harvey J. 1995. *Conflicting Paths: Growing Up in America.* Cambridge, MA: Harvard University Press.

Gordon, Michael, ed. 1978. *The American Family in Social-Historical perspective*. 2nd ed. New York: St. Martin's Press.

Hawes, Joseph. 1997. *Children between the Wars: American Childhood, 1920–1940*. New York: Twayne Publishers.

Hawes, Joseph M., and N. Ray Hiner, eds. 1985. *American Childhood: A Research Guide and Historical Handbook*. Westport, CT: Greenwood Press.

Higonnet, Anne. 1998. *Pictures of Innocence*. New York: Thames and Hudson.

Jenkins, Henry, ed. 1998. *The Children's Culture Reader*. New York: New York University Press.

King, Wilma. 2005. *African American Childhoods: Historical Perspectives from Slavery to Civil Rights*. New York: Palgrave Macmillan.

Lindenmeyer, Kriste. 1997. *"A Right to Childhood": The U.S. Children's Bureau and Child Welfare, 1912–1946*. Urbana: University of Illinois Press.

———. 2005. *The Greatest Generation Grows Up: American Childhood in the 1930s*. Chicago: Ivan R. Dee Publisher.

Macleod, David. 1983. *Building Character in the American Boy: The Boy Scouts, the YMCA, and Their Forerunners, 1870–1920*. Madison: University of Wisconsin.

———. 1998. *The Age of the Child: Children in America, 1890–1920*. New York: Twayne.

Mintz, Steven. 2004. *Huck's Raft: A History of American Childhood*. Cambridge, MA: Belknap Press.

Nasaw, David. 1985. *Children of the City: At Work and at Play*. New York: Anchor Press/ Doubleday.

Rotundo, Anthony. 1993. *American Manhood: Transformations in Masculinity from the Revolution to the Modern Era*. New York: Basic Books.

Stearns, Peter. 2003. "Historical Perspectives on Twentieth-Century American Childhood." In *Beyond the Century of the Child: Cultural History and Developmental Psychology*, ed. William Koops and Michael Zuckerman, 96–111. Philadelphia: University of Pennsylvania Press.

Tuttle, William. 1993. *Daddy's Gone to War: The Second World War in the Lives of America's Children*. New York: Oxford University Press.

Vallone, Lynne, and Claudia Nelson, eds. 1994. *The Girl's Own: Cultural Histories of the Anglo-American Girl, 1830–1915*. Athens: University of Georgia Press.

West, Elliott, and Paula Petrik, eds. 1992. *Small Worlds: Children and Adolescents in America, 1850–1950*. Lawrence: University of Kansas Press.

Wishy, Bernard. 1968. *The Child and the Republic: The Dawn of Modern American Child Nurture*. Philadelphia: University of Pennsylvania Press.

Zelizer, Viviana. 1985. *Pricing the Priceless Child: The Changing Social Value of Children*. New York: Basic Books.

HISTORY OF THE FAMILY, PARENTING, AND CHILDREARING

Apple, Rima. 2006. *Perfect Motherhood: Science and Childrearing in America*. New Brunswick, NJ: Rutgers University Press.

Apple, Rima, and Janet Golden, eds. 1997. *Mothers and Motherhood: Readings in American History*. Columbus: Ohio State University Press.

Coontz, Stephanie. 1988. *The Social Origins of Private Life: A History of American Families, 1600–1900*. New York: Verso.

————. 1992. *The Way We Never Were: American Families and the Nostalgia Trap.* New York: Basic Books.

————. 1997. *The Way We Really Are: Coming to Terms with America's Changing Families.* New York: Basic Books.

Graebner, William. 1980. "The Unstable World of Benjamin Spock: Social Engineering in a Democratic Culture, 1917–1950." *Journal of American History* 67: 612–29.

Grant, Julia. 1998. *Raising Baby by the Book: The Education of American Mothers.* New Haven: Yale University Press.

Griswold, Robert. 1993. *Fatherhood in America: A History.* New York: Basic Books.

Horn, Margo. 1989. *Before It's Too Late: The Child Guidance Movement in the United States, 1922–1945.* Philadelphia: Temple University Press.

Hulbert, Ann, 2003. *Raising America: Experts, Parents, and a Century of Advice about Children.* New York: Knopf.

Jabour, Anya, ed. 2005. *Major Problems in the History of American Families and Children: Documents and Essays.* Boston: Houghton Mifflin Company.

Jones, Kathleen W. 1999. *Taming the Troublesome Child: American Families, Child Guidance, and the Limits of Psychiatric Authority.* Cambridge, MA: Harvard University Press.

Koops, William, and Michael Zuckerman, eds. 2003. *Beyond the Century of the Child: Cultural History and Developmental Psychology.* Philadelphia: University of Pennsylvania Press.

Ladd-Taylor, Molly. 1986. *Raising a Baby the Government Way: Mothers' Letters to the Children's Bureau, 1915–1932.* New Brunswick, NJ: Rutgers University Press.

La Rossa, Ralph. 1996. *The Modernization of Fatherhood: A Social and Political History.* Chicago: University of Chicago Press.

Lasch, Christopher. 1977. *Haven in a Heartless World: The Family Besieged.* New York: Basic Books.

May, Elaine Tyler. 1988. *Homeward Bound: American Families in the Cold War Era.* New York: Basic Books.

Mintz, Stephen, and Susan Kellogg. 1988. *Domestic Revolutions: A Social History of American Family Life.* New York: The Free Press.

Postman, Neil. 1982. *The Disappearance of Childhood.* New York: Delacorte Press.

Skolnick, Arlene S. 1991. *Embattled Paradise: The American Family in an Age of Uncertainty.* New York: Basic Books.

Stearns, Peter. 2003. *Anxious Parents: A History of Modern American Childrearing.* New York: New York University Press.

Wolfenstein, Martha. 1955. "Fun Morality: An Analysis of Recent American Child-training Literature." In *Childhood in Contemporary Cultures,* ed. Margaret Mead and Martha Wolfenstein, 168–78. Chicago: University of Chicago Press.

Index

About the Editor and Contributors

LISA JACOBSON is associate professor of history at the University of California, Santa Barbara, where she teaches courses on American social and cultural history. She is the author of *Raising Consumers: Children and the American Mass Market in the Early Twentieth Century* (Columbia University Press, 2004) and is presently working on a book about alcohol promotion and consumption after the repeal of Prohibition.

AMANDA BRUCE received her PhD in history at the State University of New York (SUNY) at Stony Brook for her dissertation, "Strangers in the Living Room: Debating Radio and Early Television for Family." Bruce is currently an instructor at SUNY–Stony Brook, where she teaches courses on the history of women and popular culture in the United States.

PAUL RINGEL is assistant professor of history at High Point University in High Point, North Carolina. He received his PhD in 2005 from Brandeis University, where he completed a dissertation titled "Conceiving Childhood: Juvenile Magazines and the Acculturation of American Children, 1823–1918." He served as a historical content advisor for the new animated children's television show, "The Time Warp Trio," which airs Saturday mornings on Discovery Kids.